Voices From the Prairies

The Extraordinary Stories of Ordinary Ranch Women

Dorothy Louise Beasley

PROMINENCE
PUBLISHING

Published by Prominence Publishing, Inc. ISBN: 978-1-990830-59-4

The author can be reached as follows:

Dorothy Louise Beasley
Box 193, Patricia, Alberta, Canada T0J 2K0
Email: mrs.bee09@gmail.com
Website: www.grandmaskitchen.ca

Disclaimer from the Author:

These extraordinary stories from the ranch women co-authors have been meticulously
compiled with loving care and respect by Dorothy Louise Beasley. In many instances, Louise
has gone to great lengths—even transcribing live interviews and dialogues—to accurately
capture the narratives of women who, for various reasons, were unable to document their
own experiences.

Interviews are also recorded differently than stories written by the co-authors. The stories do not have to be in chronological order according to dates or years, etc.... The story unfolds as per questions asked of the interviewee.

In the retelling of memories and life stories, it is natural for discrepancies to arise, as different individuals may recall events differently. Those familiar with the individuals and their narratives may notice such variations within these pages. Family members may even encounter stories they have not heard before, as was mentioned when Louise talked with one of the 16 co-authors in the book. A co-author's son mentioned that he had never heard one of the stories and so she told him that of course they hadn't heard it, and yes, they are more stories they haven't heard her talk about. She told him they were ordinary stories from the past and it didn't seem important enough to tell up until now.

Throughout this endeavour, Louise has made it a priority to pay homage to the women who generously shared their stories. Every effort has been made to preserve the integrity of their recollections and experiences. Any perceived discrepancies or inaccuracies are unintended and do not reflect upon Dorothy Louise Beasley's dedication to this project. It is essential to recognize that, in capturing these stories, Dorothy Louise Beasley has aimed to respect the voices and memories of the women involved. The decision to present their stories in their own words, rather than imposing a single narrative, is a deliberate choice made to honour their individuality.

Therefore, any critique directed towards Dorothy Louise Beasley regarding the methodology employed in compiling these stories should be approached with the understanding that Dorothy Louise Beasley has acted with integrity and sensitivity in preserving the authenticity and completeness of these narratives.

All co-authors have signed a written document stating that they have given Louise permission to write their stories as previously corrected by them. The family of the co-authors were asked to get permission from the co-author family member herself, before the family could make any changes to any of the stories. The permission documents were given out and signed, by Louise and the co-author, which made it a legally binding document. Editors left stories as written or told to the author. correcting only punctuation, grammar and sentence structure.

The co-authors have also given Louise permission to promote the book. However, the co-authors retain the copyright for their own stories: no other person/people are allowed to copy any of these stories without express written permission from the co-authors and Dorothy Louise Beasley. Co-authors do not receive any monetary compensation for their stories in this book. However, they will receive a 40% discount when purchasing any books for their families. They will also receive one free book for themselves.

Endorsements

"Dive into the captivating world of Canadian ranch life with 'Voices from the Prairies: Extraordinary Stories of Ordinary Canadian Ranch Women'. Within its pages, you'll encounter the inspiring tales of 16 remarkable ranch women who embody resilience, resourcefulness, and unwavering dedication. From mastering ranch tasks to balancing family responsibilities, these women exemplify the true essence of strength and determination. This book is a testament to their invaluable contributions and a celebration of their indomitable spirit. A must-read for anyone seeking inspiration from the heart of the western Canadian prairies."

—Mary Morrissey, Founder of the Brave Thinking Institute
and author of *Brave Thinking:
The Art and Science of Creating a Life You Love*

"A must-read for anyone seeking inspiration from extraordinary women in the heartland of Western Canada. This book offers profound insights into leadership, resilience, and the power of community."

—John Boggs, Co-Founder & CEO Brave Thinking Institute,
Leadership Expert / Speaker / Consultant

"Immerse yourself in the captivating stories of 'Voices from the Prairies' and uncover the remarkable determination of Canadian ranch women. This book offers a profound journey of inspiration, empowering readers to embrace their own challenges with newfound courage and appreciation for the extraordinary spirit of these amazing stories about ordinary women. I will also add that when it feels like our world is moving in so many directions at once, there can be peace in reflecting on where powerful women once held roots."

—Karie Cassell, #1 International Bestseller of
The Domino Diet: How to Heal You from the Inside Out,
Dietitian and Life Mastery Consultant.

Dorothy is a powerful and caring coach and author. Her unique life experience as a ranch woman brought into her coaching a wealth of knowledge and perspectives on life. The stories in this book are both inspirational and informative! It truly shows the resiliency and resourcefulness of these ranch women, which I believe represents the True Human Potential! I admire Dorothy's work, and her way of living life!

— Lin Yuan-Su,
Success Coach, Founder, Enlightened Success Institute

Table of Contents

Introduction & Purpose

These stories are set in the heartland of Western Canada, where vast prairies meet rugged Badlands, and the Red Deer River converges with the Cypress Hills landscape of southwestern Saskatchewan, towards the South Saskatchewan River. This is where the resilient spirit of livestock ranching thrives, a time-honoured way of life that has shaped the nation's character for generations. While many often think of cowboys as the iconic figures in this industry, there's another essential yet often overlooked group that deserves equal recognition: ranch women.

This book showcases the remarkable lives led by these women. Some may claim they have "nothing special to share" and see themselves as ordinary, but I disagree. I have heard women from other walks of life talk about ranch women. They've emphasized that without ranch women actively contributing their time and effort towards the rural communities and livestock ranching, neither industry would be as robust in Canada as it is up to the present day.

This anthology of true-life stories introduces 16 ranch women who have dedicated their lives to their family-owned livestock ranches. Some stories are about mothers and daughters as ranch women, some are stories written by themselves and their partners, and some of the stories were done as interviews. The interviews were transcribed into words through a transcribing website.

Their unwavering commitment, resilience, bravery, and deep passion have not only sustained their families but also strengthened the ranching industry. These women may not be famous, but their everyday adaptability shines through in their humble determination.

INTRODUCTION & PURPOSE

In the past, positive or happy stories about women were rarely found in history books. Most of society viewed such stories as "bragging" and accused those who shared their stories of exaggerating or ignoring the truth. As a result, few of these stories were valued or preserved. However, in this book, we share both the happy and sad moments in these women's lives. Exploring their entire life experiences makes them relatable and helps us connect with their emotions at different points in time.

As you delve into their stories, you will uncover the challenges they've faced, the wisdom they've gained, and the empowerment they've achieved. Each story highlights the enduring human spirit, the strength of community support, the significance of family, and the preservation of our precious prairie ranch lands.

In the early 1900s, John Palliser, an explorer, was hired by the Canadian government to check out the lands in Western Canada and see if they were fit for farming. Palliser noted that this land was better suited for grazing cattle and sheep than farming. The government really wanted the western provinces to be occupied, and so, regardless of Palliser calling the area unfit for farming, the Canadian government and the railroad companies led immigrants from all over the world to come here and farm. For example, in the Special Areas #2, 3, 4, which is a part of the Palliser Triangle, that area had 29689 people in it in 1921. Settlers began homesteading within that area in 1909 and were mostly gone to greener lands by 1938-39. Almost every quarter section of land had a family living on it during that influx of homesteading. Today there are only about 4000 people living there. Although more than 100 years have gone by, we are still working through ways to deal with drought, winds, colder temperatures in winter, warmer temperatures in the summer, plus government interference/control issues. The ranching way of life still plays a vital role in our lives and that of our families, as it did with our predecessors. These prairie landscapes and livestock ranching somehow go together and we make it work as best as we can.

I found some interesting information on a Canadian Government Website Prairies Ecozone, www.prairiesecozone.ca On that website it states: "The Prairies Ecozone, spanning an area of 520 000 square kilometres, is larger than the Yukon Territory and is one of the Canadian regions most altered by human activity. Farmland dominates the ecozone, covering nearly 94% of the land base." The original prairie land comprises of only 6% of that land base, so it is crucial that we preserve this prairie landscape for grazing cattle and other livestock, as the native grasses provide food for the wildlife that live on the prairies, as well as the livestock we raise. Another quote from the above website states: "Termed the Breadbasket of Canada, the Prairies Ecozone contains the majority of the country's productive agricultural cropland, rangeland, and pasture. The area is the source of much of our food and, as a result of the export of grains, oilseeds, and animal products, is an important source of foreign exchange." The family run ranch families make this happen, and are proud of what they have accomplished over the past 100 years.

Presently, some of these families have lived here for generations, over 100 years. Families who encompass the land areas from Brandon, Manitoba, to the Rocky Mountains in the southern prairies have made a living from this land. Through various modifications to the land—adding fertilizer, harnessing water from the creeks to feed the land, planting trees to stop the wind from blowing all the soil away and tilling in fibre to also keep the soil in place when the winds blow—the ranchers and farmers have made this land very productive.

INTRODUCTION & PURPOSE

Recent droughts in 2020-2023 have affected these prairies, turning the natural grasses brown and leaving no runoff or rainwater in dugouts to water cattle. Ranchers, who have been on this land for more than a century, handle it with care during these dry periods. They pray for rain in the late spring, summer, and fall seasons and hope for snow in the winter to replenish the prairie grass in the early spring months. Wild birds, animals, insects, and reptiles also share the land with the domesticated livestock. These ranchers coexist with all life on the prairies, including endangered species like the burrowing owl. The ranchers prioritize the well-being of all creatures, maintaining the natural habitat and allowing species at risk to thrive without disruption. Love for this land is deeply ingrained in our hearts and souls, driving us to be dedicated stewards of this cherished place we call home.

Bald Eagle near Steveville, AB, Canada on 01/01/24
-35 C. with wind chill of -45 C. Photo by Dorothy Louise Beasley.

And so, we invite you to join us on a journey. A journey through the Canadian prairies, where these extraordinary ranch women defy stereotypes. They prove to be ordinary women who formed an everlasting and loving bond with the land and all its inhabitants, including the livestock they raise. This love has been passed down through generations of ranch women who are happy and grateful for all that they have become, all that they do, and all that they have. It is my desire that these stories from my fellow ranch women will inspire, empower, and remind all of us about the true power of women, from all walks of life.

Indeed, I believe that ranch women are the glue that holds ranches and families together. Their ongoing dedication and determination to bring their best foot forward—whether during the upturns or living through the down price shifts in the livestock markets—creates a solid foundation of support. Family-owned livestock ranches' main income is derived from the livestock they raise, so it is of utmost importance that the little tasks, as well as the big tasks, are looked after. It takes many people to run a ranch: mom, dad, children, hired help and the next generations. You also want valuable money management, positive relationships that promote teamwork, ongoing leadership, and learning from the ground up to make a ranch work. Decision-making from the ground up means everyone having a say, sharing some ideas, and throwing others out so that everyone learns to do by doing.

In many traditional ranching communities, an entrenched cultural bias designates men as the unquestioned heads of households. This deep-seated mindset, passed down through generations, results in some ranch women feeling undervalued, overlooked, and unheard. The pressure to continually prove themselves, coupled with societal expectations discouraging emotional expression, creates a challenging environment.

These experiences, not limited to any specific individual, span decades and reflect a broader narrative. The generational influence, particularly among men born before and during the 1940s, 50s, and 60s, perpetuates the belief that a man's perspective should dictate family life. Emotional suppression becomes ingrained, deeming vulnerability—especially in women—a sign of weakness. Some of these beliefs are passed down to the next generation, perpetuating the mistreatment of women, as well as some men. This book is about the women.

The challenges faced by ranch women are not isolated incidents but part of a systemic issue. Stories of feeling unseen, unheard, undervalued, and the pressure to meet unrealistic expectations resonate across various contexts, encompassing different family structures, cultural backgrounds, and societal expectations. This highlights the universality of struggles faced by individuals in similar situations.

Not all families experience these kinds of struggles: some families have no experience with these emotional games people play and are surprised when they hear that it has been happening for many generations in other ranch families. These struggles feed into who you are as a human being now, they attack the core of who you are, rather than your behavior.

I encourage those who resonate with feelings of humiliation, embarrassment, frustration, and unworthiness to recognize that they are not alone. Thousands of women from all over the world suffer from these feelings. I am here to let you know that the opinions of others do not diminish our intrinsic worth. Let me also mention that blame causes pain and inefficiency, when you blame yourself and/or others, straining relationships and diverting focus from resolving issues.

Let me reassure individuals that their experiences are shared and that their worth remains intact. I ask you to believe that our worthiness definitely remains intact, we are far more powerful and capable than we are aware of up until now. All the things that happen to us over a lifetime, all the hardships, fun, faulty beliefs, sorrows, and joys were meant to be lived during our childhood on up into adulthood. Once we become aware that our total number of experiences, good and bad, equal up to create a wealth of information so that we may help others through similar difficult circumstances and begin to heal each other.

I welcome you all to the indomitable spirit of these ordinary ranch women as their inspiring true-life stories unfold right here in the following pages. Below is a short story of this spirit as an example of what drives us ranch women to learn to do by doing.

Over half a century ago, at the tender age of 16, I found myself alone in a field with a flat tire on my father's truck. The vastness of the prairie engulfed me, and a mix of nervousness and fear coursed through my veins. "What am I going to do now? It will be dark soon. Am I going to be able to change this tire by myself?"

As tears welled up, I faced a moment of doubt, questioning my abilities. The isolation was deafening, and the realization that there was no one else around added to my apprehension. But it was in this solitary moment, amidst the golden grass and endless skies, that I summoned an inner strength I didn't know I possessed.

With grit and courage, I decided to try it on and get the tire changed. Retrieving the heavy jack from the back of the truck I checked to see if the spare tire had air. I located solid ground to safely jack up the truck and then placed rocks strategically behind the other tires, to prevent the truck from rolling. The lug nuts, tightly affixed by time and wear, posed a challenge. I tried to leverage the tire iron to loosen the nuts off, but they wouldn't budge. A moment of fear again cropped up. Darn it, why didn't my dad look in his back mirror and come back to see what happened to me? Now I was mad at him, wishing he would come back. Yet, I knew that wishing wasn't going to get this tire off before dark. It was then that another thought popped into my head. Why not jump onto the tire iron by hanging onto the edge of the truck box? Maybe the nuts would come loose that way. As luck would have it, they did move, and I was able to remove all the nuts this way. It took quite a while, and it was getting dark outside. Coyotes were beginning to howl. It was scary out there by myself, but I had a job to do and concentrated on that instead of what was going on around me.

As I recount this pivotal moment, my chest still swells up with the same determination I felt that day. I removed the flat tire and wrestled the spare into place. Then I tightened the nuts, relieved that they went on much better than they came off. So it was that with my heart racing, my spirit unbroken, I drove home. My father learned about my experience, and all he said was, "I knew you could do it. I didn't worry about you having trouble, but with that said, I am sorry I didn't look back."

This story, etched into the annals of ranching history, illustrates that within every ranch woman lies an unyielding resolve. It symbolizes their adaptability, their ability to take on any task that the ranch demands, whether inside the house, in the fields, on a horse, or out on the road. These women are true janes of all trades, using whatever they have on hand, along with the gifts of their higher power, to do what they want to do.

In sharing my story, I seek to honour the resilience of all ranch women and celebrate their ability to face the unknown with unwavering determination and grit. These characteristics empower them to fulfil their role as essential pillars within the ranching community. The tire story is but a glimpse into the extraordinary lives hidden behind the ordinary façade of ranch women, setting the stage for the inspiring stories that await within these pages. The use of many names within the stories is necessary to provide a legacy of community within these stories. Everyone within the community is of vital importance, so bear with us as we wander through these stories. In fact, we invite you to put yourself into these stories and relive these women's lives with them. See what can be taken with you on your journey. We're confident that you will glean insights about who you can become and what you can do with what you have from where you are right now. Begin it! There is a quote someone once said, "The present is a gift we give ourselves." It is an opportunity to live each moment in perfect harmony.

Chapter I

Endurance & Resilience

Eleanor Gillespie—Interviewed by Dorothy Louise Beasley

The following story was recorded while Dorothy "Louise" Beasley was visiting Eleanor in her apartment in Bassano in April and May of 2021. Another interview was performed when Eleanor was staying with her granddaughter, Joanna Slorstad, in the summer of 2021. Some of the stories in this book were taken from the Gem History book, Dreams and Ditchbanks, under the Delbert Gillespie family history (starting on page 211) and the Augustus (Slim) William Sonnie family histories (beginning page 423), as well as other interviews in 2022 and 2023. There are many names in this story, so bear with me. It is a story of community and family support, handed down as a legacy from one generation to another.

This is Eleanor's unabridged account of her life over the past 90+ years. She dedicated herself to supporting her family alongside her husband, Delbert, in the cattle ranching business in Alberta, Canada. Through both challenging and prosperous times, she lived and is still living a life devoted to her loved ones as a daughter, wife, mother, and grandmother.

Mary (Eleanor) Sonnie was born in the High River Hospital on March 14, 1930. She is the oldest of 5 children born to Augustus William (nicknamed "Slim") Sonnie and Ruth (Betts) Sonnie. Her parents were married in 1929.

Delbert & Eleanor- Australia Olympics- 2000

Eleanor's father was born in Galletzen, Pennsylvania, U.S.A., on April 15, 1893, to John and Matilda Sonnie. Their family was of Swedish descent. Slim's father was a coal miner in the Alleghenny Mountains and rose to be foreman of the coking plant. Not wanting their sons to be coal miners, Slim's parents decided to come west after hearing glowing reports of free land and great opportunities in Western Canada. They packed up and travelled to Canada, on the train, with seven children. They bought land in the Diamond Valley area, west of Red Deer, and broke it up to use as farmland.

Eleanor's father wanted to be a cowboy, so he kept running away from the farm, until his parents let him go. He became an excellent horseman: he could rope a cow out in the open prairie and learned how to train horses. At the age of 14, 1907-1909, he worked with Charlie McKinnon Sr., who was the boss for the Cattle Roundup for the Bar U Ranch. He then began working with Herb Millar, who also worked for the Bar U Ranch, which was owned by George Lane. He worked there for many years.

Corralling Calves—Wolves Bad

In 1911, he went home to Diamond Valley for a visit and went to work for the Gaetz boys for the summer. Slim's job was to butcher fat cattle wherever they could be bought to supply the Alberta Central Railway construction crews with meat. He had to butcher the animals "on the spot" and then deliver the meat each day to the camps. He also worked with the Dick Bros on Willow Creek for 2 years from 1913-15 and remembers working alone all winter, seeing no one except a solitary native for 72 days. He had to corral the calves every night, as the wolves were so bad in those days. Slim went to work for the Bar U again until 1916, when he began working for Jack Drumheller. He and Jack were together for the next 32 years.

Eleanor's mother, Ruth Betts, was born and raised in Raymond, Alberta. She was the daughter of Richard S. and Julia Ann (Hale) Betts. Ruth's dad and her mom, Julia Ann, had 7 children together, and then Ruth's mother died. Her dad married again, and so he and his second wife had 5 more children. Ruth had 12 brothers and sisters. (One of her step-nephews, Ing Betts, was well-known to all the folks living in Gem. He was a community cattle lease rider for Gem Community Lease. Ing's Dad was Alma Betts, Ruth's half-brother.)

Ruth and Slim Sonnie met at one of the Jack Drumheller Ranches while she was visiting her sister Pearl. Slim and Jack formed a great friendship and became partners in the ranches in 1928. Slim married Ruth Betts, Eleanor's mom, in 1929. Slim and Ruth had five children.

Mary Eleanor was born in 1930, the eldest of the family, and she married Delbert Gillespie in 1952. They had three children. Delbert was the son of Alex Gillespie. Augustus William (Bud) was born in 1931; he married Eileen Cornelson of Bassano in 1972.

They lived in South Gem, Alberta, and had three children. Elizabeth Jane (Betty) was born in 1932. She married Eric Berg of Millicent in 1957, and they had four children. Second youngest in the family is Julia Ann, named after her grandmother. Born in 1933, Julia Ann married Gene Christianson in 1955, they lived north of Duchess, Alberta, along the Matzihwin Creek. They had three children. Eleanor's youngest sister was Joan Viola, born in 1934, who married Frank Andrus in 1958. They lived in Standard, Alberta, and had six children. Frank was a son of Andy and Alice Andrus of Finnegan, Alberta.

The Augustus (Slim) William Sonnie Family lived out in the "boondocks" in Happy Valley. Their closest neighbours were 7 miles away, and that was almost 40 miles from the nearest town of Nanton. It was too far to walk, so there was no way to get there other than horse and buggy. There were always people around the Sonnie house—working girls who helped in the house and men who worked on the ranch. Eleanor's mom had rheumatic fever when she was 12 years old and almost died. She was never very healthy after that. Her dad hired a young woman in the area to help with the household chores, such as cooking and cleaning and outdoor chores. There were always hired hands to feed, plus the five children to look after. Eleanor says her mother was a wonderful cook and homemaker. Her mother worked inside and outside the house, helping with the main herd of cattle, doing chores in the barnyard, feeding the pigs, sheep, and chickens, tending to the garden, raising the children, keeping food on the table, and cleaning the house. Ruth loved her sheep. She had help, but there was a lot of work to be done every day. Her hands were never idle. There were clothes to mend and material to sew into clothing for the children, socks to knit, and many tasks to fulfil on a regular daily basis. Eleanor and her siblings helped her and their dad whenever they could.

Eleanor's Recollections of Horses

Eleanor remembers learning how to ride horseback and having a horse named Dolly. She recalls that she used Dolly when learning how to ride at the young age of 5 years old. She remembers her dad having many horses and training all the horses they rode over her lifetime. Dolly would bend down her head and let Eleanor climb up her neck and onto her back. She never had to ride close to fences and climb onto the fence to get on the horse. Dolly knew lots about cattle, too, and so with a little help from Eleanor, she brought the cows back to the corral. Her dad would leave her out on the prairie with Dolly and know they would both come home and that the cattle would all be there, too. She was a good horse and never tried to buck Eleanor off or run away with her. Dolly was trained by Eleanor's dad to be an excellent kid's horse. Her brother and sisters had other good horses, too, though some not so good.

Eleanor remembers they also had a little Shetland pony. Some of her younger siblings rode her. Judy was her name, and her dad had a harness to put on her, a harness which had absolutely everything on it. But this little pony was the orneriest piece of meat that walked on four legs. Once, the family was going to a neighbour's place, the McFarlands', to attend their branding. Her mother had got all five kids in white clothes, placing the youngest four in the buggy. Eleanor's dad got the harness on, hooked up to a top-of-the-line cutter, and everything was ready to go. It looked so beautiful on the little pony, like a million-dollar outfit. Well!

Her mother came out wearing her white dress, and Eleanor was sitting there on her horse in her white dress. She was about seven years old, looking at all the younger children in the cutter, all with their nice white outfits on. Her mother got into the cutter and picked up the lines to move the pony. The Shetland Pony took off at full speed and hit Eleanor's horse's back leg with a wheel, which tipped the cutter over, and everybody went out. (Her mother was trying to get a hold of Joan because she was the youngest; she didn't want her to be run over.)

They all watched as the pony kept on running around the yard. She just never stopped. She was hitting stuff as she went around by the corrals and the buildings, as they had a huge yard. Her dad attempted to stop the pony, but she ran so fast he couldn't catch up. The cutter was all ripped to shreds, totally torn apart. Not one piece was unbroken. She had deliberately brushed against the corral railings and the buildings to rid herself of the harness and the cutter, wiping everything off, even the bridle. All the pieces of the beautiful harness and the cutter were lying in tatters all over the yard. Afterwards, she stood in the middle of the yard and looked back at the entire family as if to say, "Fooled you!"

Eleanor said, "So, help me God, nobody was hurt, but everybody was dumped out and rolled in the gravel and stuff. Their dignity was torn to shreds, right?" Eleanor's mother was so mad. Yeah, and this darn little Shetland Pony stood there so proud of herself for doing what she did that day. She stood there, daring them to think she would take anyone anywhere.

They were all going in the cutter because it was supposed to be a nice outing. It turned out to be a big mess. All the children and their mother were mussed up and dirty. The white outfits were no longer white, as they had all been rolled in the dirt. So, Eleanor went to the branding with her dad, about seven miles south of where they lived. He always used Eleanor's horse to rope the calves and pull them up to that part of the corral where the men were wrestling them to the ground. The other men could then brand them with a hot iron, and her dad did the castrating of the bull calves as necessary. The McFarland's had a boy a year older than Bud. As a result of the pony wreck, Bud didn't come because he got dumped out and rolled in the dirt in his white shirt and pants.

When she and her dad arrived, no girls were allowed to go to the branding corrals. No women allowed, as they might witness the castrating and such, right? So, she went to the house, and the women told her to sit in a chair, and that's what she did. They wouldn't let her do anything. She sat there all day. When she got home again, the kids were all so mad that they wouldn't talk to her. And her dad asked her if she had fun. "No," she said. "I wish I had stayed home." He said he needed the horse to do what he had to do at the branding, so she had to go, too. Later that day, they all picked up the bits and pieces of harness and cutter parts strewn around the yard, put them in a pile in the yard, and burned everything because it was all broken apart. What a day that was!

Another story about this pony shows how determined she was to do what she wanted. Eleanor's dad had made a bull rail corral. A stout, wide, wood fence around the house to keep the animals from coming close to the home. Her mother had baked pies, opened a window in the house and stuck them on the windowsill to cool. That Shetland Pony smelled the pies, crawled under the fence, and ate the pies. Eleanor's mother couldn't believe what a miserable little beast that pony was.

Eleanor's dad on Tiny Toes (rope horse)

Around this same time, her mom was not feeling well, and the doctor discovered she had a goitre growth, growing on her right side, next to her collar bone. She went into the hospital and when they removed the outer goitre, they found an inner goitre underneath it, and so removed it too. She was in the hospital for 3 months to heal, as the operation had taken its toll, weakening her heart. Eleanor remembers that was not a fun time at home. Her dad had hired young women to come in to look after the kids, and they also helped with the cooking and house cleaning. It wasn't the same as having their mom there, and three months is a long time in the life of a kid. That was in 1937, when Eleanor's youngest sister was only three years old, the others aged four, five, six, and then Eleanor at seven years of age. It was a hard life, with no time to be sitting around feeling sorry for oneself.

Eleanor says her mother taught them all about the flowers that grew in the foothills of southern Alberta. The shooting stars, tiger lilies, lilacs, crocuses, all the lady slippers, the ferns as well as the names of the trees and the smaller bushes in the area. In the spring and summer, the hills were covered with all colours of blossoms from the beautiful flowers that grew there. She knew about the roots of plants that could be used for medicines. The neighbours used to come to Eleanor's mother to treat them for wounds and sickness using these chopped up roots, to help them get well again. This was in the 1930s and penicillin had not been invented yet. (Eleanor continued to be interested in the flowers, trees and bushes and worked with the University of Alberta to count and keep track of the flowers, trees, and bushes in the area, as did her daughter Debbie many years later.)

Eleanor's Mom

Eleanor's mom cooked three meals a day for all the hired men who worked on the Drumheller ranch. The owner, Jack Drumheller, lived in Calgary and only came out occasionally to see what was happening at the ranches. Jack had a wife and two children, but the Drumheller family never lived on the ranch. There was a ranch at the Gregory Place and a farm at Cayley owned by the Drumheller family. (Drumheller, Alberta is named after this family.) Eleanor recalls some of the men and women who worked with them at the Drumheller place. She remembers them as good people, and most of them remained friends throughout their lives.

The children in those days grew up faster than they do now, as they were more independent at an early age. Her mother also taught her how to cook and can berries. She remembers canning 32 quarts of raspberries. There were honeybees at the neighbour's house, and so they were able to harvest the honey. They used honey instead of sugar for all their baking. During the War, there was no sugar available, so Eleanor recalls they got a 5-gallon pail of honey instead. They had a milk cow, so they made butter and had fresh cream as well as milk. They also collected eggs from the chickens and ate chicken, pork, and lamb.

Eleanor recalls, through a quote from the history book, *Dreams and Ditchbanks*, "School was a big problem for us; I boarded in Nanton or places closer to school." Eleanor and her brother Bud were away getting their schooling while their mother was in the hospital. They boarded out in High River at the young ages of 6-7 years old. Can you imagine having to board out at that age, being away from your family for months on end? They only came home for Christmas. Her dad wanted his children to be well-educated, not having to rely on others to make and pay their way into the world. Eleanor's father hired schoolteachers to stay at the ranch and teach there for a few years, too. There were bullies at some of the schools they attended, older boys who bullied both the teachers and the other children.

The Sonnie family moved closer to Nanton in 1941, to the Dew Place. She and her younger brother, Bud, boarded in a house they had rented, staying with the schoolteacher, Mary Skeen. Eleanor remembers she was good to them. Eleanor said they lived 3 miles north of the Sunset School, and then that closed because of a lack of students. Eleanor's mother died in 1942. It was a sad time for all of them. Eleanor was 12 years old. Her dad was lost, wondering how to look after 5 little kids. Eleanor became a caregiver, along with the help of some hired girls and her dad. They moved away from Happy Valley at about that time.

Then the Sonnie children attended the Basin School, which was 3 miles south of their place. There was lots of snow, and they rode their horses to school. Sometimes, the temperatures fell 20-30 degrees below zero Fahrenheit. There was always a potbellied stove at the school, which would be hot by the time they got to the one-room school, so they all sat around it to warm up. The schools were not insulated in those days, which meant that they were cold during the winter months and hot during the summer months. There was always a barn nearby to put the horses in for the day.

Her dad was a great horse-trainer. Eleanor recalls the names of other horses she had: Buck, Kate, and Tiny Toes. Tiny Toes was a purebred Thoroughbred horse, and Eleanor could rope and do anything on him. She said she raised him on a bottle, as his mother Kate died of sleeping sickness, a disease from infected mosquitoes, in 1943-4. They had called the veterinarian from High River, but he couldn't do anything for the horse.

She had other horses, too, but she has since forgotten all their names. She said people saw her riding the horses and always wanted to buy them. Sometimes, her dad would sell one as he said she was "horse poor." But he never sold Tiny Toes: he came to the Finnegan ranch with the family.

Eleanor and her siblings rode horses all their lives growing up. She continued to ride horseback when she got married and had children. Eleanor says her mother rode horses, too. She helped to chase cattle and had the best saddle horses on the place. Eleanor also learned at a young age how to open and shut the big wire gates, even though the gate was bigger than her sometimes. The cattle would get out of the field and be in the neighbours' pasture if she failed to close the gates. The Drumheller family in partnership with Slim raised Hereford and Shorthorn cattle. They had longer hair than the Longhorn cattle and more meat on them. The Longhorn cattle came up from Texas back in the 1800s.

When Eleanor was 14 years old, she was responsible to cook meals for hay camp workers while they did the haying. She enlisted the help of her younger sisters to help her. This task lasted from July until September. They hayed the prairie wool with mowers and made up stooks, gathered piles of hay that looked like witches' hats in the fields. The hay was then gathered up with dump rakes or loaded on hayracks using handheld pitchforks and then hauled to a yard and stacked into big piles of hay. Eleanor said her dad had the haying contract for the Cross ranch, so the hay was put into stacks loose.

Recollections of Wonderful Neighbour Ranch Women

Eleanor says she has known some very wonderful women that helped run their ranch with family and hired help. Edith Ings was a neighbour lady, who was very English and an only child from down east. When her husband passed away in 1934, she looked after their farm in Nanton. It had a huge stone house full of the most beautiful antique furniture. Eleanor says, "Edith was a big support to me after mother died." She had a summer place next to the Sonnies. During the Second World War, Edith took in Dudes—airmen from all over the word, mostly Australian and English descent, who were learning how to fly planes at High River and Claresholm airports. These men didn't know how to ride a horse nor how to saddle them up, but they learned with help from Edith and Eleanor.

Eleanor remembers Ann Clifford and her husband Raymond. Ann cooked for the hired help and looked after their ranch while her husband was away looking after his cousin Pat Burns' cattle. (Pat Burns had 7-8 ranches all over the area.) The cowboys always stayed the night when they passed the Sonnies' ranch during the summer, moving cattle from one field to the next. Eleanor's dad had a hold-up field that they used to put the cattle in for the night. Ann was a very lovely lady, and Eleanor helped Ann do the cooking for these cowboys, too.

Another woman was Elsie Lane Gordon, George Lane's daughter. She rode side-saddle and drove a car. Elsie was married to Cook Gordon, and they had three children—two daughters and one son. The family lived about 10 miles from the Sonnies. Cook's family had a packing house down east in Winnipeg, Manitoba. He left Elsie at the ranch and returned to Winnipeg to live with his family, taking their son Jim with him. Elsie and her two daughters remained on the ranch. From then on Elsie ran it, another hard-working ranch-woman who took their marital separation in her stride.

By the time she was 15, Eleanor was a woman, with lots of experience in looking after a house—cleaning, washing, patching the clothes—and riding a horse to help gather the cattle. There wasn't much time for fun or being a child during that period. She did enjoy riding horseback, though, and rode horseback everywhere. They used to ride out and pick saskatoons in the hills. Her dad used to bring the horse and buggy so they could bring the containers of saskatoons home. She said she remembers her brother Bud seeing bear tracks and then they saw the bear. Her dad jumped on a horse and chased the bear, thinking he might rope it if he got close enough. Luckily, he didn't get close enough to it. Then they just went back to picking saskatoons, took them home, washed them off, and then canned them for winter use.

Eleanor recalls working for the Cross Family at Nanton when she was 16 years old. They had bought the Gregory Place which Jack Drumheller had owned previously. She cleaned the house when the Cross family came out and lived there for the summer months. Eleanor's brother and sisters were still at home, and Eleanor's dad was looking after them. At that point the Second World War was happening, so there was no one around to work.

The Canadian government closed all the country schools. The schools around their area had already been closed, as there weren't enough children around to keep them open. The schoolteachers were young and able, so they went off to join the war effort. Some men and women travelled by train to the west coast and east into Ontario to work in factories. They made bullets for the guns used during the war. So, Eleanor remembers no longer having access to girls in the neighbourhood who could work in the house and look after the children. There were no extra men to help with the extra chores around the ranch, either.

Eleanor-16 yrs

Eleanor's Dad Harvesting—Eleanor Mending Jeans & Cooking

Eleanor remembers her father having one tractor and towing 3 mowers, spaced out so they could mow three times as much hay as they would have with only one mower. Alex Gillespie then purchased the first 3 hay balers in the district, and they baled the prairie wool from then on. Her dad was working for Alex Gillespie at that time. Alex had a very good friend who owned the Farm Dealership in Picture Butte, Harry Watson, so they bought haying equipment there and used them at the Gillespie ranch at Thumbhill. (The Thumbhill ranch took in a large area 7 miles north of Dorothy to Fish Lake, part of our Alberta Ranch History, a well-known ranch and still referred to by that name to this day.)

These were little rectangular bales weighing about 50-60 pounds each (up to 23 kgs), which were loaded onto a stone boat. Pulled behind a team of horses, the stone boat was a long square or rectangular platform of wood planks nailed together to make a flat bed. The men lifted bales onto the stone boat, using their knees and legs to boost them up higher onto the load. Their blue jeans got thin around the knees due to the hay rubbing against them, and Eleanor had more mending to do to keep their knees safe from the rough texture of the prairie wool hay. Eleanor says one of the stacks of hay bales was ¼ mile long. After being stacked there, it was hauled down to Dorothy and then to Finnegan on the ice of the Red Deer River in the wintertime. The cattle were fed near Finnegan during the winter months.

Eleanor on horse- 16 yrs. old

Eleanor's dad worked at the feedlot in Picture Butte and helped at the ranch at Thumbhill, too. Many other men were employed by Alex Gillespie after the war was over. This was in 1948-49: men came from down east, Ontario and other provinces, to work in the fields. There was a team of workers that came from Drumheller, and they knew what they were doing in the hay camp. The men had a very large tent where they slept. Delbert Gillespie, Alex's son, was the foreman for the haying crew. Eleanor was one of the cooks and she had her own tent, which she shared with another cook, Betty Ferguson. Eleanor was 18 years old then. She and Delbert got to know each other; however, they were both too busy to form any other relationship at that time.

It was a lot of work making hay in those days: long days of cutting the hay, waiting for it to dry, and then baling it and stacking it by hand. It was hard work every single day, and the men were tired when they went to bed at night. Eleanor remembers being tired at the end of the day, too, as she was part of the cooking crew.

She went to bed when all the washing up was done, and the food was ready to cook the meals the next day. Most times, it took until midnight to finish all this work, as everything was done by hand, and they were in the middle of a hay field, living in a tent. They provided breakfast, lunch, and supper for the haying crews, which meant getting up before the men—around 4 am most mornings—so that breakfast would be ready when the haying crew got up. Eleanor never complained as it was work that needed to be done. Each person contributed their share towards the winter-feeding program for the cattle and for the animals around their yard.

After haying was done, Eleanor remembers having chickens, pigs, sheep, and cattle to look after. She had a faraway look in her eye as she was speaking to me, remembering a time when they sold a cow/calf pair for $12.50. The Pat Burns Company out of Calgary bought them for that price. She recalls a cattle buyer who came and stayed overnight at their place. One of the cattle buyers was Bud Sewell, Tom Sewell's dad. (Tom Sewall was a veterinarian who lived and worked around Brooks, the closest town.) Bud Sewall, the cattle buyer, would eat breakfast with the Sonnie Family, borrowing a horse and riding out to see the cattle they were wanting to sell. Then he would come back to the house and let her dad know what he would pay for them. From there, Eleanor's dad would trail them with a saddle horse to the railroad corrals and load the cattle onto the train. Then, the cattle were dropped off at the Burns Packing Plant in Calgary, where they were butchered for meat and sold in grocery stores. The life of a livestock rancher means selling cattle to pay for expenses on the ranch, such as housekeepers, groceries, schooling for the children, taxes, and other living expenses.

Eleanor's Dad Moved So the Kids Could Have an Education

Eleanor says her dad moved all the time so the kids could get an education. They left the good places, too. Eleanor didn't finish high school as her dad couldn't find anyone to look after her younger siblings; that was now Eleanor's job. There was a woman who came and stayed for a year or so, but she wanted Eleanor's dad to marry her, and he said NO, so she left. So, Eleanor worked to help make money for the family. The family finally moved to Calgary, and she went to Henderson Business School to take a secretarial course. She had an apartment and shared it with another girl who was also attending the college. The apartment was close to the college: they could walk to school every morning and back home at night. (An elderly couple from Hanna had fixed up the house, and they were able to rent it.)

One of her younger sisters, Julia, got a job at the telephone company. Joan, another younger sister, was in high school and ended up sick in a sanitorium with rheumatic fever and lung problems. She got it from school. All the kids were tested, too, but none of the others got it. Joan did get better after that. Years later, the same thing happened when Frank Andrus, Joan's husband, was working on building the bridge at Emerson, off Highway 36. He got rheumatic fever from the water. They all had to get shots and stuff to stay healthy. After that, they boiled all the water, and the other workers wouldn't let Frank drink it.

After graduating from secretarial school, Eleanor went around looking for a job. The offices were dingy, dismal, and dark, which didn't look appealing to her. She didn't think she could work under those conditions, so a girlfriend of hers from Claresholm asked if she would like to go to work at a Bag Factory in Calgary. Eleanor was then 20 years old and knew how to sew, so she joined her girlfriend as they worked, sewing up cotton and jute bags to hold sugar. They sewed up many different types of bags, including cotton bags and fancy bags. Eleanor worked there for 2 to 3 years and made good money, much more than she would have made as a secretary.

After that, Eleanor married Delbert Gillespie on November 15, 1952. She said they had been dating for 3 years; she was 23 years old. Delbert was a workaholic; he loved working on the ranches; Eleanor had known him for a long time. After getting married, Eleanor and Delbert first lived on the farm where Delbert's mother was born, the Lewis homestead. This farm was located near Conrich, Alberta, east of Calgary. The exact location was 2 ½ miles east, 1 mile north of the Calgary Airport. (At that time, it was the Calgary Airport and Barlow Trail.) After that, they moved to the cattle ranch out at Finnegan in 1955. Delbert worked for his dad, hauling bulls, haying, and looking after the cows, etc. Eleanor remembers that it was beautiful in the Red Deer River Valley, with the saskatoon and chokecherry bushes blooming in the coulees and the river running by.

Their first child, a daughter named Debbie, was born September 10, 1953. Debbie was 18 months old when they moved to the ranch at Finnegan, where they lived for the next 60 years. Marshall was born November 4, 1956, and Cameron arrived March 8, 1959. The family was complete. Eleanor and Delbert enjoyed having the children: they brought so much joy to them.

Eleanor's father moved out to the Finnegan ranch in 1957 to help Delbert and Eleanor, and he stayed until his death in 1980. He helped with the ranch work and the children. Eleanor says he enjoyed the children, and the children loved him so much. He followed his grandsons while they played hockey and was enthusiastic about all their sporting events. He also helped his son Bud and Eileen and their family. He assisted Eleanor when she was calving out the cows in the early spring months, while Delbert was busy getting the fields ready for crops.

Debbie- 18 months old on Tiny Toes, her mom's horse

L-R- Delbert, Eleanor, Slim (Gus) Sonnie- 1958

Delbert recalls that Slim was "Old School" —a cowboy who liked to do things the old way and, most times, his way. Slim, or "Gus" as Delbert called him, was a very caring man, very willing, and one of the hardest workers Delbert knew. Slim liked to tell stories and enjoyed visiting with people. He attended the Old-Time Range men's dinner at the Palliser Hotel in Calgary every fall, a place where old friends gathered once a year to visit. Delbert remembered Slim telling a story about camping at the bottom of Lake McGregor while working on the Bar U. He and some other cowboys were moving cattle, setting up camp for the night, and settling down for a good night's sleep. Slim remembers some of the horses getting loose and leaving in the middle of the night to go home. The next morning, Slim was sent back to the Bar U to fetch them. It was nine miles back to the Bar U, and the horses beat him back by about two hours. Slim also remembered coming through Brooks, Alberta, in 1903, before Alberta was a province. There was only a railway siding with a railway car for the section-men to live in. Eleanor said her dad rode a horse right up until the spring of 1980 and died as he had lived on August 11, 1980, 87 years young. Slim was a great asset to the Gillespie ranch near Finnegan and helped them as much as he could, wherever he was needed, whether it was helping to haul water or dig a water well.

No Running Water, Gillespie Children

Eleanor recalls they had no running water and no modern conveniences when they first moved to the Finnegan ranch. For the first three years, they hauled water to drink and cook with and used river water to wash their clothes. They drilled three water wells and could not separate the water from the quicksand in any of those wells. From there, Delbert dug three more water wells by hand, 25 feet deep, pulling the dirt out of the hole using 5-gallon pails. He eventually came up with a good water well in 1958. The new well pumped 7 gallons per minute. They dug another water well down by the cattle corrals.

Original Gillespie Log House 1903-1964

Delbert and Eleanor hired people to come in and put the plumbing lines into their log house in the fall of 1958. Eleanor cooked extra food for her family and the 6 men who came in to put in the plumbing lines/pipes. Those men were there for 1 week to get all the pipes into the house. It was well worth the effort: they no longer had to go to the river for water to wash dishes and got to use the toilet in the house instead of the outdoor privy. This wonderful improvement occurred just a few months before Cameron was born. It was so good to have water to wash the baby's diapers and other laundry, not to mention the luxury of flush toilets, water for the dishes, and water for bathing. They lived in this original old log house up until 1964.

This log house burned to the ground on May 21, 1964. Luckily, none of them were harmed. However, they lost all their belongings. Neighbours, friends, and family gathered and made life bearable by providing them with clothing, food and furniture. All the neighbours helped build a new house, along with a good building contractor. The family moved into their new home on Halloween Day, October 31, 1964.

One time during a cold winter day, an older friend, Bob Hale Sr., was driving to feed cows, and his truck quit. He ended up walking to their place, 7 miles at least, and was almost frozen when he knocked on the door. He had a summer ball cap on his head, a scarf, and overshoes, but wasn't really dressed for cold weather, even though it was -30 degrees Fahrenheit that day. He only had a pair of gloves, no warm mitts on his hands. Eleanor brought him into the house and warmed him up. Bob lived in Bassano and worked for the McKinnon family then. He drove to the Whitney place at Dorothy from Bassano to open the water holes and feed the cattle. (He lived in Bassano, which was 64 km/40 miles, or about one hour of driving one way, which he drove every day during the winter months.)

The Finnegan Ferry, which was used to bring vehicles and people across the Red Deer River, had to be crossed whenever they wanted to do anything in Gem or Bassano. They had many interesting characters running the Ferry over the years: some good ones, some not so dependable. In the winter, they crossed the river on an ice road. Sometimes, that was scary, as the ice would melt or move, and water would be on top of the ice. They would drive through the water to get to the other side.

During most of their children's growing up years, all three of them were in the Gem 4-H Beef Club, which was on the south side of the river, about 22 miles from Finnegan, and 30 miles from their ranch, which was on the north side of the Red Deer River. Debbie was in the 4-H sewing club as well. Marshall and Cameron played hockey with the Gem and Bassano boys all through their school years. Eleanor says they all enjoyed being members of the Gem Community through the school, the Presbyterian Church, and all the other activities they helped with.

Debbie, their oldest child, attended school in Gem for Grades 1-3, then a bus came for her to take her to Homestead Coulee School. Debbie and Marshal attended school at Homestead Coulee for 3 years. The school board had not figured out what to do yet, so the schooling atmosphere was not so good there. After that, they attended the Gem school. Eleanor and Delbert attempted to get their children to attend school in Cessford, as it was the closest school. However, the school board members at that time said they didn't need any more students.

Eleanor and Delbert decided to take the children across the Red Deer River for their high school education too. They met the school bus at the home of D.W. "Jappy" and Martha Douglass, 7 miles from the Finnegan Ferry, on the south side of the river. Either Delbert or Eleanor drove the children there, where they boarded the bus along with Jappy and Martha's children and travelled to the Bassano School. Whomever wasn't busy when the children needed to be picked up after school brought them home. They did this for their high school years, though Marshall decided he wanted to take his last two years of high school in Drumheller.

After high school, Debbie attended Kelsey College for two years and then the Veterinary College, both of which were in Saskatoon, Saskatchewan. Debbie then worked in Edmonton for three years in the science program at the University of Alberta. She also worked at the Lakeside Packing Plant in Brooks for one year as a meat inspector.

Delbert, Debbie, Marshal, Eleanor, Cameron Gillespie Family

Next Generation & Third Generation Ranching

In 1977, Debbie married Sheldon Peake, the second son of Richard and Cassie Peake of Finnegan. They ranched 10 miles/16 km from the Gillespie ranch. Debbie and Sheldon have three daughters. Lauren was born in 1980, and she is now married to Lars Nielson. They have two sons, both of whom Lauren home-schools. Jocelyn was born in 1982 and married Kevin Stangowitz; they now have two children. Joanna was born in 1985, married to Carson Slorstad, and they now have three girls. Debbie and Sheldon lived on his parent's livestock ranch near Finnegan, and the children went to school in Cessford, at the Berry Creek Community School. (School board members changed and now they wanted students to attend the school.) Joanna and Carson and Lauren and Lars are third-generation livestock ranchers. Carson also came from a ranching background near Sunnynook, Alberta.

l-r Cameron, Laurie, Sheldon, Debbie, Donna, Marshall, Eleanor & Delbert -28 yrs service-East Central Gas Co-op

Marshall went to Southern Alberta Institute of Technology (S.A.I.T.) in Calgary and received his welding and pressure tickets. He worked for L.K. Ranches in Bassano for several years before coming home to help on the Gillespie ranch. He married Donna Annett, daughter of Kilburn and Bertha Annett of Bassano, in 1985. They have two children, Valerie and Jordy. Donna and Marshall moved a house from the Hudson's Bay Plant at Cessford, Alberta, to the ranch to live in. Cameron, their youngest son, married Laurie Hood of Bassano, daughter of Rod and Jean Hood, in 1982. They had three children: Ryan, Allison, and Brent. They bought Fred Linn's place at Finnegan in 1983 and moved there to live.

The land joins his parents' ranch to the west. Cameron levelled the ground and irrigated the crops using water from the Red Deer River. He also operated the Finnegan Ferry in the summer months. Cameron also helped Eleanor and Delbert on the ranch, feeding cattle, and farmed his land too. His wife Laurie worked at the post office in Finnegan. Their children attended school in Homestead

Coulee, then the Berry Creek Community School in Cessford. Their daughter, Allison, passed away suddenly in 1994 on the way to school from an epileptic attack, which was quite a blow to the families.

Marshall and Donna moved to Bow City in 2015, six months before Delbert and Eleanor decided to move as well. They lived in the same yard as Marshall and Donna, in a manufactured home, which suited them well. Cameron and Laurie moved to live in the house they had built in 1964, the main house at the ranch. One of Cameron and Laurie's sons moved into his parents' former home near the Finnegan Ferry.

Tragedy Strikes the Gillespie Family

Life marches on, and sad things happen—unexpected things, unimaginable things. Eleanor watched helplessly as Debbie, her only daughter, got sick, weak, and then passed away from a long bout with cancer in 2012. Louise sees tears come to Eleanor's eyes as she recalls the love she had for Debbie. A mother-daughter bond that is bound together with love. Debbie's beloved husband Sheldon passed away after a long bout with cancer as well on January 27, 2017. Sometimes, no matter how hard we pray for recovery, God seems to have other plans for our loved ones.

Very sad times for the Gillespie and Peake families. Eleanor lost most of her siblings to cancer: her youngest sister Joan, her brother Bud, and her sister Betty. Her only remaining sibling is Julia, who lives in Nanton, Alberta. The premature deaths of those people she loved left big holes in her heart, but she kept on moving, going forward, as that is what ranch women do. They keep busy, as there is always work to be done. It never finishes, until they moved away from the ranch.

The author believes one never knows when it will be our last breath, when God takes us home. So, as a ranch woman herself, her motto is, "Live life to the fullest, spend quality time with your loved ones, and make happy memories, as every present moment together counts as love for one another."

Delbert began to have mini-strokes two years after they moved off the ranch, so they moved into the New Brook Lodge in Brooks, Alberta. Eleanor says she got sick shortly afterwards with bladder and kidney infections that went into her bloodstream. She fell in 2019 and broke her shoulder. She said she had a good doctor, a specialist out of Medicine Hat, who kept checking up on her to make sure she would have mobility in the shoulder afterwards. She has full mobility in that shoulder.

Delbert had a major stroke about the same time as Eleanor's shoulder was healing, and he went into long-term care for six months in the hospital in Brooks. He could no longer walk, so he was in a wheelchair. He was transferred to the Sunrise Personal Care Facility in Brooks, where he lived for another one-and-a-half years. Eleanor remained in the New Brook Lodge and visited him every day at Sunrise Gardens. She never missed a day going to see him and stayed most every day, visiting and making new friends with families and other patients in the Personal Care Home.

Eleanor hired Helping Hands Caregivers to help him and keep him company when she couldn't be there. He loved it when visitors came and always recognized the author of this book. Louise has known Eleanor and Delbert since she was a little girl. Growing up with their children, she always had a great relationship with the Gillespie families. Delbert adored his loving wife, Eleanor, and was well-known as a gentle, caring man during his time in the Sunrise Personal Care Home.

Delbert passed away on April 27, 2020, during the Covid-19 pandemic. It was a sad time for the Gillespie families, as he had contracted Covid from one of the nurses in the personal care home, and the Gillespie families were never allowed to see him in person again. It is a great shame and disgrace that a man so humble, caring, and gentle and who was such a family man was never given the chance to say good-bye to his loving wife, his grown children, and their families in person. They saw each other via Facetime, a poor substitute for in-person visiting.

Louise mentions that many tragedies like this happened, and it makes her realize she never wants to be in a home care facility. When something like the COVID pandemic happens, our elderly folks become pawns for the government in power. Our federal and provincial governments worked "against the people" instead of governing the laws "of the people, by the people, for the people," a partial quote from Abe Lincoln. (There was no reason to keep family away from their precious elderly parents, who were dying on their own. Our elderly folks everywhere, hold the wisdom through their life experiences that would help to heal our world. They deserve more from us, from our society, and our governments, and have the God-given right to die with family around them.)

As Eleanor says, Delbert was a good, kind man, a great husband and father, a friend to many, and a wonderful provider. He and Eleanor's dad were like father and son: they were very good friends. Delbert and Eleanor also had a special kind of relationship that endured many hardships and many happy times with friends and family. True love, valuing each other as equal partners on the ranch, working together as a team to create a well-run, successful ranch legacy.

At 93 years young in 2023, Eleanor drives her own vehicle, has her own apartment, and spends time with her grandchildren and great grandchildren. She helps her sons, their wives, and her granddaughters, who live on livestock ranches of their own. There she babysits her great grandchildren and helps their mothers preserve fruits and vegetables by canning them in quart sealers. She bakes cookies and cakes for them, still making her own traditional Christmas fruit cakes from scratch. She also sews quilts for her great-grandchildren and weaves shawls and scarves, using her weaving machine and spinning wheel to make yarn. She entertains guests in her apartment, discussing life over a cup of tea and a homemade meal. Eleanor manages to keep healthy and busy. She loves the outdoors, loves horses, loves cattle, and loves nature—just as her dad did while he was alive.

Eleanor is a great example of what being a ranch woman is all about. She loves being out in the open, loves the land where they made their home, and loves the life she has lived. She truly exemplifies the life of a rancher's daughter, a wife, a mother, a grandmother, a great-grandmother, a loving sister, and a friend to many. Eleanor says she wouldn't have traded any of the years that she has lived for all the riches in the world. She is the real deal, a remarkable woman who truly exemplifies an Ordinary Canadian Ranch Woman who is still living an extraordinary life.

These recipes below were submitted by Eleanor, some of her favourites. She makes up goodies to take with her when she visits friends or freezes them when people visit her.

COCONUT CRUNCH

¾ cup butter or margarine	1 tablespoon baking powder
3 cups brown sugar, packed	1 teaspoon salt
1¾ cups flour, sifted	1½ teaspoons vanilla
3 eggs, unbeaten	1 cup coconut

1 cup chopped pecans

Set oven at 350° and grease 9x12-inch pan. Melt butter; stir in sugar. Add all other ingredients. Bake 45 minutes. Cut in squares.

MRS. FRANK G. TURPIN

PUMPKIN DESSERT BREAD — Maud Knight

3 c. flour	2 c. sugar
1 tsp. baking soda	1/2 c. nuts
1 tsp. salt	2 c. pumpkin
3 tsp. cinnamon	4 eggs, beaten
1 tsp. cloves	1 1/4 c. cooking oil
1 tsp. nutmeg	

Place all dry ingredients in a large bowl. Make a deep well in the centre and add all liquid ingredients. Stir carefully, just enough to dampen all dry ingredients. Grease and flour 2 loaf pans. Pour into loaf pans.

Bake at 350 degrees F for 1 hour, until done.

Chicken in Wine

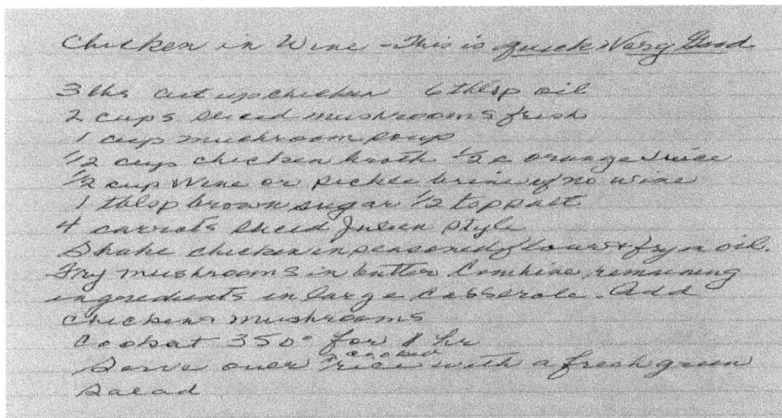

Chicken in Wine — This is quick & Very Good

3 lbs cut up chicken   6 tblsp oil
2 cups sliced mushrooms fresh
1 cup mushroom soup
1/2 cup chicken broth 1/2 c orange juice
1/2 cup Wine or pickle brine if no wine
1 tblsp brown sugar 1/2 tsp salt
4 carrots sliced French style
Shake chicken in seasoned flour & fry in oil.
Fry mushrooms in butter. Combine remaining
ingredients in large casserole. Add
chicken & mushrooms
Cook at 350° for 1 hr
Serve over rice with a fresh green
Salad

Apple Cake

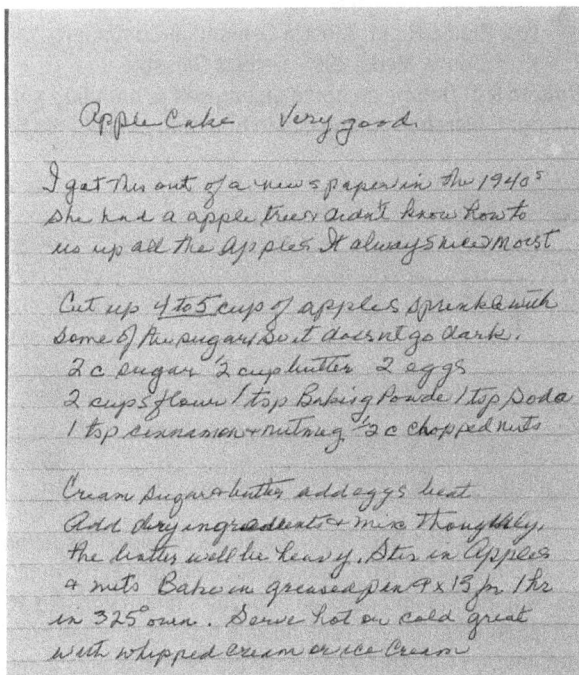

Apple Cake   Very good.

I got this out of a newspaper in the 1940s
She had a apple tree & didn't know how to
use up all the apples It always stays moist

Cut up 4 to 5 cups of apples sprinkle with
some of the sugar so it doesn't go dark.
2 c sugar 2 cups butter 2 eggs
2 cups flour 1 tsp Baking Powder 1 tsp soda
1 tsp cinnamon + nutmeg 1/2 c chopped nuts

Cream sugar & butter add eggs beat
Add dry ingredients & mix thoughtly.
the batter will be heavy. Stir in apples
& nuts Bake in greased pan 9 x 13 for 1 hr
in 325° oven. Serve hot or cold great
with whipped cream or ice cream

Top Left: Evelyn Burton & Eleanor Gillespie.
Top Middle/Right: Alberta Centennial Community
Serv. Medal 2005- Delbert Gillespie.
Bottom left: Debbie on horse pulling calf to branding pot.
Bottom right: Marshall pulling calf to branding pot with his horse.

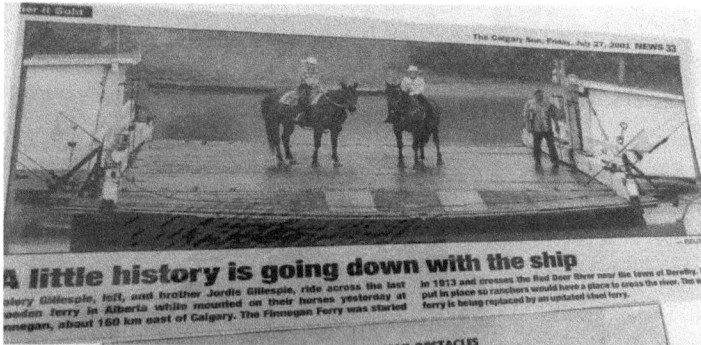

Finnegan Ferry across Red Deer River. Valerie & Jordie Gillespie on board on the last day of old wooden ferry being used. Finnegan Ferry went onto this piece of the river in 1913 and used up until 2001. It was updated at this time with a much larger steel ferry. Everyone who wanted to cross the river right here used it. Cameron Gillespie was one of the Ferryman who manned it for a few years as well. In a Calgary Herald Article July 27, 2001.

Chapter II

Ranch & Community Advocate

Laurel Schlaht—Story by Laurel

Like many ranch women, I became part of the agricultural community as a young schoolteacher and never left. After meeting Alan, an amicable cowboy on a cruise to Australia in 1978, I knew I would probably choose the road less taken. For me, that meant living in cattle country.

Before that fateful meeting, Alan had never travelled outside of Alberta. Six of his friends thought they should all go on an adventure to Australia. I, on the other hand, was tired of university life and convinced my friend Donna to join me on a cruise to Australia. My cousin lived in the rural town of Armidale, NSW, and that was our destination. Donna met Patrick on the cruise, and they got engaged a couple of months later in Tasmania. Alan and I dated for three years and then married in 1982. This year will be our 40th wedding anniversary. In 1985, Jenna was born, and then our son Carter was born in 1986. Sadly, Carter passed away in 2018.

I am the daughter of a grain farmer. Grandpa Maley began a homestead 28 miles southeast of Swift Current, near McMahon, Saskatchewan, in 1906. Dad took over the farm in 1945 after serving in the Royal Canadian Air Force during WWII. Dad farmed for 40 years before he sold out.

In 1951, Mom and Dad decided to become suitcase farmers. They bought a house a block away from a school and then would run back and forth to the farm during the work season. I was born in 1958 and had the best of both worlds: a farm with a lake, a horse to ride, and the amenities of the little city of Swift Current. I grew up playing a lot of sports within a competitive southern Saskatchewan league. In the summer, I would help Dad by picking rocks in the springtime, driving the truck at harvest, or shovelling grain when the quota was open. There used to be four grain elevators in McMahon; now there are none. Helping my dad was way more fun than doing housework. I must give credit to Mom because she never complained. In fact, she told me I had my whole life to keep house and sent me out to enjoy the sunshine!

Throughout my life, sports and the outdoors have been a continuous theme. I played university basketball for the U of Saskatchewan Huskiettes and competed in martial arts tournaments from 1998–2003. At the age of 45, I won my last sparring tournament, held in Medicine Hat. Overnight canoe trips, trail riding with my horse, and entering and winning a 15-mile endurance race with my paint horse Leota were some of the highlights.

When Alan and I met, I understood farming but had no experience in ranching. Since then, I've learned a lot of barnyard language and know my way around cattle.

At first glance the Bindloss district looks bleak. People joke that you must be blind and lost to live there. Sometimes looks are deceiving. There is more to the picture than meets the eye. What we do have is freedom. We're free to do pretty much whatever we want within the beauty of a grassland ecosystem surrounded by two rivers—the mighty South Saskatchewan and the meandering Red Deer. The confluence of these two rivers is just east of the town of Empress, Alberta, where Alan was born. The beauty of the living sky never ceases to amaze me. Peace and quiet is paramount. Nature abounds. Many endangered species still survive, and several archaeological features, like medicine wheels, can be found. Duck-billed dinosaurs have been exhumed at Sandy Point and can be found on display at the Royal Tyrrell Museum in Drumheller.

Bindloss & Government Accountability

Bindloss is a hamlet named after a turn-of-the-century English poet and writer, Harold Bindloss. In 1914, when the railroad went through, perhaps a worker was reading an H. Bindloss novel and thus named the town. Our rail line was known as the Royal Line since communities such as Empress, Cavendish, Patricia, Countess, and Duchess possess royal names.

Our land is located near the northeast corner of Canadian Forces Base (CFB) Suffield. Alan's grandparents, Dave and Molly Sturm, came here in 1925.

Alan and I live in a small community called Social Plains, where we have many good neighbours. We operate about 7,000 acres of grassland and rent out our cultivated land. The grassland in our area is a good hard grass on which our cattle and horses do well. Over the years, we needed both the farm and ranch to support a living. We used horses to work our cattle up until 2021 when surgery forced us to use quads.

The lumber for our 1913 home and red hip-roofed barn came 90 miles down the South Saskatchewan River by barge from Medicine Hat in 1912. A team of horses pulled a skid loaded with lumber out of the river hills to supply materials for our home. The old blacksmith shop and other historic buildings still exist. Many of our friends' ancestors were affected by the introduction of CFB Suffield. In 1941, under the War Measures Act, the Canadian Government expropriated many farms to create what we refer to as the British Block. About 130 families were given short notice to get out. They were unfairly compensated. A newspaper article wrote, "His Majesty's settlement was $1.00 per acre for raw land, 5 cents per acre for each unexpired year on lease, 4 cents per acre for moving livestock and no definite offer for buildings, fences, or improvements.

Laurel with cat, 2 dogs- cow in background

Moving expenses other than $2.00 for livestock would be on their own." The settlers had to get out, and they did. But the way they were treated will never be forgotten. There was a big rush to get them out, and then the area just sat unused for many months.

In the fall of 1993, I remember our neighbour was contacted by a friend who worked at CFB Suffield. He stated that the military was interested in having the 1,200 head of wild horses removed from CFB Suffield commonly called the British Block.

The herds were the descendants of the horses that our grandparents had set loose years ago, since tractors had replaced these once-valuable animals. Alan and I were part of ten families that joined together to apply for the contract. We really didn't want to see the horses removed but knew one way or another it was going to happen. Our group was called the Social Plains Homesteaders, and we believed we could do this task, paying mind to ethics and safety.

Another group from the Buffalo area formed together and applied for a contract independent of ours. We were awarded a contract, and so were they. Each operated independently. The men used skidoos, horses, and an airplane to gather the wild horses into corrals.

The gathering and adoption of the horses took place just outside of the corner of the British Block, where a neighbour was gracious enough to lend his handling facilities.

I remember that some of the stallions were scarred up from fighting over the herds. When the studs were gathered in the big pen, they quieted down and became like an old boys' club. Many mares had given birth, and some of the yearlings were stunted. There were separate pens for mares with foals and yearlings. People came from all over Canada to adopt horses for $350.00 each. A number sticker on their rump defined each horse. The buyers then chose which horse they wanted. The horses were cut out, moved into a chute, and then loaded onto horse trailers. In all, there were 1,201 horses sold. Only one was lost.

Alan and I still say that taking all the horses out of the block was a big mistake. The herd could have been culled back and managed at a reasonable number. At least the horses respected the fences, unlike the herds of Elk that we have now.

Canadian Forces Base (CFB) Suffield Fire - Disaster to Ranch

In 2017 disaster struck our Social Plains and Bindloss communities. CFB Suffield started a fire that burned out of control and consumed 90,000 acres. Alan and I had two sections of winter grass that burned, including miles of fence, some damaged machinery, and some singed cattle. Alan's cousin Ivan had over 80 cow-calf pairs burned to death. It was a gruesome sight. When we applied for compensation, I attempted to explain to the Federal Government that a ranch is like a giant jigsaw puzzle. All the pieces must fit together so a ranch can run efficiently. If you remove an integral part, the whole operation suffers. Without our winter field, we had to relocate our cattle, drill a water well, purchase windbreaks, and buy extra feed.

Dealing with the government was one of the most frustrating and disappointing things I've ever had to endure. We had to involve the media to get our point across. We participated in talk shows, wrote news articles, and even went on national news, but our efforts were to no avail.

Dealing with urban people who know nothing about agriculture is an exercise in frustration. For example, one government rep thought a cattle-guard was a person hired to watch the cattle, and they weren't going to pay for that!

Laurel with baby chick.

Over the years, I juggled raising our children, teaching at a local school, and volunteering in the community, all while doing my fair share of farm and ranch work. My teaching job helped cover the cost of extras for the family and allowed me to travel.

The most devastating challenge in our lives is the loss of our beloved son, Carter. Alan and I and his sister Jenna miss him every day. There is a quote that I'd like to share: "There must be those among us whom we can sit down and weep with, and still be counted as warriors." We need to make it just as normal to talk about our pain as it is to talk about our joy.

I appreciate this opportunity to share a bit of my life's story. I'm very grateful and privileged to have spent my entire life connected to the land.

Laurel with her horse.

Chapter III

Traditional Autocratic Leadership Versus Collective Leadership

Written by Dorothy Louise Beasley

Autocratic Leadership: Boss/Owner Decides All:

One person, like the ranch owner, makes decisions without asking others. It's quick but doesn't use everyone's ideas.

"There is a difference between being a leader and being a boss. Both are based on authority. A boss demands blind obedience; a leader earns his authority through understanding and trust."
—Klaus Balkenhol

The drawbacks of Autocratic Leadership highlight the importance of considering various opinions for better decision-making.

Old Ways Stick Around:

Many ranches followed autocratic leadership because it worked for a long time. People didn't know another way, and if it works, why change it?

Family Ranches and Change:

As families grew, kids wanted to join in decisions. Some ranchers let them, but others kept deciding everything. This can make it hard for everyone to share ideas.

Downside of Autocratic Leadership:

Autocratic leadership in family-run livestock ranching businesses may impede innovation and the ability to adapt to necessary changes. While suitable for larger corporations, it proved problematic in Laurel's story above of government intervention using the War Measures Act. It was almost like dictatorship within a government organization when they **forced** Canadian livestock ranchers from the **ranches** that were their **livelihood** in 1941, during the Second World War.

This is only one example of poor decisions made by Autocratic Leadership: Autocratic Leadership challenges include a lack of consideration for affected families, and exclusion of various viewpoints (Canadian livestock ranchers were given 26 days to move their houses, barns, feed for their cattle, the cattle herds, other buildings, other livestock, machinery, etc., off the land). Local family history in Gem Community history book, *Dreams & Ditchbanks*, tells above information, plus how the ranchers were harassed by RCMP to make sure they got out within that time frame. The land then sat for months without anything happening and a very small amount of compensation for any of their property, livestock, livelihood was paid back by government.

Collective/Collaborative Leadership:

Teamwork Makes the Dream Work

In collective leadership, a diverse group collaborates to achieve common goals.

- Decisions involve everyone, empowering those with expertise.
- It prioritizes collaboration, teamwork, and shared responsibility.
- Ideal for family-run livestock ranching businesses.

Why Collective Leadership Matters:

- In today's complex world, no one leader knows everything.
- Collective leadership taps into the team's intelligence and expertise.
- Involving everyone creates ownership, engagement, and commitment.
- Encourages innovation by leveraging diverse perspectives.
- Leads to sustainable solutions benefiting the ranch and family.

Book Recommendation:

- *Generation To Generation: Life Cycles of the Family Business — This book offers insights into family business life cycles.*
- *The Leadership Mindset Weekly:52 weekly practices to transform your leadership mindset.*

Challenges in Family Businesses:

- Family businesses have overlapping subsystems: "The Family" and "The Business."
- Challenges arise as family members navigate both roles.
- Good business practices involve collaboration and feedback.

Unique Environment of Family Work:

- Working with family offers a unique, rewarding experience.
- Elements keeping the ranch moving forward:
  - Collaboration
  - Adaptability to challenges
  - Transparency and trust-building
  - Preserving Tradition & Embracing Change
  - Business-Minded Approach
- Promoting Accountability:
  - Make clear agreements and stick to them to keep everyone responsible.
  - Make sure that everyone in the family is accountable for their actions.
  - Regularly discuss family values, decisions, and how you communicate.

Leveraging Personality Traits:

- Learn about each family member's strengths and preferences.
- Build relationships by understanding and respecting each other.

- Assign tasks based on what each person is good at and enjoys.

Leadership Development:

- Practice being a good leader by facing challenges and learning.
- Spend time and effort solving problems and planning for the future.
- Inspire everyone by having a clear vision for the ranch.

- In *The Leadership Mindset Weekly* by Blaine Bartlett, he says as follows: "Effective Leadership is not for the faint of heart. It requires courage and discipline. As a leader, I am called on to move into the unknown, to go places I'm not certain of, and that others fear to tread. Not foolishly...but with discernment and a clear understanding of the "for the sake of what" I am undertaking this journey." With this quote in mind, have a clear understanding "for the sake of what" results you are working towards.

- Louise has learned through this leadership program, taught as *The Hidden Laws of Leadership* with John Boggs and Blaine Bartlett, through BTI, that awareness allows us to move forward with more choices. These choices were made visible through my new awareness that "If I can dream it, I can be and do it." (I have dreamed of writing a book for years; now I have become an author and written this book about ranch women.)

Continuous Education:

- Keep learning about how to run the ranch and improve it.

- Develop your "superpower," as Blaine Bartlett suggests, and develop your imagination as to what can be done through this leadership tool. Learn to develop your imagination as it is an empowering method to manifest what you want the business to look and feel like and who should be involved with it to help it to grow and prosper.

- Share knowledge within the family to help everyone grow.

- Invest time in overcoming challenges together for the ranch's success.

- Attend livestock producers' meetings to keep up with new industry knowledge.

In a nutshell, **autocratic leadership** may be quick, but it's not the best for a family-run ranch, unless a decision needs to be made in the "spur of the moment." For example, repairing a tractor right away, rather than stopping harvesting to discuss the situation.

Collaborative leadership allows a family-run ranching business to respect traditions while also being open to change. Any customers or neighbours that have ideas as to what changes might work if given a chance, improves the way people feel about your ranch too. Everyone on the team, all employees, all family members, right down to the children, have ideas and opinions that deserve to be heard and listened to. When the whole team talks and votes on decisions, everyone feels like they have contributed to the well-being of the ranch and its team members. Working together brings pride and puts your ranch in the best position to succeed.

"Outstanding leaders go out of their way to boost the self-esteem of their personnel. If people believe in themselves, it's amazing what they can accomplish."
—Sam Walton

Chapter IV

Gender Roles Don't Matter

Story of Rosemary Doonan

I was born in 1942, at Maple Creek, Saskatchewan, in late November and raised at Murraydale, Saskatchewan, for the first seven years of my life. Murraydale is 20 miles southeast of Maple Creek, up on the bench that runs from Elkwater, Alberta, to Eastend, Saskatchewan. The town of Eastend derived its name from being the "east end" of the bench. The bench, which rests above the Cypress Hills, is a high structure of land that is cooler in the summer and very cold, with deep snow, in wintertime.

My grandparents homesteaded at Murraydale in 1909. My father was born in 1914, the second of ten children. Times were tough during the First World War. Only the very determined were able to survive. Although my father only had a Grade 5 education—

because he was needed to help on the farm—he proved to be very intelligent and possessed many natural talents. He even learned to speak Cree fluently since he only had native children to play with while growing up. The Doonan farm adjoined the Nekaneet Reservation.

My parents, Robert (Bob) and Norah (Udal), were married in 1939 and lived at Murraydale until 1948. At that time, they were able to buy a place below the Cypress Hills, which was much more comfortable than living on the bench. I attended Murraydale country school for my first couple of years of school. It was a two-mile hike, so I rode an old, reliable horse as transportation.

Growing up, we did not have running water or power in our homes until 1955. The family bathed once a week in a square aluminium tub, and we shared the water, which was heated on the wood-burning kitchen stove. We had outdoor toilets, and I must say that they were not comfortable in the winter months.

When we moved from Murraydale to our home below the Cypress Hills, I attended Hay Creek country school. Again, transportation was on horseback, except in winter, when we drove a pony hitched to a cutter sleigh because it was warmer.

There were no boys in the family, so I was designated to help my father with outside work. I enjoyed these tasks because I am an outdoor person. When summer holidays arrived, I got on a 1947 John Deere tractor with a seven-foot mower attached and mowed hay at both properties all summer. The tractor had a hand clutch. Since I was too small to reach it, I would partially slide off the seat and push it in with my foot. That was my job until I returned to school in the fall. My salary was 25 cents per week. With that money, I could go to a movie in Maple Creek on Saturday night.

The movie cost 15 cents, popcorn was 5 cents, and a pop or chocolate bar was another 5 cents.

While attending Hay Creek school, I rode green (untamed) horses for my (Udal) cousins as they were too young to train them. Horses were used extensively then. Loping them over the hills to school every day soon got them trained. The country schools closed in 1958, at which time we were bussed to school in Maple Creek.

I graduated from high school in 1962 and then moved to Medicine Hat, Alberta, to attend Business College. I graduated from Business College in April 1963 with a Gold Seal Certificate, which meant all my marks were over 90 percent. Three days later, I secured my first job at Eaton's department store, which I endured for 15 years. I got married in 1975, after which my husband and I managed a 1,500-head feedlot, west of Medicine Hat. It was great being back in the country, but unfortunately, the marriage ended in 1982 in a brutal divorce.

After that, I purchased a home in Medicine Hat where I lived for 15 years. I got a job on a 2,500-head feedlot known as JOG Management and worked for John Gay. When that feedlot sold, John saw an ad in the newspaper wanting financial planners. With his persuasion I applied, took a securities course, and spent the next 27 years with Investor's Group. I retired from that career January 30, 2013.

John and I purchased a quarter of land in the Many Islands district, northeast of Medicine Hat, in 1994. Between the two of us, we cleaned and dismantled all the old buildings and built the place where I still reside today. Unfortunately, John had to leave in 2002 due to poor health. He passed away in 2019. In 2004, I purchased an adjoining quarter and ran purebred black Angus cattle for a few years.

Rosemary loving her land check round up cattle at 83 yrs young.

After my parents passed, I was able to buy out my two sisters' shares of the home place at Maple Creek. I now purchase yearling steers in the Spring and graze them: some at the Maple Creek home place and some here where I live. I sell the cattle in early fall. I also feed and enjoy riding a couple of horses all year round.

Open country is my life. I will be 82 years old this November, and if my health holds, I intend to continue to do what I love. I enjoy carpentry, riding horses, checking my cattle, breathing fresh air, and enjoying the scenery of both my places. Freedom at its best.

I appreciate this opportunity to share a briefing of my life, which has been an experience to say the least. While I have experienced severe tragedy, I have lived through it and manage to rise above it each and every day.

Rosemary's black angus grass fed yearling steers, 2023

Chapter V

Innovation & Life on Horseback

Pat Suitor's story, as told by Pat herself.

This story all started on January 7, 1939. I was the youngest of three kids, born to Jim and Georgie Brodie. First, Kenneth (K.O.), Donna, and then me, Pat. My life has kind of centred around the Red Deer River, from as far north as the Thumbhill Ranch at Dorothy and east to the Atlee district. I'm 83 years old now, so I better get writing!

K.O., Donna & Patsy Brodie on Whistler (Horse)

Jim, my dad, was foreman on the Thumbhill Ranch from 1940 to 1946. Georgie, my mom, cooked for the men, helped with the riding, and looked after us three kids. She made most of our clothes by hand, mostly out of old jeans, shirts, and dresses. And sometimes flour and sugar sacks! We rode to a school located on the ranch hayfield, and I started Grade 1 there. In the winter, Georgie and us kids moved into a small house by the railroad track in Dorothy, and we attended the Dorothy School. Everything at the ranch was done by horses: riding horses for cattle work and heavy horses for haying. Us kids had horses we could ride, but the favourite was Whistler. Donna could help K.O. onto him, and I could help Donna on, but there was no one to help me on! Sometimes, they'd let me hold on to his tail and walk along with them—but only if they wanted me to. And then we had a smaller kind of a pony given to us. We could ride it, but it would go under the clothesline and wipe us off. It was one of the ponies used in the coal mines at Drumheller to pull the coal cars from underground up to the loading area. These ponies were kept underground, and some would go blind from the light when they were brought out. Our pony was totally blind.

There was a lot of haying to do as the winters are long and cold there, all done by hand. But somehow, there was time for a little fun. Occasionally, there'd be a keg of beer at the table, and ranch hands and neighbours would come over. Jim would play his banjo, Georgie a mandolin, and Delbert Gillespie, with his banjo, would entertain. Alex Gillespie owned the ranch. He lived in Calgary, and when he came out to the ranch, us kids were excited. He always had chocolate bars for us in the glove compartment of his car.

We left Dorothy in 1946, and Jim worked for Cliff Sewall at the Cowoki Ranch near Brooks. Us kids attended the One Tree School, which was six miles north of the ranch. We drove Teddy, a workhorse-type, on a toboggan and later a sleigh in the winter. Our sandwiches, usually made of fried eggs, would be frozen when we got there. The teacher, Mr. Block, would not let us bring our lunch bucket into the classroom to thaw by the coal-fired heater. Frozen egg sandwiches weren't that good. And in the spring, after the snow was gone, we'd drive Teddy on a democrat. He didn't like the shafts on either side of him and would run away with us. K.O. wasn't strong enough to hold him. We'd usually bail out of the democrat, and he'd run into the schoolyard. One time, he even ripped a wheel off. That teacher never even came out of the school. We survived and never got hurt.

Carrots or Carrot Pie

Georgie cooked for the men there, too, and one day, she served carrots as the vegetable. The men didn't eat them all, so the next day, she mashed them, added sugar and spices, and served them as pie. They didn't even realize it until she told them. Next time she served turnips, and one of the men said, "Eat them up or we'll get them in a pie tomorrow!"

From there, we moved on to Calgary, where Jim was a brand inspector at the old Calgary Stockyard. He was able to take his horses there and enjoyed the job and the people. Georgie and us kids didn't like city living, even though we could just walk to school. K.O. had to fight with the kids who didn't understand our country ways. So, Calgary was a short stay. We moved back to Jenner country and attended Jenner School. We were at the Keay Ranch, only a mile or so away from Jenner, so we could walk to school. It was good to be back with country people and near the Red Deer River.

In 1948, and Jim took the job of running the Atlee Buffalo Community Pasture for the Special Areas. Local ranchers and farmers could graze a given amount of cattle in there during the summers. It was about 90 sections, broken into 4 pastures, so there was a lot of riding and fencing. That's where us kids really learned to be cowboys (and cowgirls): lots of long, hot rides looking after cattle. Sometimes, my sister Donna and I would ride about 30 miles to visit our friends, the Campbell family, for the weekend. Our folks never knew if we made it or not until we returned home Sunday evening. One time, we were late leaving Campbells, and it got dark on us. But Jim, our dad, always taught us that if we were ever lost, give your horse his head, and he'll bring you home. We did, and we made it home. In the summer, we mostly rode horses to school. Again, six miles north in the morning and six miles home in the evening. Sometimes, if the weather was too bad, Jim would drive us in. K.O. went to stay at our grandparents' place in Jenner and went to school and helped with the farm. In the winters we moved to Atlee, so we were close to school.

The Atlee store was the hub of the community—the post office and the train depot—so groceries were bought there. Things like canned milk, canned vegetables, SPAM (a not-very-good, canned meat), cheese, bologna, flour, potatoes, etc. And, of course, Georgie canned lots of antelope and deer. That was a lot of work. Butchering was done by Jim, and Georgie did the rest. And in the summer, hauling water up from the spring and into a boiler to boil the jars full of cut-up meat on the wood cookstove, usually fuelled by old fence posts sawed and chopped to fit. No big deal, that's just the way it was. There were a lot of good times there at Atlee, with playing canasta, going to the show in Buffalo occasionally, and sometimes dances with the local music makers.

I took my last years of school (8, 9, and part of 10) by correspondence. The lessons were sent out by mail from Edmonton and supervised at school by a lower grades' teacher, then sent back to Edmonton to be checked and graded. I did get my grade 9 diploma. And drama class was the Christmas concerts! Oh, and bath time before the Christmas concert. Water was hauled up in a pail from the spring, heated on the wood stove, and poured into a galvanized bathtub. The youngest child, being me, bathed first, then the next oldest, and so on. We were at Atlee for six years! A long time for us. Such good friends and neighbours.

Ranch & Rodeo Queen

Then Jim got offered the job of cow foreman at the V Bar V Ranch at Wardlow, owned by Credit Foncier out of Montreal. The ranch had land on both sides of the Red Deer River, North of Jenner. We moved to the Cow Camp, the old Tom Owens place where Art and Frances Klassen now live. We were able to take our horses there, and it was also a great place to live. We had a kerosene fridge and a large generator for power. Credit Foncier paid for groceries that we ordered off a very long list. We ate well there. Georgie got paid for any hired men that needed to be fed. One day, she set an extra plate because headquarters was sending the farmhand down. But the farmhand was a machine! The hired men at the Cow Camp lived in a bunkhouse in the yard. They were good hands and fun to be around. Jim had bought a little old army jeep, and Donna and I drove it mostly to Wardlow or to Patricia to visit the family of friend Alice Owen for some weekends of fun. It was open air, so in the winter, we would cover up with a buffalo robe to keep us warm.

We met many more good neighbours at Wardlow, and JoLee Anderson (Godfrey) would ride 7 miles through 7 gates to visit us. While there, Dirk Scholten came out with cattle buyers to buy the 2-year-old steers. We had corralled them at the Halisbury Stock Yards to be loaded onto cattle cars on the Canadian Pacific Railway. They were shipped East to Ontario. Dirk saw Donna and me riding and wanted one of us to run for Medicine Hat Rodeo Queen. I did, and became Rodeo Princess in 1956, and Medicine Hat Rodeo Queen in 1957. My daughter, Connie, was Brooks Rodeo Queen in 1978. I met more people during the contests and appearances and made more good friends.

In 1955, the V Bar V Ranch sold to a Calgary syndicate. They had started farming some of the land. The 78,000-acre V Bar V Ranch, and cattle, sold for a half million dollars. This didn't sit well with Jim, so he went to work for Gene Burton South of Medicine Hat.

"Results"

Poem written by Pat 1955

White face cattle, grass growing high
Was once the scene that met the eye
Cowboys riding across the hills
Alone with their numerous thrills and spills.

Horses bucking and running loose
Free from the feel of a cowboy's noose
But now with the outfit changing hands
There's a different outlook of the lands.

Big red tractors, wheat growing high
Is now the scene that meets the eye
Plows, combines, harrows and cats
Turning up sod along the flats.

Fences, machines, and people near
Have taken the freedom that once was here
Someday it may change again
And the cattle country will once more reign.

I moved to Brooks to work and lived with my grandmother there. While in Brooks, I started going out with Shorty Suitor. He and his parents ranched on the Red Deer River at the Hutton Ferry. We were married on June 9, 1958. Now, again, I was on the Red Deer River. The Hutton Ferry was just down the road past the ranch house. The ranch house had been a stopping house for the stagecoach from Bassano to Richfield, which was driven by Felix Warren. The stopping house was called the Glenview. Shorty bought a house at Wayne near Drumheller, and it had to be moved across the river. But the bridge was too narrow. We had to wait until the river was low enough for the mover to ford it across the river. Then we had a home! And 32-volt power that could run lights. And if the wind blew or the Delco was running, we could use a 32-volt iron, toaster, and other utilities! There were cisterns on the hill to haul river water into, so we had running water and sewers. Pretty modern!

Anyway, we ran a cow-calf operation and raised horses. We sold the grade mares and bought registered quarter horse mares and studs. We got into King Leo Bar and Two Eyed Jack breeding. Had a lot of fun with the horses, going to many sales, selling, and buying a few. I would ride the broken horses and show them in the sale ring and lead the unbroken ones (usually yearlings) while Shorty was getting them all ready to go through the sale. Sold at many Alberta auction marts, and into B.C. to Kamloops and Williams Lake.

"Life on a Ranch"

Poem by Pat

What does ranching mean to me?
It's a way of life I'd say
A cup of coffee with a neighbour
That stopped as he passed this way.

It's the quiet and calm of an early morn
As I saddle my horse and ride
Checking that heifer, it's calving time
The calf's up and feeding at her side.

It's seeing spring happen, grass turning green
A new little colt being born
While the anxious mother, with nervous eyes
Watches the coyotes so forlorn.

It's starting to ride a 3-year-old colt
He'll be a good one, of course
There's nothing more rewarding
Than working with a horse.

It's waiting for the rains to come
To make the hay grow tall
Cutting and baling and hauling it in
But the works never done in the fall.

Cause then it's time to start feeding again
And through the winter I'll try
To catch up on my housework
Do the books, maybe make a pie
(etc...)

Yes, ranching is my way of life
It's busy, there's many a task
But I live the life that I like best
And I'm happy, what more could I ask!

Pat & Shorty's Children

On Feb 9, 1961, our daughter Connie was born in Brooks Hospital. At that time, mother and baby were kept in the hospital for several days to make sure all was well with both. When Shorty came to take us home, the roads north of the river were pretty much snowed in. So, he decided we'd travel the river. It was frozen over solid—we hoped. So, with the Oldsmobile car and new baby, we drove as fast as possible through snow drifts and made it home just fine. It was a little more work now with our baby girl, and cloth diapers were used. I'd rinse them after each diaper change. Then, after most were used, I machine-washed them all and hung them out to dry. Now that was cold on the hands! And then brought in the frozen diapers to dry on a rack. Just the way it was, and all was good.

Our son, Murray, was born on October 4th, 1963. Since I got a lot of baby practice with Connie, it was easier the second time around. I sure had Connie potty trained before Murray was born—doing diapers in winter wasn't fun. Shorty's mom was very good to help with the kids, so I still did a lot of riding and outside work. Shorty's dad, Andy Suitor, passed away in 1964. And so, before too long, Mrs. Suitor left the ranch to live with her other son, Lloyd. So, then we moved into the big ranch house, and our extra help, Ken and Marg Olmstead, moved into ours.

We had a bad blizzard just before Christmas that blocked all our roads. We didn't have our Christmas shopping done, or any extra food in, but Marg and I found whatever we could to wrap for gifts, just something to open anyway. And Ken Suitor got as far as Flanagan's, our neighbours, borrowed their tractor and a toboggan and brought a turkey, a tree, and my parents over the snow drifts, down the hills, and we had a great Christmas.

It was probably later that year that Gordon Douglass (the Author's dad) came with his Caterpillar to plow snow off the roads and brought us an orphaned pig. It thought it was a dog, running around the house outside, playing with the dogs. They'd make three laps around while Piglet made one lap. I had never liked pigs and was kind of scared of them. But Piglet made me realize that pigs were quite smart and even had a bit of personality.

Connie and Murray attended Cessford School, about 15-20 miles east of us. They were picked up and brought home by the big yellow school bus. Sure, beats the transportation I used to get to school! They had good, fun bus drivers, so it was pretty much fun for them going to school. Thanks to Lou Nester and Stanley Andrus, as they were the bus drivers. New Cessford School taught from Grade 1 through 12, and it still does. I joined the Women's Institute mostly for the chance to meet all the neighbours. Meetings were held and hosted in a different member's home each meeting, so I not only met neighbours, but I also got to go to their places and see where they lived.

Most kids had horses and rode, and a horse 4-H Club was formed. I was elected by the members to be their leader after Art Klassen quit. Quite an honour for me! Albert McBride was my assistant and taught the kids how to make cowhide into braided reins and mohair cinches, breast collars, leather hobbles, and much more. We all learned about riding and teaching horses. We had practice days, trail rides along the river, and the grand finale, achievement day with certified judges. We went to rodeo parades with 15-20 members and won our classes in Brooks and Medicine Hat. A lot of good times, like tobogganing on the Red Deer River hills in winter. What a great set of parents and kids to work with. We all had fun and learned to do by doing. 4-H helped my kids to prepare for showing their horses at horse shows, and they did well. Connie with her horse K.C., and Murray with Tabby.

Pat & Team Roping

But then I started team roping in 1974. So, after 5 years at 4-H, I quit being a leader and went on to be an aspiring team roper. First, using Connie's horse, K.C., then later riding my black horse, B.J. (a colt from Murray's mare, Tabby). Connie and Murray both roped, but by then, Connie was through school and out working, so she didn't have much time for roping. Murray did quite a bit on Tabby. I roped in the Canadian Girls Rodeo Association and won the

Canadian Championship saddle in 1977. I also won the Cowgirl of the Year award in 1982.

Back to ranching and branding, between 4-H and roping. Branding was always a big community affair, with neighbours helping neighbours. Some work and a lot of fun. The prairie oysters were served in the corral during the branding as hors d'oeuvres before the big meal. The meal was mostly made ahead of time so the women could help with roping, vaccinating, or whatever. Everyone had a cold one during branding breaks and after with the meal.

Pat's Prairie Oysters (Recipe)

Collect the calf-fries in clean, cold water and clean immediately, taking off all gristle until only the ball is left and put into more clean, cold water.

Butterfly each one from end to end.

Put into flour, seasoned with seasoning salt, garlic salt, and pepper.

Put into the frying pan that has melted butter on medium heat. Add butter if needed.

Fry on all sides by turning each one over as it browns. Cook well.

Serve in an easy to carry container. Offer toothpicks to the crew to stab the fries for eating!

Then to the hayrides. February 9, to celebrate Connie's birthday. These were pulled by the tractor on the hay-hauling wagon with a lot of straw. There would be a contest for the best booze holder, prizes hid along the trail to be found first, and a bonfire on the river. The rides went upriver to the Bullpound Bridge and back either on the ice or the riverbanks. Ages of people from 1 to 75!

We hosted trail rides for the neighbouring ladies. We rode from Richard and Cassie Peake's place down the Bullpound Coulee to our ranch. And another from our place downriver to Emerson Bridge on Highway 36. Eleanor Gillespie from Finnegan was with us, too. Some of the ladies said they hadn't ridden since they rode to school.

1983 was the year of weddings and anniversaries. Both kids got married, and Shorty and I celebrated our 25th wedding anniversary. And my parents, Jim and Georgie, celebrated their 50th anniversary. Our kids gave Shorty and me plane tickets to Hawaii. It was a great trip.

Irrigation became available with water pumped out of the Red Deer River for the Deadfish Irrigation Project. We put a pivot system at the old Hutton townsite and put in grass and alfalfa, so we were finally able to know we would have feed. We had been using a small square baler, and on the dry grassland I could help with handling bales. They'd weigh about 50lbs. But now the bales off the pivot field were too heavy. And so, one less job for me! That was good 'cause now I had become a grandmother!

Krista was born on August 18th, 1984, to Ivan and Connie Gomke. But she was only a few days old when she was diagnosed with a heart problem, Truncus Arteriosus. The only doctor doing the needed operation was in San Francisco, California. So, parents and grandparents (Shorty and I) went with her. It was a very stressful time for all our families, but she came through the operation, and as I'm writing this, she is preparing for her wedding.

Unwanted Changes…. We Carried Onwards

Shorty had not been well for a while, and we lost him in December of 1984. Tough times for our family. Murray, Carrie, and I carried on with the ranch. Doing business with cattle buyers, oil patch, horse business, and all. But we found most people very fair with all the dealings, and all seemed to go ok. We cut down the size of the brood mare band but kept about 15 mares and a stud. We sold by auction and a sale at the ranch in 1986. We maintained the cattle herd. Murray and Carrie had set up their home about a quarter mile from the ranch yard, down in the trees by the river. So, we decided it was time for them to move up into the yard and into the ranch house. I bought a new house trailer and set up down in their yard, moved in a little building and made it into a barn, and built a corral and pen. Then me and my horses moved in, in 1987. This worked well for all of us. I lost both my parents that spring, Georgie in March and Jim in May. They had retired into Duchess, where Jim kept his two saddle horses and rode until he died. Georgie, even with poor eyesight, enjoyed friends and family and playing her banjo. They lived in their own house right to the end.

By now, Charlie Chick had come into my life. He had bought some of the mares from our 1986 horse sale, and he just kept visiting me after that. Everyone liked Charlie, and we had some good times together. And I became Grandma again to Laci Louise Suitor, born to Murray and Carrie on April 2, 1989. We had good hired help, and it freed up time for us to go south to Arizona in our motorhomes for the winter holidays. We took quads down and learned a lot about the Yuma, Maricopa, and Quartzite areas. I spent quite a bit of time in Maricopa, and had good friends there, most all from Canada. We called it Little Canada. It was fun to be home at the ranch, too, for skidooing and tobogganing down the river hills behind the house. Neighbours would join in, and there were quite a few visiting the chiropractor after.

In 1996 the Western Stockgrowers were having a cattle drive to commemorate 100 years since being formed. They were starting their drive from the Rafter T Cattle Company at Buffalo across the British Block, an area of land with no fences or buildings for 40 miles, south toward Medicine Hat. Rafter T was owned by Tom Osadczuk and family, and Tom and I were together now, so I was able to go on this drive. I phoned my sister Donna, living in Savona, B.C., to come join me! I had a horse for her to ride and asked her to please come! And she did! It was the first we had ridden together in 35 years. It was great, and the cattle drive was very successful. Then, on July 14, 1997, my grandson Chance was born to Don and Connie Edelmann. So now I'm grandma to three grandkids!

Tom and I went to Arizona and stayed in Doug and Irene Gray's yard at Maricopa. Then, we bought the acreage across the road from them in 1998. We spent winters there, and at the ranch in Jenner in summers. Leaving the Red Deer River and the ranch, my home for 40 years, was very hard for me. As the saying goes, "You do what you got to do," and I did it.

Life at Tom's was good, still living on a ranch and doing ranch work. And I'd taken two of my saddle horses with me and kept on riding and even roped a bit again. I had my house trailer from the Suitor ranch moved to the acreage in Arizona. It was still furnished just the way I'd left it, and it made Maricopa feel more at home. So, let's see... I moved to Tom's in 1997... now it's 2022.

That makes it 25 years of living in Jenner. And still go to the Jenner rodeo grounds for rodeos and points days, still along the Red Deer River. Murray, Carrie, and Laci sold the Suitor Ranch, and bought an acreage East of Red Deer, still on the Red Deer River. And I still enjoy family, friends, and fun. Life's good.

Photo: Tom standing beside horse, Pat on horse, branding day

Chapter VI

Home on the Range & Teamwork...

Kerrie (Armstrong) Kusler

I was born in 1954 to Arnold and Shirley Armstrong of the East and West Ranch, located south of Bassano. Mom was raised at Countess, Alberta, and Dad was raised on the original East & West Ranch in the Cypress Hills. Grandpa George, Dad, and his two brothers—Bob and Peter—expanded to Bassano in 1946 and continued to ranch together until 1983. For the record, the East and West was so named because one of the original Faucett brothers started that ranch and lived in Nova Scotia.

We lived on the Teigland place, which was purchased by the Armstrong brothers in 1952. It was near the Bow River, straight south of Bassano, about 15 miles. In those days, the roads were not great. Dad and Mom had an old one-ton truck to drive. One time, Mom and I went into Bassano with the "old Grey Ghost," as we referred to it. Mom shifted up and managed to stall the truck right on the railroad crossing. Of course, there was a train coming, so she gave it one chance and managed to get the truck started and off the tracks. Mom was fully prepared to grab me and run. In those days there were no safety seats, so extricating me would not have been as difficult as it would be now.

I remember the old International WD9 tractor that was used for many things, including to run the "farmhand"—a giant pitchfork-like tool used to gather hay stooks or, eventually, bales to be stacked by a hard-working crew. I'm old enough to remember stooked oats. Dad hired boys from the Blackfoot Reserve to do the stacking.

When Sam Wilson was employed at the ranch, Dad decided it would be a great idea to drill a water well. Dad had a drill bit made at the local welding shop, and they rented a pump from the E.I.D. The farmhand was used to hold up the pipe. About 40 feet down, they hit a rock. Dad, being a dynamite "expert," decided to try and move the rock. The resulting explosion lifted the ground about a foot and sent a sand geyser about 200 feet into the air. After bailing sand out of the hole for two days, they decided to try a second hole in the middle of the yard. Everything was running quite successfully when the two-inch pipe blew apart and flew around like a snake, spewing mud through the open window of my mom's new green '54 Plymouth. After that, they were ready to quit drilling for wells. In the evening, Grandfather Armstrong showed up. He suggested to Sam that the next time Dad came up with one of these ideas, he should try and talk him out of it.

I did not see very many children my age except for my cousins. Uncle Bob would bring Gena and sometimes Kathy or George along to play while he and Dad talked over their plans for the farm and ranch operation.

Further down the Bow River, we had our summer range, referred to as "Scottie's Camp." The camp yard consisted of a two-room shack with a cook stove and kitchen cupboard. There was also a small barn. Our ranch employed an "old country Scotsman" named Ed Lewis (Scottie), who oversaw the cattle during calving season and on into the summer and fall. We kids loved a trip down to see Scottie. We delivered the weekly supply of groceries and checked on how things were going. He did not own a vehicle and relied solely on his horse for transportation. We delighted in a bucket full of clam shells he'd gathered from the riverbed for us, and miraculously, he always had a stick of Wrigley's gum handy. I remember the old pot-bellied stove used to heat the social room at the Bassano Curling rink. Dad purchased it to heat the shop.

In the winter, we had hired men to help feed with a team and hay rack on sleigh runners. They had a little bunkhouse in the yard with a coal and wood stove for heat. Scottie wintered there as well and would become very ornery by spring. Mom had to have had a pretty good sense of humour. Scottie told Dad he had better give the preacher another $10.00 because Mom was such a good cook. Sam Wilson, from Eastern Canada, was great at carpentry. We kids were outfitted with a lovely set of bunk beds and a little wooden rocking horse. He remained a close family friend until his passing.

Funny Recollections

Mom raised chickens, and I can still remember the odious process of butchering. One time, my parents decided to get rid of some tough old laying hens, so they threw them into the slough. Well, much to their surprise, the chickens swam to shore. I, being about four years old at the time, thought this was the most hilarious thing ever!

Our ranch yard was situated in line with the river crossing that the cowboys from the XL Ranch (McKinnon's) used to cross on the ice. This meant that our place was a great stop-over for a meal and a visit on their way by. It was always a treat to have company because we lived far from town. It's funny how the Fuller Brush man, the Electrolux vacuum cleaner salesman, and the Jehovah's Witnesses were always able to find us.

Our garden was about a quarter of a mile east of the yard, beside a dugout from which Mom could pump water. When they first started the garden patch, Mom suggested that it was time to work it up for planting. Dad was on his way back to the yard after seeding oats and decided to run the Surflex Disk Tiller over the garden. He neglected to disconnect the seed box. This resulted in Mom having to weed oats out of her vegetables all summer. I have no idea how she managed to get any produce, as there would have been a lot of competition out there.

Though antelope were the most abundant, we did not have deer in the area back then. Once, when I was probably three, I was down at the garden, and a curious antelope appeared. I remember holding out my hand and gently encouraging him to come closer. He was maybe twenty feet away when our dogs came running and scared him away. I was very disappointed, but Dad said that he may have attacked me. Fortunately, I lived to tell the story. Dad brought home an orphaned baby antelope one time. I was very sad when Dad decided that he could get in trouble with Fish and Game, so he took it back out on the prairie. Another time, he brought home a coyote pup. The little fellow would yip and howl if he heard me crying in the house.

We had a 32-volt wind charger and a fence line telephone that connected to Uncle Bob and Aunt Verna's house south of Bassano. Mom used a gas iron that had a kerosene tank, which she pumped up so that the little burner would heat the iron. We had what was referred to as the "washhouse" about 50 feet from the main house. It had a bathroom with hot running water and a claw-foot bathtub that I later installed in my new home on the Q Ranch. In that washhouse was mom's wringer washer. In the basement was a propane water heater. One time, when I was quite small, Mom was having trouble with it. I remember watching over the edge of the basement opening when Mom lit the heater. There had been a propane leak, which caused a huge bubbly fireball. Fortunately for Mom and me, it extinguished itself. Mom sustained burns on her ankles, but otherwise, she was all right. In the winter, she would hang the wash out; it would freeze stiff, and then she'd bring it in and hang it on a clothes horse. I never did understand the wisdom in all that work. She said that they dried faster and that the clothes being outside were sanitized by the sun. The clothes that needed to be ironed were "sprinkled" with water and rolled up to be kept damp because there were no steam irons.

We had a cistern in the yard that brought cold running water into the kitchen sink, and Mom had a propane fridge and stove. The house was originally two granaries pulled together. A porch and a sun porch with glass all around were add-ons. I loved to sleep in the sun porch in the summer.

Little Frogs

One year, it rained at just the right time, resulting in an explosion of little frogs. They were everywhere! My playground included an old straw stack (which I used as a slide), a well-built barn with a loft, and a sheep shed with a page wire and straw roof. I remember a giant snowy owl that lived in the trees. His huge wingspan made him look ominous to a four-year-old. Eventually it was time for me to go to school, so the ranch expanded to include the Ben Plumer place just south of where my cousins lived. This included irrigation, so we were able to grow more hay. Mom always regretted the move, but there were many advantages to living closer to Bassano. School, sports, church, and community activities were much easier to participate in. My brother Bill was born in 1956, and Grant came in 1959, right before we moved in 1960.

Bill and Grant were both characters. Bill started collecting antiques at about age six. They both loved guns, and Bill collected many throughout his short life. He taught himself how to load his own ammo and skin and tan coyotes, badgers, and beavers. He trapped muskrats and sold coyote pelts to supplement his hobbies. The love of flying was passed down from our dad, who learned to fly later in life. Bill and Grant both became very good pilots. Bill took great delight in striking terror into the hearts of his flying instructors. He went on to become an airplane maintenance engineer and had almost completed his apprenticeship when tragedy struck. He was fatally injured when he and our cousin, Pete Burrows, crashed Dad's Aeronca on the Bow River. It was a very sad time for our family, to say the least.

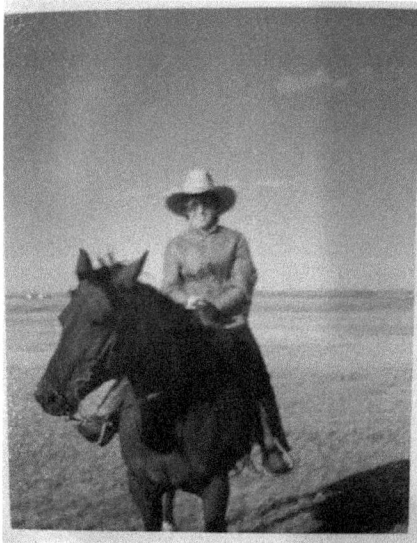

Grant used his Super Cub for many things, including visiting friends near and far, going to brandings, checking cows, and helping the RCMP "get their man," plus search and rescue. He could land anywhere because he had large tundra tires. One time, he landed too hard on a river sandbar and broke a bungee cord. He happened to have his fencing "come along" on board, so he rigged it to hold the wheels in position. He flew it that way for quite a while.

During the month of July, my dad ran an artificial insemination (AI) program. That created many good times as he and my brothers set up a camp and corrals about 20 miles south of the main ranch. I did not get to help a lot. I stayed back at the home place to assist with Mom's huge garden and yard. Mom and I took meals down on Sundays and usually spent the afternoon swimming at Snake Lake. There were many good times and practical jokes. Sometimes, they would get "surprise" visitors. On one occasion, some pranksters decided to turn their horses loose and remove the keys from Dad's truck. Mysteriously, some domestic chickens got locked in the truck as well. One can only imagine the mess. Grant had an ornery mare named Suzie that was not discovered in her secluded pen, so Grant was able to use her to find the rest of their horses. Another time, Bill and Grant dyed some gophers black with the dye used to mark cattle. It was funny when some biologists showed up to study these strange gophers.

I had a very smooth horse named Rocky during my high school years. Dad did not encourage us to take part in riding clubs. He wanted the horses reserved for "ranch work."

We all had 4-H calves, which was a great experience. One highlight was that Dad and some neighbours organized a trail ride in the Cypress Hills. Our base camp was at Graburn Gap. We had a great time swimming our horses in Battle Creek at Fort Walsh. We kids spent many hours at the Bassano swimming pool each summer. Mom and Aunt Verna would take turns running us into town for the afternoon. In return, they could have some peace and quiet. My girl cousins and I all went on to pass our Royal lifesaving and instructor classes. These certifications allowed us to work at the pool in the summer, teaching swimming lessons and lifeguarding. It was a great way to raise some money for college.

I studied Animal Health Technology at the Saskatchewan Institute of Applied Arts and Sciences and at the WCVM in Saskatoon. Many lifelong friends were made, and our AHT class has managed, up until the Covid situation, to hold a reunion every five years. I worked for a short time at a clinic in Lethbridge and then joined an Embryo Transplant team west of Claresholm. My long-time school friend, Marilyn Wood, worked for Lucasia Ranches near the Transplant Centre. We really enjoyed life in the Porcupine Hills and working with livestock.

Bruce Kusler and I were married in 1977. The Kusler family had ranched near Walsh, Alberta, but in 1971, purchased the Q Ranch at Wildhorse. Bruce and I were fortunate to be able to live in the historical old house for two years. It had been added onto many times. The original part was built by the Day Brothers and then added onto by the Gilchrist family. It was unique, with four bedrooms, two bathrooms, a dining room, an L-shaped living room, an office, and a landing that served as a hallway. Every space between the bedroom doors was turned into drawers and tiny closets. The house was log and plaster, with a dirt basement and a foundation that was not in great condition. Several layers of shingles on the roof kept the rain out. There were so many porches we lost count. I believe there were nine doors to the outside, all together. The most significant was the porch where they fed the hired men. Food was served through an opening from the kitchen. I discovered a bullet hole in the window casing in the kitchen. There were layers of wallpaper from bygone days. The house was equipped with two walk-in coolers, complete with big, heavy, insulated doors and a place to hold large blocks of ice. There were canning shelves in the basement with doors that could be locked. We were surprised to discover two cement hot tubs that Mr. Gilchrist had built in the sun porch. There was a heated water system rigged so that he could run hot water into the cement tubs to ease the pain of his arthritis. There was a gas collection system set up to supply fuel to the antiquated hot water tank.

Kerrie's Jackhammer Experience

Bruce and I weren't married very long when I asked if there was a way to turn up the hot water. So that evening, he went down and adjusted the gas feed. The next morning, I went to use the washroom and flushed the toilet. The whole place started to rumble and shudder, sounding like a jackhammer. I went racing back to wake up Bruce, screaming. "Do something!" I'm sure my eyes were as big as saucers. He got up, and we turned on all the taps. There was steam coming out of the hot water and the cold-water faucets. We were so lucky that the old plumbing held.

Because the Sage Creek flooded our land in the spring, there were few locations on the ranch where we could build our new homes. When we had to tear down the original Q ranch house, it broke my heart. The Days, the Gilchrists, and many other families had history in that home. Eventually, Bruce and I built a new yard and home on the west side of the lake. Our son Winston was born in 1981, followed by Daniel in 1984. When we were expecting Winston, we were living in the little tin house in the main yard. My sister-in-law referred to it as the honey-moon shack because we all got a turn in it. It had tin siding and windows that would rattle during a windstorm. One particularly hot, dry, windy April, I remember thinking, "After two long days of listening to those windows go tack-tack-tack, that weather was enough to send any pioneer woman running into this desert, screaming and tearing her hair." I was thinking of the women who lived in sod huts with terrible windows and doors, trying to endure a two or three-day windstorm with dust sifting down from the ceiling. Many endured bone-aching loneliness as well. Someone said that this country was hard on women and horses. They weren't wrong.

When Winston was a baby, the Alberta Health Unit had a home visitation program. It was funny because we had just moved into our "new" home. The nurse had brought her husband along because she thought she may get lost in the "wilderness." When she came in, the first thing out of her mouth was, "You have running water!" I retorted, "Yes, and I also have a built-in vacuum system!"

I love cross-country skiing and skied on the prairie and lake when there was enough snow. One very cold morning, I remember skiing up onto the hill north of our lake. Over the rise were about 300 antelope resting there. The deafening silence and crisp morning light made it an incredible moment. We did not have many neighbours. The One Four Research station to the west had several families employed. There was a good-sized community hall at which our Ladies' Club met once a month to do various projects and visit. We always held a large community Christmas dinner, complete with a Santa and our local dance band. One of the best projects was our two-volume cookbook, *Home on The Range*.

Two particularly memorable winters were my first, 1977-78 and 78-79. The wind blew every day in February. We had an old caterpillar, which Bruce used to break trail down to the cows every day and then back again as the trail would be blown in again. It had no heater. I remember helping to feed out some old hay frozen into solid chunks one could barely manage with a pitchfork. Shovelling out troughs for the calves was another fun job during those winters. The winters could be very long, and occasionally we would be snowed in. I was very upset when I could not go to my Grandparent's fiftieth wedding anniversary celebration.

Living on the #41 highway was interesting in that the Port of Wildhorse, U.S.A., closed at 5:00 p.m. in the winter and 9:00 p.m. in the summer, so there was not a lot of traffic at night. If one got stranded, they were generally on their own. That first winter, snow drifts were so deep that we could only see out the top of the window in the living room of the old house. One afternoon, I heard something walking on the roof and discovered it was a deer. He had been pawing for forage on our lawn and decided he'd try the roof, even though the season for Rudolph was over. It was nothing to have a couple hundred pheasants feeding on the leftovers in the calf fence. The cows were eating hay off the top of the feed bunks that had eight-foot plywood walls.

The following spring was memorable. The creek came down early and caught us by surprise. Some of the calves were trapped on the other side, and of course, the guys needed help, so I was on a horse. Riding in the cold water, with ice cakes, I was very afraid we'd wind up swimming, as I had no sense of where the creek was and where I should go to avoid slipping in with my horse. Needless to say, I really was not much help that day.

It was a challenge every spring to predict exactly when the water would arrive. We always liked to have the yearling calves sorted and moved to higher ground along with all the heifers and cows. Once the cattle were moved, the guys could proceed to irrigate, which they did by managing the water with a series of dikes and culverts. It was really something to see so much water in the spring. Sage Creek was higher than the land, and that enabled the flood irrigation system to work. If I stood on the Dam Bridge, and looked south, it looked like there was water clear to the border.

All Cattle Work Done on Horseback

For most of our ranching career, we did all our cattle work on horseback. We purchased a side-by-side in 2009, which was a nice addition for fencing and moving bulls, etc. Two great additions to my gear were a nice light bullwhip (I did not enjoy moving bulls) and muck boots. The person who came up with that idea deserves a medal! My feet were never cold while riding and sorting again.

Kerrie on Badger, her very smart horse

I had not learned to handle a rope when I was young. One of my first experiences on the ranch with Bruce was to go and help as he and his brother Dennis loaded up a lame bull in the middle of a large field. Bruce and Dennis captured the bull, and then Bruce pulled the rope through the trailer and out of the front and then handed it to me to dally onto my saddle horn. I was petrified, but the horse knew what to do. I managed not to lose any fingers as the bull was encouraged from behind and my horse pulled him into the trailer.

The first few years, I rode a sure-footed horse that was aptly named "Badger." He had some Thoroughbred in him. Our cattle were still skittish from being handled harshly by the previous owner. On occasion, we would have a breakaway where the cattle would spook and start to run. Badger was always up for the challenge, and he would outrun the leaders every time. He thought it was so much fun that I'd have a heck of a time to get him to slow down and turn the cattle. Badger never once hit a hole. Good thing I was young. He lived to be a ripe old age, and our son Daniel used him for a 4-H Horse. One of my more "unfavourite things" was sorting calves in the spring. I usually "got" to run a gate right beside the water trough. Our water trough made a lot of noise because of the gas pushing the artesian water through the pipes. It would make huge gurgling and splashing sounds. Mix that with a bit of wind and then have the various husbands give hand signals and holler instructions for the gatekeepers, all the while having groups of five or more yearlings running toward you at break-neck speed. Suffice to say, it made for a long day. Sometimes, we had to do this in a foot of mud and manure on top of ice. Other years, the dirt and manure were dry and blowing in our eyes. On more than one occasion, I was tempted to stomp off to the house and tell them to do the job without me. That was a piece of advice I generously shared with any young ranch bride who would listen to me.

My favourite thing was moving cattle. Our fields were huge, so there were usually four or five of us riding. We often used the Sweet Grass Mountains as our point of reference. Most times, the only thing one could hear was the breeze, the meadowlarks, and the odd time we would hear antelope make their blowing sound, which is hard to describe. I could tell where the next rider was by the movements of the antelope as they would run ahead before you could see cattle appear on the horizon. The last few years that we were on the Q, my friend Laurel Schlaht liked to come and help gather bulls. We had a lot of fun singing to pass the time. We were sure no one could hear us, and the bulls didn't complain, though I'm sure it was painful for them. One time, Bruce, Dennis, Dennis's wife Arlene, and I went to what we referred to as the Cutbank field to gather some cows. The men failed to tell us what exactly their plan was, and we had neglected to ask. (There was a lot of communication by "osmosis" on our ranch.) The guys rode off, not bothering to look back. Meanwhile, Arlene's horse blew up. He tried to buck her off, but she managed to ride him. By the time we turned our attention to our work, we had no idea which direction we were supposed to head. We eventually found our way and got the job done.

In 1996, the Western Stock Growers Association celebrated one hundred years by organizing the most wonderful trail ride from Buffalo, across the British Block (CFB Suffield) to Medicine Hat. My dad organized two wagons. Arnold and Shirley, my sister-in–law (Marilyn Armstrong), our nieces (Alisha, Laura, and Rae-Lynn), Bruce and I, our boys (Winston and Daniel), Dad's cousin (Ashmore Reesor), and two of his friends were a family unit. My sister-in-law, Marilyn Kusler, and her son, Lyndon, were along as well, but in a different circle. We were in Leo Maynard's Wagon Boss Circle, which meant we were the first crew up, packed, fed, watered, harnessed, and hitched and on the trail by first light every day. About the third morning, Ashmore was heard to ask, "Somebody remind me, are we putting up or taking down these tents?" My mom said it was one of the best things that she had ever done in her life. I agreed with her. The journey and experience could only be described as epic. If anyone had a video of that first morning, it would be priceless. There were buck-offs and wagon run-aways galore. I heard one of the lady doctors say that she had never seen so many blisters in "unmentionable" places before. Lots of people who had not ridden were feeling the stress by the third day. The fun and experience could not be duplicated, even though we had a second trail ride about five years later. It just wasn't the same.

Our Children's Education

Getting our boys educated was a challenge on the ranch. It was 48 miles to Manyberries. We had wonderful bus drivers, Helen Flaig and her husband Phil. If we had to go to town early in the morning, I would let Helen know, and she would arrive early just in case Winston and Dan were not ready. Helen had to drive in some nasty weather. One year, it rained in the fall, and the roads were a nightmare. Still, she persevered, and the kids always got to school. The boys were on the bus for an hour and 20 minutes each way.

Our boys played school sports. With the generous help of community members to coach and drive, we had great teams and a lot of fun. Winston and Dan played in the spring league volleyball in Medicine Hat. I put on an extra 4,000 kilometres in those years. Winston also joined the high school rodeo, and I went with him for the first three years. The fourth year we sent him on his own. The school and the curling rink were the hub of our Manyberries community. There was a community association and an Ag Society to help keep things going. I—along with the help of Gladys Stryker, Shannon Ulrich, Val King, and Debbie Saville—managed to have a light-horse 4-H club. We evolved to include beef and some other projects depending on what interested the kids. It was a bit difficult organizing meetings to fit everyone's schedule. We showed our cattle with the Hoping Club at Foremost, Alberta. The benefits of 4-H are exponential. Our key leader, Maureen Laidlaw, shared a very profound quote: "If you don't do a good job raising your family, nothing else in this world really matters." The community dwindled, which resulted in the complete closure of the Manyberries school. We were fortunate, over the years, to have some great teachers and support staff. Our little school turned out some of the most successful and independent students at any small school in Alberta.

My two sisters-in-law and I spent many hours and kilometres volunteering our time to make sure that our kids got the best education possible. There were endless Parent Council meetings, plus our ECS (Kindergarten), which was privately operated. This took a lot of administration time on the part of the parents. Along with the community, we managed to fundraise and build a playground for the school. We raised $25,000 for that project. A few years later, our government decided that cedar playgrounds caused slivers, and it had to be taken down.

Branding Crews & Cattle Processing

Another huge project that we helped make happen was our *Forgotten Corner* history book. We had to pre-sell and fundraise to gather $26,000 so we could complete the book. We went on to do at least two extra printings. Probably the busiest but most fun time of the year on the ranch was branding season. We girls were lucky because we had each other to share the work and the cooking, where most of our friends were on their own to do it all. The family hosting the dinner would get their place ready in advance of riding week because we had to spend about three days gathering. We also sorted off the *dry cows at this time. Sometimes, it was very hot and dusty. In those years, the guys would get a water truck to come and dampen down the corral so that it would not be so dusty for the workers. The day before branding, we girls would get together and do all our salads and prep work so that we only had to make sure that the meat, beans, and potatoes were cooked on the day. We made all our desserts, squares, etc., well in advance. It would take about three trips to gather all the groceries and refreshments needed. (Keep in mind that town was eighty-five miles away.) In today's world, the young ranchers are hiring caterers or food trucks. Times are changing for sure. This enables the gals to work in the corral, which is great.

The Q Branding was an all-day event. We usually started the branding fires at 7:30 am for the larger herd. The riders showed up early to gather the cows and calves and push them from the holding pen into the corral. We ran two pots, and then at break time, there were sandwiches, cookies, coffee, and beer. We girls always managed to get to the corral for a visit and to take a few photos.

A small crew would go and gather the heifers and their calves at the other corral. The rest of the gang would move to that corral after finishing at the first. Often, some of the ladies and kids would clean the oysters at the corral. This made the oyster cooking process less work after lunch. Branding would be finished between 1:00 and 2:00. The crew and families would come in for dinner and spend the afternoon visiting, playing cards and horseshoes. Prairie Oysters were always a delicacy at our place. Our friends Kathy and Heather devised a way to cook them in a turkey fryer. (So much easier to clean up.) We would then add Frank's hot sauce, and the little morsels would disappear quickly. It was a huge relief when the day was done. We enjoyed having our neighbours and friends come to the ranch for the occasion. We did get rained out at least one year, and that was quite a production. Fortunately, we had enough food to carry the crew through the two days. The spring that we were in the process of landscaping, we had tons of rotted manure brought in from the feed yard and worked it into the soil around the house. For branding day, I had made five or six pies and set them on the counter to cool. About that time, a hot, dry wind swirled around the house and blew manure dust into my kitchen, covering the pie with the lovely stuff. It was a good thing they had top crusts, so I took my vacuum cleaner and put my fingers between the nozzle and the crust, and managed to suck most of the dust away. I figured the guys wouldn't notice and a dollop of ice cream can fix anything. I told one of my cousins this story, and she thought it was the most hilarious thing she'd ever heard! Quote: "Just a second, honey, I have to vacuum the pies."

Bruce & Kerrie taking a much-needed rest with other ranchers during a cattle branding event.

*Weaning and pregnancy-checking the cows was another two-day event at our ranch. We would have several extra men each day. Often, we would wait until there was a bit of snow on the ground to keep the dust down, so it was very cold. We ran a lot of cattle through the chute in a day. Our veterinarian was very efficient at getting it all done by dark.

Shipping cattle could be a stressful morning. We managed to get the yearlings into the corral in a timely manner as the liners were rolling into the yard. It was quite a sight, the steam and frost rising off the steers as we headed them into the corral just after sunrise. I carried my camera in my shirt pocket, but it was difficult to get good photos while we were on the move.

The Q Ranch was unique in that we had five artesian wells approximately 1300 feet deep. This meant that we did not have many water holes to chop in the winter as the wells (56 degrees) maintained a constant flow, winter and summer. We were isolated but not as remote as some, and for that, I was grateful. Bruce and I took the boys skiing in the winter months. In the summer, the family had a cottage at Elkwater, so we did get up there occasionally. Winston and Dan got to spend time with my folks and take swimming lessons as well. I had a garden and raised great raspberries, asparagus, tomatoes, carrots, potatoes, peppers, beets, onions, and lettuce or spinach. We found that cold crops like cabbage, cauliflower, and broccoli were a waste of time due to bugs. My sister-in-law Marilyn is a Master Gardener and a great source of knowledge. Her yard was and is a showpiece. Bruce and I were fortunate to get to travel, though there are many places that we still have not seen. I'm afraid that our world is growing smaller with the political issues of the day. One thing we did get to do was go to Australia and visit folks that live in true isolation near Thargomindah, Queensland. They must drive for two days to see a dentist or buy shoes for the children, so that put our eighty-five-mile drive for groceries into perspective.

Prairie Fires & Retirement

One of the last prairie fires that happened before we left the ranch was quite large. Bruce and I were the only ones at home that day, and so I wound up having to drive while he ran the sprayer. It was awful! There were times I could not see. At one point, the fire was **burning in fingers, and we looked back to see that there was another fire coming up behind us. I wound up driving through a bone pile, and as they popped, I was sure the tires would be ruined. We generally used my garden pump to fill the sprayer tank. All the while, we were trying to alert the neighbours by phone. It was very awkward trying to explain the location of a prairie fire to a dispatcher in Red Deer, which is about 7 hours away. No cell service is also a huge disadvantage.

Before 9/11, our neighbours to the south would come if the fire was huge. They brought water on a semi, which was a welcome sight. Fire season was always stressful. On several occasions, Bruce used his Super Cub airplane to locate a fire, as it was often very hard to tell the exact location from the ground. One memorable June, there were lightning strikes every evening for a couple of weeks. Because it was so dry, the folks from OneFour Ranch, Bruce, and I started going out on the ridge west of Hwy 41 to watch for fires.

Bruce used his plane to check fences and cows during calving season and make sure the bulls were all in. The plane saved us many hours of bouncing around in the truck. Each Monday through breeding season, he would fly early in the morning, and then we would take our horses to the summer field and move all the cattle north. This helped to keep the field evenly grazed and make sure that the bulls were spread out.

In the early years, pre-9/11, we had a problem with people running the border. May long weekend was particularly troublesome as often, our fences were cut and cattle would escape into Montana. Our cattle did not enjoy being handled with quad runners and that created quite a lot of stress.

Bruce and I retired to Elkwater when we sold the ranch in 2012. I enjoy kayaking, flower arranging, a bit of art, hiking, cross-country skiing, and more photography. However, there are things that I miss. Riding. The sunrises and sunsets. Being able to shoot pesky rodents. The sound of the geese in the spring and fall, plus the shore birds, nighthawks, meadowlarks, and coyotes. (Even though they ate the last of my carrots right out of the garden.) The cactus flowers. The smell of the prairie after a rain. And, most of all, my 360-degree view.

In 2019, we moved to Medicine Hat. We get to see our four grandboys more often and our nieces stop in occasionally with their kids. We enjoy watching them participate in sports and rodeo.

Bruce, Owen, Luke, Kerrie, Kooper, Ashton

Louise's Add-on Insights to explain weaning of the calves and pregnancy testing the cows for people who are reading the book and are not associated with the cattle ranching industry.

* Weaning: cows and calves are brought into the corrals, and the calves are taken away from their mothers in the fall. This allows their mothers to dry up and no longer have milk in their udders, so they can put on weight before the cold weather of winter comes. We also either sell the calves in the fall or put them on feed for the winter, to either sell in the spring or put them out on grass for one more year. If we put them back on grass, then we would bring them back to sell as grass fed beef or fatten in a feedlot from October to February and sell as fat cattle—grain-fed meat.

Pregnancy Testing: We test all the cows to see if they got bred over the summer months. A veterinarian is hired to come out with a machine to see if each cow came into heat at the correct time and the bull was able to breed her. (The cows are unharmed during this procedure.) If they are not bred during this time from July 1-August 30, or whatever time of year the rancher wants to be calving (it takes 9 months for a calf to develop in the mother's womb), then the cow is described as "open" or "dry." She can then be fattened up on grass for another couple months and sold as grass-fed beef.

**Burning in fingers: If you can imagine your fingers splayed out and having fire come up behind you on all sides, the fingers would be on fire in lines, with spaces in between.

Recipes below that Kerrie uses quite often, as they are old-time favourites.

Calico Beans—Kerrie Kusler

CALICO BEANS

½ lb. ground beef   ½ lb. bacon
1 pound mushrooms
Brown all of the above and add the following:
1 onion, chopped   1 Tbsp. vinegar
½ cup ketchup   1 can lima beans, drained
3/4 cup brown sugar   1 can pork and beans
1 Tbsp. dry mustard   1 can kidney beans
Bake ½ hour at 350°F.

GRAMMA BURROW'S LEMON LOAF   Kerrie Kusler

½ cup butter   2¼ tsp. baking powder
1 cup sugar   ½ cup milk
2 eggs   ½ cup chopped pecans or walnuts
1½ cups flour   grated rind of 1 lemon
½ tsp. salt

Cream butter and sugar, beat in eggs [one at a time].
Sift dry ingredients and add alternately with milk into
creamed mixture. Add lemon rind and nuts. Stir well.
Put into greased loaf pans and bake at 350' for about
45 minutes. Mix ½ cup sugar and juice of 1 lemon. *Do not double this - too much*
Spoon over loaf while still hot.

Buttermilk Biscuits

By The Canadian Living Test Kitchen

These buttermilk biscuits are delectably scrumptious and sure to start your day off right. They're a great make-ahead pastry to keep in the freezer, too!

This recipe makes 12 servings

To change the number of servings, enter the number of servings you'd like in the box below, then press "calculate".

portions

Ingredients

2-1/2 cups (625 mL) all-purpose flour
2 tbsp (25 mL) granulated sugar
2-1/2 tsp (10 mL) baking powder
1/2 tsp (2 mL) baking soda
1/2 tsp (2 mL) salt
1/2 cup (125 mL) cold butter, cubed
1 cup (250 mL) buttermilk
1 egg

Preparation:

Line rimless baking sheet with parchment paper, or grease; set aside.

In bowl, whisk flour, sugar, baking powder, baking soda and salt. Using pastry blender or 2 knives, cut in butter until in coarse crumbs. In small bowl, whisk buttermilk with egg; add to flour mixture and stir with fork to make soft dough.

With lightly floured hands, press dough into ball. On lightly floured surface, knead gently 10 times. Pat into 3/4-inch (2 cm) thick round. Using 2-1/2-inch (6 cm) floured round cutter, cut out rounds. Place on prepared baking sheet.

Bake in centre of 400°F (200°C) oven until golden, 12 to 15 minutes. (Make-ahead: Let cool. Store in airtight container for up to 1 day or wrap individually

---

Cheddar Corn Casserole - Kathy Bradbu
(Serves 6)

bakes 30 min ti puffed
+ golden.

½ c butter - melt.
1 lrge onion chop.
1 sm grn pepper   chop saute fr
1 sm red pepp.   2 T butter til soft.

3 eggs   - Combine next ingreds
1 cup sr crm   - whisk - mix into corn
1 can cream corn   corn meal salt + pep.
⅓ cup yellow corn meal   - stir in cheese + onion
¼ tsp salt   mix - (buttered)
¼ tsp pepper   - put in cassrole
1 cup cheddar chees shedd   350 - 30 min.

Chapter VII

Family Relationships

Written by Dorothy Louise Beasley

In the vast expanse of ranch life—where the land stretches as far as the eye can see and the rhythm of nature dictates the ebb and flow of daily routines—family relationships take on a unique texture. Within this tapestry, the dynamics between boys and girls, as well as men and women, weave a rich story of interconnected lives.

The sun rises over the prairie landscape, casting golden hues upon the sprawling pastures. It reveals more than just the physical vastness of the ranch. It illuminates the diverse perspectives that shape the experiences of those who call this land home. In the world of ranch women, motherhood does not come with a manual. Mothers may want to understand the distinct differences in how boys and girls perceive their roles on the ranch.

It may also come to light that men and women approach the challenges of daily life differently. In this chapter, I share some insights about what to expect in such relationships. I believe this knowledge becomes essential for healthy relationships to form on any given ranch home life, even when you are my age. Elderly ranch women can learn and apply new knowledge, too. I changed up some actions in my relationships once I learned about some of the information in this chapter.

From the spirited aspirations of ranch girls to the steadfast determination of ranch women, the pages ahead unfold stories of unity in diversity—a testament to the resilience of family ties in the heart of the livestock ranching industry.

Little Girls

Recently, I read the book *Children Are from Heaven* by John Gray, Ph.D. (He is also the author of *Men Are from Mars, Women Are from Venus*.) In this book, he focuses on positive parenting skills. He emphasizes that boys and girls have different ways of thinking. When a girl is upset and complaining, she benefits from unwinding, reflecting on her day, and having a conversation about it. Girls need a parent's undivided attention and a listening ear to release any stress from their day.

Little Boys

In the realm of youthful exuberance, akin to their grown counterparts, young boys often find themselves absorbed in one pursuit, inadvertently forgetting the tasks at hand. To help them remember, parents can engage their sons in positive conversations and seek their input.

When a parent endeavours to imprint a task in their son's memory, they might first inquire if he's ready to listen and then proceed with an affirmative and encouraging dialogue. Similarly, when parents express their viewpoints, they can invite their children to share their own perspectives.

This practice not only cultivates an atmosphere where diverse opinions are embraced but also instils in children the confidence to make independent choices rather than succumbing to conformity. This nurturing environment lays the groundwork for a positive, open-minded upbringing.

Parents' Ability to Understand Children & Their Temperaments

Every child is unique: recognizing and respecting their individual temperaments is essential for effective parenting. There are four fundamental temperament behavioural factors that can help parents better understand their children and provide the right support:

- **Sensitive Children.** These youngsters often exhibit intelligence, intense emotions, deep thinking, and a serious demeanour.

- **Active Children.** These children tend to be strong-willed, intelligent risk-takers who thrive on being the centre of attention.

- **Responsive Children.** They require stimulation, thrive on interaction, and possess intelligence. They tend to move quickly from one activity to another. may have shorter attention spans.

- **Receptive Children.** Intelligent and pleasant to be around, they are cooperative and enjoy routines but are opposed to change.

Most children display a mix of these temperamental qualities, with one or two dominant traits. To nurture children effectively, parents may identify their child's primary temperament(s) and tailor their approach accordingly with respect and kindness.

Parents may also find that their children have different temperaments than their own, highlighting the importance of understanding and respecting these four temperamental types.

When parents adapt their parenting style to align with their child's temperament, it fosters an environment where children can grow, thrive, and ultimately become happier individuals. I was particularly struck by five actions recommended in Dr John Gray's book:

- **Celebrate Differences.** It's perfectly fine for our kids to be unique and act differently from one another.

- **Embrace Mistakes.** Mistakes are opportunities for growth. They are nothing more than feedback. They help our kids learn what to do better next time.

- **Express Feelings.** It's okay for our children to express their negative emotions openly, like anger, disappointment, or worry. Encourage them to release these feelings in healthy ways, like talking or using a pillow to beat on a couch or on the floor. (Just make sure they don't use your feather pillows.)

- **Encourage Ambition.** It's more than okay for our kids to desire more in life. Encourage them to want to achieve and experience more of what they love.

- **Respect Their Voice.** Teach our children to say "NO" when needed. To share their opinions with their parents. And to understand that we, as parents and/or grandparents, are doing our best with the knowledge we have to help them become responsible, knowledge-seeking adults.

In addition, remember that children learn best by doing and experiencing. Work together as a family towards common goals. Nurture responsibility. Encourage open discussions. Most of all, pay attention to what works and what doesn't. By giving our children the freedom to be themselves and express their feelings, we're giving them the precious gift of becoming the greatest version of themselves.

**Families working together during ranch branding.
Moms, dads and children work.**

Differences in the way Men and Women Think

Understanding the relational dynamics between men and women is akin to navigating a diverse landscape. In this intricate dance, individuals can benefit from gender insights, fostering tolerance and forgiveness when responses diverge from expectations. The essence of this understanding lies in recognizing that men often navigate the relationship terrain using a "dead reckoning" approach, relying on calculations of direction and distance, while women tend to anchor themselves with landmarks. This metaphor serves as a metaphorical guide, shedding light on the nuanced differences in thinking between the sexes.

Mat Boggs wrote a book called *Project Everlasting*, and in it, he has stories of husbands and wives from all over the U.S.A. He and his friend/co-author interviewed couples to find out about their marriages and how they were still married after many years. He also has developed a course called *Cracking the Man Code* which describes some of the differences between men's and women's thinking, of which I share some of his research in this chapter. John Gray's book *Men Are from Mars, Women Are from Venus* was also a source of some of the following information.

The journey toward better communication involves a transformative shift in how one communicates, reacts, and responds to a partner. Armed with new insights, individuals possess the wisdom to adapt their approaches. This transformation facilitates more effective support exchange and fosters harmonious connections. I have learned many ways to communicate with my husband, too. I need a reminder occasionally so I don't repeat the same pattern of reacting to whatever pushes my anger buttons. Once I remember the lessons I have learned about men and women thinking differently, I can then respond and avoid conflicting actions.

1st Observation: Understanding how men and women think differently in relationships is like figuring out a puzzle.

1st Insight: Recognizing and accepting these differences can help avoid unnecessary misunderstandings.

1st Teaching Point: Talk openly with your partner about how you both perceive and approach things. Understanding each other's perspectives can lead to better communication.

2nd Observation: In relationships, men sometimes don't realize that women aren't looking for solutions when they share their problems after the day is over. Women, your partner is looking to want to fix your problems, as that is what he does all day long, and he thinks that it is his job to fix your problems, too.

2nd Insight: Women value emotional support and connection in conversations, not a Mr. Fix-it.

2nd Teaching Point: Women, let him know you only want him to listen, understand, give emotional support, and acknowledge that you have a problem to work out. This is how women build dopamine in their brains at night; by talking with someone else. They need to talk about their day and what happened.

3rd Observation: Did you know that men have a compartment in their brains where they can go and veg out? There is no thinking done in that compartment; it is a nothing zone. Their brain gives them access at the end of the day so they can destress after work.

3rd Insight: In ancient times, as a caveman, he could go to his cave and replenish his mind, sleep, think of nothing, meditate, watch his kids play, etc. Meanwhile, the woman/women would be out gathering berries, talking amongst themselves. It is the same today: he goes to the living room or his mancave and rests, watches sports on T.V., reads, or flips through Facebook videos and articles, things he doesn't have to think about or solve anything.

3rd Teaching Point: Women, if you need to talk with your partner when the day is done, don't do it while your partner is in his man cave. He may have to be in his "no thinking" compartment for at least 30 minutes to rebuild the dopamine in his brain. Then he will be happier and less likely to bark at you as he might have done in the past when you wanted him to talk before he went to his man cave. He will then be able to function mentally for the rest of the evening.

4th Observation: Women may often try to change or improve their partners, thinking it comes from a caring place. In relationships, women often feel a deep sense of responsibility for the growth and well-being of their partners. Men don't like changes or improvements, as they like things to stay the same.

4th Insight: Women often seek improvement by nurturing and caring for their partners, ensuring their well-being and happiness. Men like the saying, "If it's working, don't change it."

4th Teaching Point: Women, refrain from trying to change or improve your partners or what they do daily. Concentrate more on yourselves and what you can do to create a win-win situation. Let your partner do what he chooses to do for himself. Consider the poem, *The Difference*: "God grant me the serenity to accept the things I cannot change, the courage to change the things I can, and the wisdom to know the difference."

5th Observation: Did you ever notice that when a woman asks a man to get something from the fridge, he invariably comes back without it, as he couldn't find it? "Men and women search the fridge differently due to their ancestral roles. Women, as natural gatherers, excel at spotting stationary objects like fruits on trees or bushes. Men, as hunters, focus better on moving targets. Women notice everything in the fridge, while men might miss things, reflecting our evolved survival instincts—women's 180 degrees sight broadened their vision for gathering, while men singled out specific targets using tunnel vision."

5th Insight: Men and women see the world differently.

5th Teaching Point: Women, it is important to pay attention when you ask your partner to do something for you, especially when going to the fridge to get something to put on the kitchen table. Make sure you explain in detail exactly where it is, what colours the lid and container are, etc.

6th Observation: Women, did you know that men have separate compartments in their brains that deal with whatever individual event they are focusing on at any given moment? For example, when a man is totally focused on doing a task, sometimes the woman in his life comes up and asks a question or wants her partner to do something for her. He is unable to come out of that compartment in a hurry. He must shut off his mind to what he was doing, which may take a few minutes. Then, once all that is settled down in his brain, he can direct his focus to you. Yet, women often think their partner hasn't heard them when he doesn't answer right away.

6th Insight: Women can multitask somewhat, as from their ancestors, they needed to be alert to many things in their environment: watching the children, picking berries, thinking ahead about what to cook for supper, etc. A man has separate compartments in his brain so he can only focus on one thing at a time.

6-2 Insight: Sometimes, my partner is startled when I go up to him to ask a question, as he is so in that other compartment in his brain. He is all in with focusing on a TV sports program that he doesn't hear me approaching. It takes him a few seconds, sometimes a minute or two, to come out of that other place in his brain. I sometimes wonder if it was a good idea to expect a proper answer, as his thoughts are still in that other compartment, even though he is looking at me. So, I have decided, in this New Year of 2024, to leave him be. so long as he is that focused, he is possibly de-stressing and needs to be left alone. When he gets hungry, he will come out of that compartment in his brain and find his evening meal waiting for him.

6th Teaching Point: In relationships, it's vital to find a balance where both partners feel understood and valued. Couples can navigate differences by embracing them and working together through knowing what is happening in each other's brains. Give your male partner time to shut down what he was thinking at any given moment. He has many compartments/apartments in his brain that he goes to and then focuses totally on what is going on in that compartment. Expect to wait a few seconds or minutes for your partner to adjust to incoming messages from you and be able to concentrate, listen and answer you.

I found a very impressive message written and spoken about by Oprah Winfrey, which came from a Chicken Soup for the Woman's Soul book published in 1996. It tells of a message about love. Oprah reminds us that within all of us lies a Queen, waiting to claim her glory."

Be A Queen

Be a queen. Dare to be different. Be a pioneer. Be a leader. Be the kind of woman who, in the face of adversity, will continue to embrace life and walk fearlessly toward the challenge. Take it on! Be a truth seeker and rule your domain, whatever it is—your home, your office, your family—with a loving heart.

Be a queen. Be tender. Continue to give birth to new ideas and rejoice in your womanhood...My prayer is that we will stop wasting time being mundane and mediocre...We are daughters of God—here to teach the world how to love...

It doesn't matter what you've been through, where you come from, who your parents are—nor your social or economic status. None of those matter. What matters is how you choose to love, how you choose to express that love through your work, through your family, through what you have to give to the world...

Be a queen. Own your power and your glory!
–Oprah Winfrey

Chapter VIII

Autonomy in All Our Relationships

Written by Dorothy Louise Beasley

Autonomy is about more than just being on your own. It's about having the freedom to make choices that respect your desires and needs. In a healthy relationship, when your partner supports your autonomy, it means they encourage your personal and relational growth. A strong relationship is built on mutual respect, support, and openness. It takes self-awareness and emotional intelligence to understand and respect each other's boundaries, embrace authenticity, and have good communication.

Studies suggest that partners who pursue their individual goals and achieve both personal and shared objectives tend to have better well-being and higher satisfaction in their relationship. Being in an "intimate" relationship shouldn't block your freedom to pursue your dreams. It's crucial to maintain your self-confidence and self-respect. Healthy relationships allow both partners to move in different directions while supporting each other lovingly.

A partner who values your autonomy might:

- Respect your personal space and boundaries.
- Share common relationship values and future goals.
- Celebrate your hobbies, achievements, and personal growth.
- Encourage you to maintain meaningful social connections and support networks.

- Make decisions that honour your desires, needs, feelings, your autonomy.

Observation: Autonomy in relationships means that each partner respects the other's personal space and boundaries. Building a strong connection in a relationship is important, but it's also crucial to keep your own feelings and independence. Finding a good balance between spending time together and having personal space is key for a happy long-term commitment.

Insight: It's not just about having autonomy; it's about creating a supportive environment where both/all partners/people actively contribute to each other's growth and happiness.

Teaching Point: Maintain a collaborative way to keep this individual autonomy for all people in the relationship. The freedom to pursue your hopes and dreams shouldn't be obstructed by being in a so-called "intimate" relationship. Keeping faith with this aspiration is pivotal to preventing your self-confidence and self-respect from eroding. **Healthy relationships, therefore, offer all parties the liberty to move in directions that the other person/ people may not share but lovingly endorse(s) and support(s).**

I found a quote that will encourage you to pursue your dreams. There is a story in a 1996 Chicken Soup book, by Robert Fulghum. He was organizing a game for 80 children, and they were to decide whether they were Dwarfs, Wizards, or Giants. A little girl asked him, "Where do the Mermaids Stand?" This is the name of the story in the book with the following quote by Eileen Caddy!

"What is right for one soul may not be right for another. It may mean having to stand on your own and do something strange in the eyes of others."

Chapter IX

The Art of Compromise in All Relationships

Written by Dorothy Louise Beasley

Balancing compromises in a relationship can be tough, but it's important for keeping things peaceful while living together. Successful communication involves effective and open talking, careful listening, and being truly open to changing plans when needed. Finding a solution that makes both/all people happy is about compromise.

Here are six practical approaches to add compromise into the interactions of shared living.

1. **Resolving Conflicts:** When conflicts arise, work together to find a resolution. Avoid letting disagreements linger, as prolonged tension can strain the relationship. Settle disputes amicably, ensuring that all parties feel heard and understood. Sometimes, agree to disagree and move forward in a friendly manner.

2. **Navigating Intimacy:** Discuss your comfort levels and establish mutually agreeable terms regarding intimacy. By openly communicating and finding common ground, you can ensure a harmonious and satisfying intimate aspect of your relationship.

3. **Managing Finances:** If you're combining finances, reach an agreement on how money will be utilized. Decide on the shared financial goals and ensure transparent communication. Joint bank accounts should be used responsibly for household needs, with clear communication before any personal expenditures.

4. **Balancing Hobbies:** Strike a balance in your leisure activities. Alternate between outdoor adventures and relaxing homestays to accommodate all partners' preferences, promoting a sense of contentment and understanding.

5. **Coordinated Parenting:** Recognize and respect the differences in your parenting styles. Develop a workable plan for parenting whereby you use **positive reinforcement in child discipline**. Establish roles and responsibilities to prevent awkward situations and ensure a healthy upbringing for your children. Look up positive parenting online at www.alldayparenting.com and find out how to use praise in child discipline.

6. **Acknowledging Different Schedules:** Understand and respect each other's daily time schedules, whether you're a morning person or a night owl. Through negotiation, find a compromise that works.

- **Observation:** Learning how to compromise helps create marital partnerships; all relationships that are fair and satisfying for everyone.

- **Insight:** Compromise serves as a great foundation for strong relationships.

- **Teaching Point**: Partners should be open to meeting halfway. It's not about hiding one's identity but discovering a harmonious balance that enriches the relationship.

Here's a quote that I believe fits here:

"We're all assigned a piece of the garden, a corner of the universe that is ours to transform. Our corner of the universe is our own life—our relationships, our homes, our work, our current circumstances—exactly as they are. Every situation we find ourselves in is an opportunity, perfectly planned by the Holy Spirit, to teach love instead of fear."
–Marianne Williamson

Chapter X

Sacrifice & Love

Stories about Julie Chickoski and her mom, Lydia Klaassen

I have adjusted a quote from Antoine De Saint-Exupery to suit my own purposes: "Only she can understand what a ranch is, who has sacrificed part of herself to that ranch, fought to save it, struggled to make it beautiful. Only then will the love of it fill her heart."

I was born on a ranch to a hard-working ranch woman, my mum, and her hard-working rancher husband, my dad. And I mean that literally: Dad, just like he had often done with animals, helped Mum to deliver me, with no medical credentials but likely with a good deal of prayer on both their parts. I consider myself completely homemade.

However, that was not my parents' original plan. Mum had been staying in the city a short distance from the local hospital, waiting for me to arrive. However, since I was late to arrive (which seemed to be a recurring theme in my life), she went back home to gather a few items and regroup. Meanwhile, the roads became blocked with snow. Dad rode a horse to a neighbour's place to use a telephone and arrange for the new chicks that they were expecting to be delivered by plane. Plan was to send Mum back into the city on that plane. But a spring storm blew in, and it came down to knowing they had to take care of things on their own. I think that could be said of many ranchers. They know that, for the most part, they must take care of things on their own, especially back then.

Julie's Mom, Lydia Klaassen

For many ranch women, it may be that we did not necessarily pick that as a career but became that by virtue of what our life partner was or became. My mum, Lydia Klaassen, was born in 1917 in Kansas, and about half of her family moved to Canada when she was one year old. She was the youngest in a large family; her older siblings stayed in the United States.

She grew up on a farm just a few miles from where I live now, got married at eighteen years of age, had a daughter at nineteen, and was widowed just before her twentieth birthday. Her husband died by drowning while their family was gathered for a reunion. She and her husband had lived with her family until they could make a start on their own. But suddenly, she was a single mother living in the 1930's. I imagine that life was very hard for her during that time.

Julie's mom, Lydia and Julie's dad on the farm, 2 dogs beside the horses.

I am glad that my dad, Eugene Martens, came along to partner with her in a new life just a couple of years later. My dad had grown up on a farm, too, and so with help and advice from, strangely enough, Mum's first husband's parents, they found and bought a ranch northeast of Swift Current, Saskatchewan, in 1944. It was a beautiful property in the Swift Current Creek valley, which would later become Martens Ranch Ltd. That is where I was born and where I now live, 67 years later.

Mum loved flowers and although she had a large vegetable garden, too, it was her flowers that gave her joy. She played the piano, and I would doubt that she would have had any kind of formal lessons. She canned almost everything, she crocheted and sewed and tried in her humble way to make our home beautiful. She taught me to have busy hands. She helped Dad in every aspect of life and worked hard despite early health struggles with arthritis. I know that she drove sometimes on the ranch, and yet she never had her driver's license. She was, however, a very good front and backseat driver! I remember one time when Mum was in a car driven by my husband. She could say things so quietly and gently yet still feel the need to say them. "For my part," she commented that day, "we don't have to pass every vehicle on the road." That has become a legendary comment within our family! But sometimes I try to imagine the inconvenience of what it was like to have to wait for Dad to make a run into the city, 25 miles away, to take care of groceries that weren't supplied by the ranch itself or to take care of appointments and other needs.

Life was Just Different

We might think life was simpler then, or harder, and yet maybe it was just different. You did what you could with what you had and made do with how life was.

To make extra money, my parents sold eggs in the city. They had horses and cows, and they grew crops and hay for feed. They believed that if you had the crops to feed the livestock, there was perhaps a slim chance you could make money from that, too! Ranching often seems to consist of being asset-rich and cash-poor. Our son, who is now an accountant and specializes in the agricultural sector, would confirm that that is so often the case, even today! I half-jokingly say that when I was a kid, I had no idea we didn't have a lot of money, and then I grew up and am still here, and now I KNOW I don't have a lot of it!

We always seemed to have extra people in our home when I was a kid. Mum adapted with grace, and I remember her saying it was just a matter of adding another cup of macaroni to the pot and getting something for them to sit on at the table. Most of the extra people were boy cousins. The only female cousin we had chose to stay with us after her parents passed away and became an integral part of the family. The boy cousins, mostly city boys, were quickly put into the work schedule, whether they wanted to be or not. But at least they weren't back home where their parents had to keep them busy and out of trouble.

I think back to what it must have been like to be my mum. All the laundry, the constant cooking, and endless dishwashing, all done in ways we would now consider primitive. I remember reading in her diary when all she wrote for one day was, "I ironed all day and killed a snake." I don't usually worry about either of those things now, and I'm very thankful for that! But I do wonder where the snake was that it needed to be killed. She didn't elaborate.

After church on Sundays, my parents would often have company. Either someone from church or from their own large extended families. Mum would usually prepare food and get it ready the night before, usually as we listened to Hockey Night in Canada on the radio until we got a television when I was about eight years old and could watch the games. Both of my parents loved to visit. Being hospitable was just part of who they were. I hope I have done credit to them by opening my own home and welcoming many people over the years.

My parents had a great heart for kids. They sold a small valley on the ranch to the Boy Scouts of Canada, the sale of which was covered by a local philanthropist's donation, left for that express purpose in his will. The camp is still here. Dad was also an ordained minister. When they bought the ranch, there had been a small Bible Camp on a location nearby and my parents volunteered to have it move to the valley where we live. It is also still here and hundreds of people—kids and families and staff—make their way to the camp every summer. In the beginning of the Bible camp, my parents were heavily involved and ran a lot of the much smaller program that it was then. West Bank Bible Camp has always been a huge part of my family's life—both the family that consists of my parents and siblings, and the family that consists of my husband and children. All of us have spent time working there, and one of my best memories is when I was able to leave the kids with family and go along on the twenty-mile trail ride that Curt led the youth age campers on.

I had two brothers and three sisters. My brothers were young teenagers when I came along, and I think I was probably a bit of a nuisance to them. The cooking and housework were usually done by the female side of the family, but that was not where I wanted to be. From an early age, I wanted to be outside. Driving the tractor while the men loaded bales. Driving the grain truck to unload the combine. Riding horses to check cows or just for pure pleasure. Playing catch with my brothers out in the yard on a summer evening.

Despite Mum being something of a worrier, she seemed to let me run wild and free, and so I did! I remember one day when I was about five years old; I was down at the barn, walking beside one of my grown-up cousins. An older milk cow that we had was usually very tame, but she took exception to the dog behind me and took a run at it. Except I was in the way. She knocked me over and knocked me out. I came to in the kitchen. I can't imagine that Mum was very happy with that whole scenario. But she probably bowed to the inevitable and let me back outside as soon as I was able.

My brothers played hockey in a small town close by during many evenings, and I would beg to go along. I could go if it wasn't colder than -20 degrees. Even -10 in that old barn of a rink was too cold. I realized why one day when I was there during a daytime game and saw all the open places in the wall at the far end of the rink. But where my brothers were, was my happy place and again, maybe it was just easier to let me go!

Mum's Extended Family & Travelling

Because my parents had large extended families that lived all over Canada and the United States, and because family was so important to them, we travelled a lot. All packed into a car with no air-conditioning! Still, I am so grateful to my parents for that. Mum might have been more cautious than Dad (I think he was more adventurous), but she loved family. So, away we would go.

Many other kids that I knew in school had not even travelled out of Saskatchewan. But I travelled to Montana, Kansas, Arizona, Oklahoma, California, Oregon, British Columbia, Ontario, and lots of places in between. We even had relatives in India and Aruba, which broadened our lives. I still remember being about 6 years old and going to see the Hoover Dam in Nevada. My brother held me up to look over the edge, and Mum nearly had a heart attack! But she was a good sport, and I survived.

My siblings all travelled to school on horseback. By the time I started, there was a school bus to take me, although it was still only a one-room schoolhouse with 11 students in the tiny hamlet of Leinan. Back in the earlier days, after my parents bought the ranch, the time came to send my oldest sister, Marina, to school a few miles away. They had a horse named Margie. They would tie my sister into the saddle and send her off. The teacher would send her home the same way. As a mom quite a few years later, I can't imagine doing that! Was Mum brave? I think so! When that teacher asked my dad if they trusted her not to fall off, Dad said, "No, I trust the horse." Wow, I think to myself. I can totally picture my dad saying that. But Mum? She must have spent a lot of time praying!

Mum created what I remember as a happy home. She loved reading books and poetry, though I'm not sure how she found time for that. My parents worked so hard. Physical, back-breaking work that had no end. But that was just part of the path they had chosen, and I never felt that they ever wanted to be anywhere else. My mum was what I think of as ladylike. She had a dignity that was just part of who she was. And yet she had new baby chicks housed in the old cistern in our basement to keep warm when they first arrived. Sometimes, mud and manure trailed through the house, probably by Mum herself, but it was cleaned up and then you carried on with a multitude of other jobs.

When I was seventeen years old, Dad died in a car accident. Mum became a widow again in an equally tragic way. But even though she experienced pain with her arthritis and may have seemed weak physically, I think I didn't realize at the time how strong a person she really was. She passed away suddenly when I was 33 years old. And I have had occasion to reflect on her life and go through things she left behind. I have come to realize that she had exceptional strength.

Her strength came with an unshakeable faith in God, who had seen her through so much. Dad died on a Saturday evening at suppertime. And the next morning Mum's wish was that we would be right where we always were on a Sunday morning. We went to church because she knew that it would be a comfort to us all. The choir sang, "Does Jesus care? His heart is touched by my grief." I still remember that moment so clearly. As usual, Mum was right. We were comforted because God provided us with a Church that surrounded us with love and buns! Church ladies back then made buns in a time of loss. Can there ever be too many homemade buns? I don't think so! I also remember Mum feeling it was important because Dad had made such an effort to have a good relationship with our neighbours and businesses that he frequented that those men were asked to be the honorary pallbearers at his funeral. I admire that Mum, in a time of loss and grief, thought of that.

I hope what I have written about my Mum is in alignment with what my siblings would say. I think sometimes stories that are told a lot or live in our memories take on legendary qualities. My siblings may see events slightly differently, but I think they would be okay with me turning Mum into a legend!

The Next Generation

As my brothers Harold and Gordon took on more ranch work, they stayed at the ranch house. Meanwhile, the rest of us—our parents and three daughters—moved to Swift Current in winter. This made it easier for me and my older sisters, Ruth and Dorothy, to attend school. I remember the last time when we left for the city, thinking that I would never really live on the ranch again. My oldest brother was now married and moved into the ranch house permanently. Surprisingly, I ended up meeting the son of a grocery store manager who had recently moved to the city and had a desire to become a rancher. What are the odds of that?

Curt and I met in high school and were married a few years later, in 1976. If he married me for the ranch, there have been a few times when he felt that he should have thought it through a bit more! But here we still are. And just like both of my parents, neither of us can honestly imagine being anywhere else.

Joining the ranch really didn't start out to be our idea. But after we were engaged, my brothers started talking to us about the possibility, and it didn't take too much to convince us. For me, it was a dream come true that I hadn't even dreamt of yet. After we got married, we went away for a week. We had bought a used mobile home, and the power was supposed to be turned on that week while we were gone. Except the power company went on strike, and we ended up living in my brother's basement for two months. It was an interesting way to start married life.

I still laugh about and remember one night when we had a bat in our room. Curt yelled for my brother to bring a broom while we kept an eye on the bat. My brother came down the stairs in his underwear, swinging a broom, and nailed that bat. When you live on a ranch you never know what kind of wildlife can end up in your house. One day, when the main door to our house stayed open a bit too long, we had a gopher sitting on the back of the couch looking quite comfortable, gazing out the window! You never know what might end up in your yard either. Escaped cows and horses are common. But one day while mowing the lawn our daughter Jill discovered a turtle as large as a dinner plate. I'm not sure which one of them was more startled.

Originally, we set our mobile home up on a bit of a hill and planted some trees. I learned two things from that experience. First, living in a windy spot with no shelter in a mobile home was not part of my dream come true! Second, getting trees to grow to provide shelter in Southwest Saskatchewan meant diligently ordering replacements every year, likely planting four trees for every one that grew. But when you're young, you tend to be hopeful and resilient, and I just kept on watering and planting as best as I could! After five years, we built a house. It was a happy day for me when we moved in, and that mobile home rolled away down the hill. Plus, I could finally see my shelter belt rows of trees developing.

Shortly after this, my brothers started to get involved in public office. One brother politically and one as a school board trustee. They were away occasionally, and so they gradually put a lot of the financial day-to-day business into our nervous hands. I took over the bookkeeping. I had always liked numbers, but the responsibility felt very big some days to both of us. I like the fact that numbers don't lie: two and two will always be four. But sometimes, when it comes to income, it would be nice if they added up to five. I think one of the most stressful things in ranching is managing your business finances, as well as your personal finances, because the amount and timing of your income are uncertain.

More and more people are talking about mental health now. Back then, we didn't know that was even a thing. You worried, but you just sucked it up and got on with life. The good thing was that we shared the greater burden with my brothers and their families. And many times, a supper together and the laughter around the table got us through the day and gave us a brighter outlook for the next. All my life, family has meant so much. And that has never changed. My parents and siblings were incredibly influential in my life, and my sister-in-law and fellow ranch woman Sylvia, being a bit older and a lot wiser, helped me navigate it in so many ways.

Our Faith, Family, Friends

The next few years were busy as we started a family. My first pregnancy ended sadly at full term when our baby boy died shortly after birth. Again, as always, faith, family, and friends got us through that difficulty, and we went on to have three girls—Loni, Jill, and Carly—and then another son. We jokingly said during that last pregnancy that it was going to be our last chance for a boy. That idea stuck, and we named him Chance. Our kids have always been involved here and now are quick to come when we need help.

Curt told our three sons-in-law that he expected two things: help with branding and help with weaning. Period. Christmas and birthdays were optional! And they have been remarkably good at keeping that expectation. But back when our kids were younger, I spent a lot of time single parenting. My husband worked long, hard hours, and I made sure to get the kids to all the things they were involved in.

Julie & Curt-cattle branding in working gear.

It was assumed that I would be at their volleyball games. But if their dad came, it was very special. I was okay, most of the time, with second place! But when he was baling, or when it was calving time, I had lonely nights.

That's when, once the kids were in bed, I spent time on the hobbies I had developed: reading, needlework, painting, photography, writing, and music. I have been so thankful that I learned about that "busy hands" policy from my mum. Being creative has always given me joy. I even became what was called a "field editor" for *Country* magazine and, among other things, had a month-long diary in one of their "Farm and Ranch Living" issues. It was fun to have a professional photographer come out and take some wonderful photos of us for that article.

After high school, I took an animal health technician course in Saskatoon. It was a great experience. However, I was only in the second graduating class, and even though now they are common in many vet clinics, I didn't get to use that training in that setting. I got a job at a jewellery store as an engraver and helped with our finances that way. Once I decided to stay at home, I got paid from the ranch for bookkeeping. I also taught evening painting classes.

Then we made a new friend, Brad Wall, who got us interested in running a tourist business, bringing guests from as far away as Europe to have a working ranch experience. At first, it was simply learning what people wanted. We found out what worked, and I ended up doing the cooking. Our guests stayed in a bunk house for the night but always seemed quite ready to spend every other moment with us! That took a bit of getting used to, but honestly, we met such wonderful people. We always joked that there had to be a bad one eventually, but that never happened. We had people from all over Canada, but mainly from Germany and Switzerland. Sometimes they spoke English, and sometimes they didn't. We hosted all manner of people: concert hall musicians, a prison psychologist, a television producer, a lingerie shop owner, and the head of a large cardiac unit, who we naturally dubbed "Doc Holliday." We had a journalist from Germany who wrote an article about her experience here when we first started, and my cousin, who lived in Germany then, saw it and was so surprised to recognize us.

These guests stayed anywhere from a day or two to a month. I remember one girl from Switzerland whose stay was open-ended. She told us she was staying till her money ran out. We had no way of really knowing how long that was! Sometimes our family of six felt very chaotic, but our guests never seemed to mind. Another girl from Switzerland came during a very busy time. We arranged for our niece to go riding every morning with her to chase some cows in where a fence had broken down. After about five days, she quietly suggested that it might be a good idea just to fix the fence. We had hoped she wouldn't think of that! She was also the one who thought nothing of the somewhat European custom of suntanning in the nude. We didn't realize what was happening till my teenage nephew was sent to check on her at the bunkhouse and came back very red-faced! That was a bit of a shock to someone who, even now, hardly leaves the ranch.

I found it helpful to make up what I considered a tasty two-week menu that I used when we had guests. It was easy then to set that in motion, allowing me to buy what was needed quickly and to delegate when I had to. This was also the time when our kids learned to help in the kitchen when necessary. If I was on the way home from picking one of them up, the ones at home knew they had to fill in—whether it was with the tourist business or just regular busy family days or when we had special events happening, like branding. Even now, if any of them are taxed with the job of helping to feed twenty people or a hundred, they just dig in and think nothing of it. I am glad I was able to teach them that it doesn't necessarily have to be fancy, although that's fun, too. It must just fill an empty stomach. I am glad that we also taught them that, as

Jane Austen said, "One cannot have too large a party." I have always wanted them to treat people hospitably.

Our Swinging Door

My daughter Loni calls it my constantly swinging door, and I have never been sorry for that. We sometimes referred to our home as Grand Central Station. I was aided in that by a husband who comes from a Ukrainian family, folks who truly are experts in food and hospitality. We both learned from the best. We did come from very different backgrounds, however, and my mother-in-law would call in the middle of a storm, with no real idea of how many cows there were, to ask if all of them were safely in the barn. We just didn't have the heart to tell her the truth! Our ranch and the camp nearby were a great place to hold family reunions. I enjoyed planning a number of those—especially for my American cousins—and as my extended family grew, we often held Christmas gatherings in our home that could be anywhere from fifty to seventy people.

After about six years in the tourist business, our friend Brad, who ran the booking and arranging part of it, wanted to enter politics and so we decided that that part of our life would end. We kept in touch with quite a few of those tourists, and some of them who were returnees became friends. Brad, whom we often made fun of when it came to ranching knowledge, went on to become Premier Brad Wall and has now become something of a rancher himself, although he would probably humbly downplay that statement.

During our days in the tourist business, I had written an article for a German magazine. As a result of this and some of the other things I wrote, once Brad became the Premier of Saskatchewan, he asked if I would become a part of his speechwriting team. What a privilege that was. It's amazing how sometimes life gives you an opportunity that you never saw coming. That was a part-time job I didn't really share about with very many people while it was happening. But sometimes, when Brad was complimented on something like a Christmas message, it felt special to know he was reading some of my words, even if no one else did. It was kind of funny to think about those words—written in the middle of nowhere by an unknown woman in her ranch house office, often in her pyjamas—being read by a person who is considered such a gifted speaker. In our busy ranching days, it was also an outlet for me that gave me a taste of the outside world that sometimes feels far away when you're mired in the busyness of what is your normal life! I also had fun writing and illustrating a children's book for my grandkids, in which they are the main characters, even though I've never had the courage to try to publish it!

Another opportunity that came along unexpectedly was when the son of some acquaintances who live a few miles from us decided he wanted to do a medical photo shoot in our local hospital. He lives in Norway and just happened to be home and wanted to do it here in Saskatchewan. He needed some extra models and asked our daughter Jill and me to do that. I never saw myself as a model or a medical person, but there I was, delivering a baby, doing a kidney transplant, and performing heart surgery! I say that facetiously. Really, all I did was stand where I was told and try to look reasonably intelligent. I had no idea where these pictures would turn up, but people have seen us in all kinds of places: on posters, in nursing magazines, and in nursing student teaching sessions. I was even surprised to see myself on Pinterest one day promoting drug-free birth, which was kind of funny considering I have had four Caesarean sections and was quite happy to take all the drugs I was given.

I think sometimes people see us as living a quiet life in the country. A simpler life than the bustling city. I still remember the day of the photo shoot. My husband had to be at the hospital early that day for a minor surgery. I went to pick him up and bring him home, drove back in twice for photo sessions, and then wondered if there would be another trip to the hospital when our four-year-old granddaughter stuck a little pebble up her nose! She said it was a piece of gold she found on Grandma's driveway! However, it was finally successfully removed by her dad without another trip. That was, along with everything else that happens on a ranch in a normal day. We had a debriefing session that evening, consisting of a lot of laughter, which usually seems to be how we try to handle things.

BSE- Mad Cow Disease & Family Health

We needed a good dose of laughter when we bought another ranch along the South Saskatchewan River in 2002. A year later, the whole BSE issue—also known as "mad cow disease"—threw our industry into a tailspin. Shortly after this, two young men came along wanting to marry two of our daughters. Wedding plans in the middle of all of that sometimes seemed bizarrely ridiculous. "Get another Visa" seemed to be the "joke" of the day. Except some days, it just wasn't funny. When you wake up one day, and BSE has entered your life, when no one wants your product, and it is worth next to nothing, that is a rude awakening indeed and a very harsh reality. But it also reminds you of what's most important.

Weather also plays such a huge part in any agricultural life. One spring, our valley was heavily flooded due to ice jams in the Swift Current creek, which runs through it. We had a couple from Germany here who had to get to the airport in Saskatoon. Curt had arranged for a dynamiter to come and blow up the jam because the flooding was causing so much damage. So, I remember driving out of the valley with our guests and wondering what I would come home to! Somehow, a dynamiter who looks like he's been a bit too close to some kind of explosion a few too many times doesn't give you a warm fuzzy feeling. But he knew what he was doing, and it was exactly what needed to happen. I was so thankful to come home to what looked almost normal!

There were also times of drought, like in 2021 and back in 1988, when the elements tested our staying power. And then when other things were added to it, it made it extra difficult. In the spring of 1988, my mother passed away unexpectedly. The day after her funeral, my brother Gordon's thirteen-year-old son was diagnosed with leukaemia. This meant that Gordon and his family had to spend a lot of time away, and it also increased the workload for the rest of us as we tried to support them through this difficult journey. My nephew Hugh, the cancer survivor, now works with us here, and we are very thankful for his recovery. Other things plagued us physically as well. I had endocarditis shortly after our son was born and spent weeks in the hospital while Curt looked after a new-born along with his three sisters. Then a year later Curt was diagnosed with Type 1 Diabetes and a couple of years later I was diagnosed with Lupus and developed a chronic heart issue. "What a gong show," as the saying goes. Again, without the help of everyone at the ranch as well as friends and other family, where would we be? A lot of those same people have endlessly helped at brandings, calf weaning days, and sale loading days. We are so grateful for all of them. As far as ranching goes, apparently it takes a community of support to keep going.

My life was often filled with cooking, cooking, and then some more cooking, and then cleaning up along with more cleaning up. But so, so many good times in the middle of all of it. Yes, hard stuff was in there too, but so was a lot of love and laughter. Working with family has its pros and cons, but for us I am so thankful that it still has many more pros than cons. My brothers have now both retired, but they each have a son living and working here. As well as my nephew Hugh and his wife Tanya, my other brother Harold's son, Joe, and his wife, Honey, are an integral part of our operation.

Family Teamwork

If every ranch woman wrote a job description based on their own experience and the dynamics of their operation, I'm sure they would all be quite different. For me I think putting it into words couldn't be done without saying it's been mostly about teamwork. Teamwork involving my brothers and their families, teamwork involving our own kids and now their families, but most of all for me, the team that Curt and I have been together. It hasn't always been easy to balance that, but I have been fortunate that it is equally important to both of us. Everyone working here at our ranch has their own area of contribution, and I am thankful for each of them. Mine has been to keep the office and our business information organized, up-to-date, and readily available. I try to fill in where needed and even sometimes when I am not. Like the time when I did my best to help fight a field fire in a skirt and flip-flops. My son-in-law Adrian was yelling at me just to get back and stay safe. I don't think I helped at all. I just burnt the bottoms of my feet a little, and even worse, had to throw out those flip-flops!

And, of course, there is always the cooking. Always the cooking! Branding was always a time when we needed huge quantities of food. I would host breakfast in my kitchen and be ready to feed fifty-plus people. The plus could be just about any number. I hadn't slept much the night before one of these breakfasts, so when I heard our dog whining by the door at four in the morning, I let him out and came face-to-face with a skunk. Well, that's not entirely true. I saw the back of it instead. That is never a welcome sight. Our dog, just a few feet away, got the worst of that experience, but I was next in line. That all took about five seconds! I had no real idea of what exactly to do next! I went and lay down on our bed, now totally exhausted. My husband mumbled sleepily, "What is that smell?" I remember laying there thinking: "Okay, God, this is likely going to be a funny story someday. But right now, it's not funny at all! Please help me because I don't know how I'm going to get through the next few hours!"

For all those days when I was a kid, trying to avoid inside work, I think I have made up for it many times over. Being ready for anything in the food department means quick lunches sent along or driving them out to a field or suddenly having extra mouths to feed. And as our family has now grown too, we needed a bigger table, because that's where we often sit visiting and solving the world's issues. We have been welcomed at other tables, too, and our kids learned to sleep wherever our truck took us, just as other kids did at our house. I remember our friends' little guy, fast asleep on his back, with a plate sitting on his stomach and a half-eaten brownie perched precariously on it! We also knew the importance of escaping the ranch occasionally, and for us, it didn't need to include trips to Disneyland, although that would have been wonderful.

A weekend in a city close by with a hotel and a waterslide and a bunch of friends was just about perfect and created lifelong memories. Our kids have reaped the benefits of all the good times and relationship building days here on the ranch, and now our grandkids are doing the same. I have a sign in my kitchen that reads: "A grandparent's house is where cousins become best friends." Apparently to do that a lot of noise is needed! But most days we're good with that. One of the biggest surprises of our time as ranchers was when our daughter Loni, a financial advisor, and her husband Adrian, a machinist, decided they wanted to move here from Alberta, in 2016, and give ranching a try. We had never even considered that as a possibility! They wanted to move into our basement with their three little girls, Charli, Molly and Finnley, until they decided for sure. So, for a little over a year, that's what we did! It was a bit strange getting used to that, but we did it, and we still like each other!

The Third Generation

Our daughter Loni became part of the third generation of ranch women here. She loves to cook, and so every supper she would use our kitchen to do that, and I would do the cleaning up. She was able to work from here at home virtually for the same company, which has been a huge asset for them. Our daughter Jill, her husband Chris, and their family—Jerry, Maci, and Wylie—live just five miles away and help a lot here, too. Our daughter Carly lives in Swift Current with her husband Ryan and their family, Lily, Eberly, and Brooks. Our son Chance moved back here from Saskatoon with his wife Kim and their family, Scotlyn and Kash. On special ranch occasions, they all turn up to help.

This place is equally important to all of them, and I consider that one of the biggest blessings of my life. Once Loni and Adrian decided to stay, they moved upstairs, and we moved out into a new "ready to move" home next door with another yard to start planting trees in all over again! But to have the next generation here has made it all worthwhile. An added benefit is that, because our daughter Loni loves to cook, I can sometimes escape from that inside life again, just like when I was a kid! I'm now the Tag Lady for branding and weaning, and I've been assured, probably with an eye roll when my back is turned, that this is a job only I can do!

Just like everyone else, my life has been full of challenges. And prayers asking for rain, good health, and safety. But living the life of a ranch woman is a life I would choose repeatedly. It is a good life, full of fresh air and plenty of homegrown benefits and privileges not everyone is fortunate enough to have. And so, I go back to the quote I started with. I have perhaps sacrificed; I know I have fought and struggled in the life I've chosen. But I can honestly say, for sure, that the love of it fills my heart.

The insights in this story are many. Doing what you can, from where you are, with what you have. Having faith to go through many trials and tribulations that life puts forth into our lives, we keep on moving forward, one day at a time. Living a purpose-driven life to teach what you live to the next generations. Instilling trust as you become a trusting role model and teach about integrity, ethical behaviour, and working as a team. Other people understand your values by the way you live daily, and they follow your lead while you walk the talk.

Rhubarb Crisp

(Simple homegrown dessert of my Mum's that is still a favourite of mine.)

Mix 4 cups of chopped rhubarb with ½ cup sugar and spread in a 9 x 13 pan.

Top with a mixture of:

1 cup oatmeal

1 cup brown sugar

1 cup flour

¾ cup melted margarine or butter

Bake at 350 degrees for 45 minutes to an hour, testing rhubarb with a fork for tenderness.

Chapter XI

Kids Will Be Kids & Animal Stories

by Betty Anne (Armstrong) Burrows

Stories growing up on the East and West in the Cypress Hills (Betty Anne is still alive and lives in Bassano.)

I was born the youngest of five to George and Anne Armstrong on July 17, 1929. My siblings were Kathryn, Bob, Peter, and Arnold.

When we were very small, Mom had a cook that we were not particularly fond of. One day, George and Anne went to town and left her in charge. We were sent out to play, and the cook commenced to wash the kitchen floor. We went down to the creek and spent the morning gathering garter snakes into a bucket, then we opened the kitchen door and spilled the snakes into the house. The cook spent the rest of the day on the kitchen table. When Mom and Dad got home, we were in big trouble and were sent to gather the snakes, which, by that time, were in every conceivable corner of the house. I don't remember if we got supper that day, but the cook definitely quit.

We ranch kids were able to ride horseback 7 miles to Evergreen School from September until the first snowstorm in the fall. Then Mom and Dad hired teachers who had some normal school training. A log schoolhouse was built at the ranch with homemade wooden desks. Regulation 4' X 8' slate blackboards were on the wall. Some of the teachers at the East and West Ranch were Annie Mack, Doris Emmard, Margaret Murray, Marie MacDonell, Helen Nelson, and Ruthie Christensen. My sister Kathryn also taught after she graduated from normal school.

Arnie's rat-tail retriever dog would sit outside and bark. The teacher would let him into the classroom to stop the noise. He would sit beside Arnie's desk and wag his tail, banging on the side of Arnie's desk, causing a terrible noise. Teacher was not happy!

Cuffie was the dog's name. One morning, Arnie and I went riding to check the cows that were calving. Arnie locked Cuffie in the barn. We were about 10 minutes away from the yard up behind the barn. The dog chewed his way out of the barn and ran and caught up with us. He grabbed Arnie's horse by the tail, and Arnie got bucked off. Arnie sat on the ground, laughing and patting his dog.

There was a forest fire in 1934 on the west end of the Cypress Hills. We all remembered being very frightened. Mom and Dad were gone for several days, George fighting fire and Anne helping to feed everyone. We kids were home with the cook and the hired men, and we could not tell where the fire was or if it might come over the hill at any time. The air was filled with smoke, and there was no way of receiving news.

Life was always exciting at the E&W ranch. Dad had about 20 Standardbred mares for breeding to an American Standard registered stallion. In the fall, it was a great sight to see them all brought in for weaning. It seemed like 100 because last year's yearlings and 2-year-olds were also with them. The spring foals were kept in for weaning, and the nicest picks were kept for two to three years to become saddle horses or were sold to neighbours. "Half Diamond-Right Angle Triangle" was the horse brand. Some blacks were sold to the RCMP for the riding academy at Regina. Soon after that, the RCMP Equestrian Training school closed.

Dad also had about a dozen heavy brood mares and a Clydesdale stallion. He was kept in a box stall when not out to pasture with the mares. Dad hired Dick Weiss, Mom's nephew, to train the young two-to-three-year-old heavy colts to harness. When they were training with a gentle older teammate, they were used for haying or harvest. They were then shipped to eastern Canada and some to England for use at the end of the 2nd World War.

Barney Crocket was a local brand inspector and often stopped in at the ranch to visit. One time, he brought two young Royal Canadian Mounted Policemen, freshly trained at Regina, for the July 1st Graburn Gap rodeo. They wanted to ride over to the rodeo grounds from the ranch. Dad asked me to take them to the barn and saddle up Doc and Robin (both 17 hands). The young RCMP fellows, red serge and shiny high-top black boots, had not ridden western saddles before. Both horses let them mount, but then they set into crow-hopping and bucked them off. The fellows then decided it was best to go to the Gap rodeo in the RCMP car. They were to lead the parade. The rodeo grounds were built on the flat below where the memorial plaque for the NWMP Captain Graburn is. He was killed in an Indian conflict. The Graburn Community Hall was built possibly 5 to 10 years before that rodeo.

In the summer, we always had four or five hired men for haying and harvest and for cutting and hauling logs off the bench. Mom also had a hired girl during the summer. There was a long dining table on the front porch, often set for 12 or more. This work crew was served three meals daily. The kitchen had a service window where food was passed out to the family and crew. My dad generally made sourdough pancakes for breakfast and put the meat in the oven for supper.

Dad butchered about once a week in the summer—a yearling lamb, heifer, or pig. We had a smokehouse where they hung pork. He made bacon as well. The smokehouse was cut out of the creek bank and lined with rocks, with a log roof and a plank floor. We also had a root cellar to store potatoes and vegetables. George grew a huge garden. We had no refrigeration in the early days before electricity at the ranch.

One year, when we kids were a little older, the hay crew decided to make chokecherry wine. They picked a lot of berries, and Dad supplied the sugar. There were two big crocks brewing in the old sod-roofed shack. It was well diluted down by the time they went to bottle their wine, as we had done a bit of sampling and made sure to keep the level of liquid up with a bit of water.

Dad put up a tall wind charger in about 1945, and it generated electricity, which was stored in batteries in the basement of the house. The telephone was on the fence line coming from the forestry ranger station on the bench. The forest ranger was George Ambrose. George and Mary Ambrose had five children: Dorothy, Flora and Chester, Jenny, and Gloria. Mary worked for Mom for a time before she was married. Entertainment at the East and West included a summer ranchers' camp that was held after haying season was over. The camp was set up at Graburn Gap. Neighbours would set up tents and spend the weekend. We had singing and poetry by Lance Brown. There was storytelling, swimming in Battle Creek, and trout fishing. Bonfires were held in the evenings. Some of the families that came were Ross and Dorothy Haig, the Good family, the Kuslers, Frank, and Hazel Reesor, and the Armstrongs. There was no such thing as a motorhome in the 40's and 50's.

As we kids got older, we rode or drove to Elkwater to the summertime dances. In the late 30's, 40's we had dances in the schoolhouse at the ranch. My dad, George Armstrong, belonged to the Cypress men's club in Medicine Hat. Sometimes the members would come out to the ranch for a weekend, unannounced. If Mom wasn't prepared for extra men to feed, she would take the 12-gauge shotgun out and shoot 8 or 10 partridges for the Sunday dinner. She was an excellent shot as well as an excellent horsewoman.

Ralph & Betty Anne Burrows

The Sarnia Ranch: The three-story brick home was built in 1901–03. They raised sheep, horses, and cattle. Mrs. Beatty was Dorothy Haig's mother. The top story of the Beatty home was full of lovely, well-dressed dolls. I remember that there were separate dolls for the children to play with, all with beautiful homemade dresses. The Haig children were Mary, Ann, and Dave. Dave became a lawyer. Another fun fact is that my Aunt Katherine, Dad's sister, would take little staycations at the Sarnia ranch. She also would stop over there before catching the train to Medicine Hat.

I remember trailing cattle, and another time sheep, to Walsh for sale or shipping. We stopped at the Sarnia ranch overnight. Ross and Dorothy were very hospitable to the extent of having a load of hay spread for our cattle when we got there if the snow was deep. We did not look forward to trailing into the Walsh stockyards because our cattle had not seen a train track, a train, a wooden bridge, or paved roads before.

One morning, as we approached with a bunch of steers, a train came through, blowing its whistle and belching steam and smoke. The steers broke back about a mile before we could get them stopped. (The air was blue, and our horses were played out.) They wouldn't go near the stockyard after that. Ed Schlenker, who lived on the flat, saw our predicament. He turned his milk cow loose and headed her our way. She was a big Holstein, apparently with a lot of charm. She trotted over, went right through the herd and out the other side, toward the stockyards, and our steers followed. Altogether, it was a long two days of hard work to get the cattle to the Walsh stockyards.

One time, we were taking sheep in. Dad employed a shepherd to help. It was very hot by the time we reached the stockyards. The shepherd tied up our overheated sheepdog to a fence. Our family went to head for home after the long day and realized that our dog was missing. Sadly, he had died of thirst and heat exhaustion, still tied to the fence. Meanwhile, the shepherd disappeared.

Chapter XII

Raising Ranch Children

by Dorothy Louise Beasley

Thanks to their pioneer childhood, children raised on ranches and homesteads established a close connection with the land. From a young age, they rode horses, helped with daily chores, and played with simple toys. These children often began working for neighbours and their ranch when they were 12 years old, instilling in them a strong work ethic. They also faced the realities of growing up quickly, often due to family losses from health issues or accidents.

Ranch children learned significantly through observation. These youngsters absorbed valuable insights by keenly observing and maximizing the resources available to them. They tended to animals, recognizing their vital contributions to their family's way of life. They witnessed the ever-present unpredictability of elements that could swiftly alter their surroundings—be it the weather, prairie fires, or illnesses affecting both humans and animals.

Life in rural areas posed unique challenges. Kids might embark on journeys in good weather but encounter blizzards on their way home, illustrating the unpredictability of rural life. In the early years, they lived far from town and relied on horses for transportation. In later years, they were still a considerable distance from town: when something serious happened, they were often a 45-minute to 60-minute drive from the nearest hospital.

Growing up in this environment, children developed an appreciation for the simplicity of life's happy times. Children had fun playing with frogs, salamanders, and baby animals. Since horses were a big part of their lives, they played games using the horses, had horse races at the local racetrack, and would ride to the river or the creek and have a picnic if friends were over. They played cowboys and natives, where some children would be riding bareback, playing the natives, building dead-wood Tepees and the others would be riding in a saddle, being the cowboys coming to find the natives.

They gained a sense of responsibility by tending to daily chores. Taking care of animals brought them pride and joy. They fed the chickens, knowing that they provided eggs for breakfast and as an ingredient in many delicious recipes. Later, the chicken itself would become a dinner table meal, too. So, it was and still is important to feed the chickens and make sure they have water every day.

Modern Homesteading

Modern homesteading has seen more women getting involved while their husbands work elsewhere. These families purchase small parcels of land called acreages. Here, they embrace a rural lifestyle, planting gardens and raising animals like cows, chickens, and turkeys. This is a little different than traditional ranching since these activities are not their main source of income. Even so, the children glean many valuable lessons about life from this homesteading culture. They learn what it means to have responsibilities that give them a sense of pride and accomplishment.

Generational family-owned and well-run livestock ranches have carried forward traditional skills: ranch children still learn to drive tractors, trucks, and other machinery to assist with planting and harvesting. Gender equality is encouraged on modern homesteads and present ranches, just as it was in the past. Boys and girls learn similar skills, breaking free from rigid gender roles. Both girls and boys drive the farm equipment, work in the fields, care for animals, and learn how to cook basic meals.

They also learned how to do their own laundry, as then they know if their clothing can be washed in cold water or hot water. They probably want their socks to stay white, so they wash them in hot water with other white items. I found that as a mother it was much easier to teach them how to do their own laundry. They appreciated the fact that their clothes were the same colour when they came out of the washer/dryer as when they went in. They got their own clothing back at the end of the day, not their brothers' clothing. They also learn how to sweep the floor and keep the house tidy. Basic life skills everyone needs to learn. Rural children also learn valuable emotional management by observing and befriending animals. They find healthy ways to cope with frustration and anger, a skill that serves them well throughout their lives. I recall times when I was a teenager and I used to catch one of the horses, put on the bridle, then jump on my horse, Star, or whichever horse was handy near the barnyard. Sometimes I would take the time to saddle up, sometimes jump on bareback. I would take my shoes and socks off and ride with my bare feet, that was the best way for me to ride horseback. Then I could ride with or against the wind, hair streaming out the back or tie it back, with my legs and feet holding onto the horse's sides like glue. The wind, the warm feel of the horse and the feeling of freedom would take my frustration and anger away with it. Sometimes I let the horse have her/his head, put the length of my body close on the horse's back, with my head next to his mane and ride as fast as we could for a bit to get as far away from the house as possible. Then bring the horse up with the reins tighter and have him/her trot the rest of the way, about 2 miles, (3 km). The horse and I were like one, he or she was my friend, my partner. I could always depend on the horse to take me away to the river breaks where I could sit for an hour or two and relax, take deep breaths, and come to terms with whatever was creating the frustration and angry feelings. Animals also help to reduce loneliness and social isolation, indirectly improving wellbeing. Animals love to be petted, fed, and talked to, which also helps the child to feel needed and calm. We always had kittens out in the barn at home and one special yellow cat named Snoopy, who was my cat and he was allowed in the house. He slept on my bed at night and he seemed to know when I needed a friend.

Innovation and resourcefulness are ingrained in ranch children's upbringing. When they grow up on ranches or modern-day homesteads, kids learn to appreciate food, its origins, and how to creatively use leftovers. Food is expensive to purchase and requires unique skills to come up with variations of recipes to cook with basic ingredients. Home-made chicken or beef hamburgers, fresh home-grown vegetables, potatoes, and salad greens. Wild berries picked from wild saskatoon bushes on top of ice cream or pumpkin pie and whipped cream, made from real pumpkins grown in the garden.

Children understand that running a farm or ranch requires the involvement of the entire family. They develop self-esteem, teamwork, and independence through these shared responsibilities. Self-discipline is cultivated by performing tasks like milking cows and gathering eggs, preparing the children for independent lives. Rural life exposes children to life-and-death experiences with animals, teaching them to accept the cycle of life and death. I remember when we raised sheep, sometimes a baby lamb would die, even though we did everything we could to save it. It is just the way life happens sometimes.

Antelope Adventures

Once, when I, Louise Douglass, was about 10-12 years old and my sister, Dulcie, was 8-10 years old, Dad found a couple of baby antelope in a field he was working in. The mother never came back for them; something must have scared her away, and then a predator got her. Anyways, Dad had watched where the twin baby antelope were all day and noticed when he went back the next day, their mother never came back. So, he brought them home in the truck. He laid them both down gently on the floor of the truck and put the heat on so they wouldn't get chilled.

We fell in love with them right away. They were so little: their legs were longer than their bodies. They were tan and white and had big ears with long and skinny faces. So cute! We fed them warm, fresh cow's milk using two glass pop bottles with lamb nipples fitted over the opening on the bottles. They would suck on the nipples until the bottles were empty.

As the little antelope grew bigger and bigger, they would follow Dulcie and me around the yard. We didn't pen them up—they just wandered around the yard, followed the dog, laid in the shade on hot days, and were with us whenever we were out in the yard. They would come to us when we called out their names. One we named Julie, and the other one was Joe. They thought they were people and would come to the bus stop with us, too. We had a cattle guard across our driveway, and it would have been dangerous for them to try crossing it. They didn't try to get out of the yard, though they watched us get on the bus and then went back to grazing in the yard. That way they didn't get onto the main roadway and get run over. We took care of them ourselves. They were our responsibility. We fed them twice a day, and the little male began to grow little stub horns.

During antelope hunting season, we asked Al Oeming (who worked at the Game Farm in Edmonton) and the Game Warden here in Brooks what we should do to keep people from shooting them. They told us to keep them in the yard and put them into a pen where they couldn't get out. Otherwise, someone would see them and shoot them, even though they were in our yard. So, we kept them safe until the antelope hunting season was over. They ate hay by then, so it was easy to feed them in the open-air pen.

However, we knew we couldn't keep them forever: they were now almost full-grown animals. We contacted Al Oeming afterwards to see if he had room to take them. He said he had the perfect spot for them, and so that is what happened. Our family went up to see them after they had been there a few weeks and got situated. Joe and Julie knew us, of course, and they came running up to the fence when we called their names. It was good to see them, and they were happy to see us too. They stuck their noses through the wire to be scratched. We noticed they looked healthy and seemed to be happy. There were some other antelope in the pen, too. It was a large enclosure that had lots of grass in it for them to eat, as well as fresh, clean water for them to drink. That is where other antelope that were incapable of living out in the wild were kept. People could see them and learn more about them from their behaviour. It was a great way to save the animals from early death.

These antelope are out in the wild in the wintertime.
They only live in Alberta, Saskatchewan, CAN, and Montana, USA.

Dulcie and I were sad to see them go after we had looked after them all spring, summer and fall of that year. They had become faithful and loving companions. We loved them, too. But we knew that they would not be safe at our place. Plus, they were still wild animals: one can never tell what a grown animal will do, even if they have been pets all their lives. It was best for them to be safe and happy at the Game Farm.

Chapter XIII

Her Own Individuality

Phyllis Rathwell Story

I grew up on a mixed farm in Southwest Saskatchewan. At the time, my older brother got to do all the "cool" chores: being outside with the animals, driving stuff, riding horses, and being treated like a grown-up. Meanwhile, I had to stay in the house to peel potatoes, help with meals, wash dishes, and keep up with housework. How I longed to swap places with him! Thirty years later, I finally had a chance to do all the cool stuff while simultaneously peeling potatoes, making meals, and doing dishes and housework! I married a rancher, moving to the ranch south of Carmichael in 1988. I had two teenage sons, a full-time job, some farmland, and stars in my eyes.

I learned so much in a short time. Before this, I had been "protected" from the grittier aspects of ranch life by being needed more in the house than in the pasture. That protection ended abruptly! I quickly learned to drive silage trucks, unload 'em, and babysit the blow deck during silaging* of the crop, all while running to the house to make meals between loads. Harvesting barley was easier: hauling truckloads to the bin, backing up, then starting the old auger and dumping itchy barley to be augered up and into the bin. Haying was a favourite time. I wasn't adept enough to be trusted with the big round baler, so I drove the old outfit to make some small square bales. There was no cab on the tractor, just a ratty old umbrella that I regularly beaned myself on. We used these small bales to feed the horses.

I finished that chore long before the rest of the haying crew, so I could get on with other summertime pursuits. That primarily meant tending to my garden: weeding, watering, picking, and preserving a variety of vegetables. I picked chokecherries and saskatoons; made pickles, jams, and jellies; and froze, cleaned, peeled, and stored all sorts of food for the winter. And I enjoyed it! It was only possible for me to do all that because, as a school-teacher, I had the luxury of summertime off work.

Weekends, Wintertime

When I went back to school, my ranch chores shifted to those that could be done after school and on weekends. I rode to help gather, ran the gate, administered meds and kept records during pregnancy testing, helped haul bales, chased bulls home, checked and fixed fences, helped bring in any critter that needed treatment for any medical calamity, and learned to give shots and assess herd health while riding through a pasture. I also helped in the feedlot, pen checking after school to assess the health of the newly weaned calves to be put on feed.

Wintertime slowed down some. The calves in the feedlot became accustomed to their rations. The bulls settled down. The cows were used to bales being rolled out, and daily chores could be handled without me. I did not have to open waterholes, thaw water tanks, start frozen equipment, or deal with the millions of cold, ugly jobs that take twice as long at forty below 0°C. Instead, I merrily drove the twenty miles to school, secure in the knowledge that most of these jobs would be done before I got home. Weekends could be a different story, as I would help bed the calves (mostly cutting twine and manning the gates) or feed cows (again, the twine**).

Spring brought the excitement, joy, and exhaustion of calving. I was spared the night checks during the week when I had to go work. But on weekend nights, it was my chore to check the heifers. I avoided the early morning pasture check, but when I got home from school, I'd saddle Tess and ride through the nearby pasture—***tagging any new babies and bringing in any that needed to be watched closely. Then came branding: planning for and feeding a crew of twenty while also riding to gather, running the gate, wrestling, inoculating, record keeping, cutting, keeping the irons hot, then helping to push moms and calves back to the correct pasture. So many parts of the job!

During all of this, I was the cook and bottlewasher, with no days off. If a ranch job required a crew on school days, I would have a roaster full of stew ready to be cooked while I was at work. A couple of loaves of sandwiches would be in the fridge, along with a cake or muffins for lunch, a salad, and pies ready ahead of time. I often made all the preparations the night before, went off to school, came home to get in on the tail end of the work, put out the supper meal, and then cleaned up as the menfolk sat on the deck to smoke and have a beer. I admit, dishes were slammed, and cussing occurred.

I kept the books, another hated job! April tax time was stressful and frustrating as I tried to reconcile the accounts and make everything balance. I did not quickly grasp the nuances of billing categories and what expenses went where. Nor could I easily decipher scribbles on the back of an envelope or intuitively understand what expense category our "quick weekend holiday" gas receipts should be filed under.

I was a gopher, driving to town to "go fer" parts, yet another hated job. Every parts man I ever met smirked as I tried to describe what I had been sent to town for. "Dipstick repair kit" and "oil pan gaskets" apparently do not exist. I often had to do these errands on the way home from school, with nobody at home to answer the parts man's questions and no chance for a re-do as repair places were closed by the time I got back home.

This may sound like I am whining. And maybe I am a little. But the fun and friendships I made were all worth it. The most pleasant day I ever had working cows was one spent sorting cow/calf pairs with our neighbour, Lyn Sauder. The two of us calmly sorted off pairs, moving them up a knoll and around the corner to where the guys waited to process them. They were swearing, yelling, and shouting. But Lyn and I had a stress-free day; just quietly riding and sorting was pure bliss! We would catch the other's eye, nod to the pair we wanted, calmly ride over, and separate that pair. No fuss, no muss, no bother!

English Teacher, Cowgirl, Poet

My life as an English teacher and my cowboy life came together after I attended a Cowboy Poetry Gathering in Maple Creek. I was hooked! Since about 1994, I have written and performed hundreds of times across the Canadian prairies and BC, Montana, Colorado, Nevada, and Arizona. Wherever cowboy folk gather, these poems and tales of life on the ranch find an audience. My poems reflect the truth, as I see it, of being a ranch wife. There is no "riding into the sunset" kind of romance on a ranch. There is hard work and frustration, comradery and joy, exultation and exhaustion, laughter, and tears. And besides, if you ride into the sunset, you end up far from home, in the dark.

I left the ranch in 1998. My ex and I have had an amicable parting and have both moved on. I am now married to a fantastic cowboy from Montana, and we live in Elkwater, Alberta, where we run the 2Lazy2 Ranch because we are too lazy to ranch now. We attend poetry gatherings and adore our families, our friends, and our life. We spend time in the USA when it suits us and consider ourselves to be too irresponsible to even own a dog.

Sortin'

"Come help me, hon, to sort some cows," the words I've come to hate.
Cause he stands way, way down the lane, and I'm stuck at the gate.
His signals are so subtle, I swear I just can't see.
He flashes left, or right, or through, or one, or two, or three.
Then he'll run a bunch right at me. "All in pen five" he'll sign.
As three tons come a pounding, and my heart beats double time.
That circle in the air means, "The first one, send 'er back."
But the others pass her on the way, and I'm trying to keep track.
Hand up means, "Whoa, turn 'em back." A wave means "Let 'em by."
But, how 'bout when he slaps his head and makes that circle in the sky?
Now another batch is coming, they're kicking up their heels.
And he's got his arms a-goin' in stupid wagon wheels.
I couldn't turn 'em quick enough so I just let them past.
Don't he know I'm getting older and just can't move that fast?
He stampedes another ten or so down the alley to my gate.
He's jumpin' up and down now, but I see 'em kinda late.
He's wavin' like a windmill; he's jumpin' on his hat!
The air around him's turning blue…What does he mean by that?
He's stomping now toward me. I think that I'll just go!
So, I flip him the birdie. It's the only sign I know!

A favourite recipe below and easy to make.

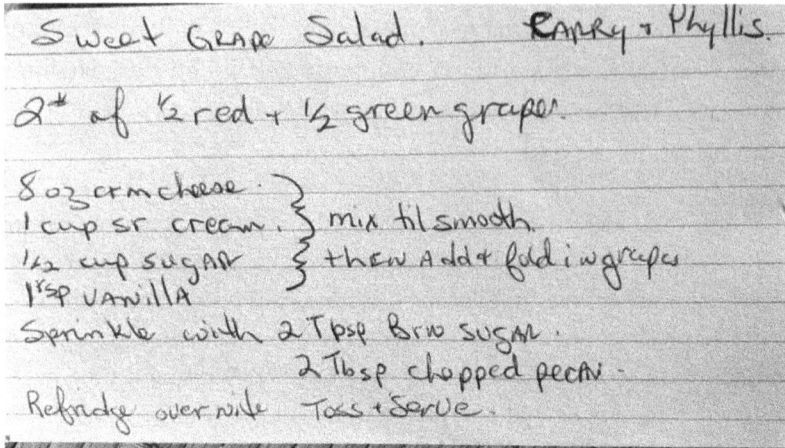

Sweet Grape Salad. Barry + Phyllis

2# of ½ red + ½ green grapes.

8 oz crm cheese.
1 cup sr cream. } mix til smooth.
1½ cup sugar } then Add + fold in grapes
1 tsp vanilla
Sprinkle with 2 Tbsp Brn sugar.
2 Tbsp chopped pecan.
Refridge over nite Toss + Serve.

Sweet Grape Salad

Louise's supplemental information:

For women who are unfamiliar with our ranch terms, here are explanations about some of the things we do and take for granted that everyone knows what we are talking about.

* Silaging of the crop is when someone swaths the grain down with a cutting machine, swather, or discbine, laying it down in rows. A silaging machine comes along and cuts the swath into little pieces, and blows it into a truck box. The truck takes the chopped grain and sheaves back to a silage pit, and dumps it onto the cement silage pit floor. A large tractor with big heavy tires tamps down the silage into a pile, taking out all the air. Once the field has been finished, the pit is then covered with plastic and old tires or heavy bales of feed to keep the plastic from blowing off. The silage then ferments until the cattle are ready to eat it in a month or so. It is good feed for weight gain and a great way to keep the grain from spoiling.

** Baling "Twine": This is a type of plastic or sisal wrap that goes around the bales to keep them together. It depends on the baler as to what type of twine one purchases and uses to wrap the bale up so it stays together for stacking purposes, as well as to store the bales longer and feed out the bales easier.

*** "Tagging" the baby calves: Phyllis said she would "tag" the baby calves after they were born. This is a method of identification for the rancher to bond the cow/calf pair, as they will then have the same numbers on their ear tags. Tags are also used for selling, sorting purposes for the paperwork, etc. Or if the calf dies during the season, it will be marked down in the calving book as "died as cow had no milk," or whatever has happened. Sometimes a cow will have twins, and so the rancher writes numbers on the plastic dangly tags that say, 23-1, 23-2, while the mother will have a tag that reads 23. There are different colours of tags for each year, so one can tell what year they were born. The tag goes into one ear usually, using a quick click of a plier, and the tag is there for identification purposes, supposedly forever. The hole in the ear is like a piercing done for our earrings.

Chapter XIV

Resourcefulness & Self Reliance

Gail (Gompf) McKillop Story as written by Gail.

I, Gail Gloria Gompf, was born on March 7, 1949, in Regina, Saskatchewan, to Henry Alvin Maxwell Gompf and Annie Elizabeth Gompf. Since our small town of Lang was snowed in, Mom was staying with her cousin in Regina to await my arrival. I am the second child out of three, with my brother Gary being four years older and my sister Colleen being four years younger than me. We grew up seven miles north of Oak Lake, Manitoba, on three quarter sections owned by our grandfather, Harry (Heinrich) Gompf.

We attended Harvey school, which was one and a half miles from our home. We had a Shetland pony that pulled a cart in which we rode to school. In the summer months, our parents bought my brother and me a bicycle to ride. We rode double, which worked fine until we were out of sight, past the trees. At that point, my brother Gary would decide that I had to walk or run while he rode the bike. I had to run two telephone pole lengths and then got to ride one telephone length. However, I was not a runner. When I was born, my left hip didn't form a hip joint. I was a year or so old when my parents took me to the doctor. Then I was off to Winnipeg to the Shriner's Hospital, where they put me in traction for six months. The doctors hoped that the socket would grow around the hip bone. I came home with a cast around my waist—down to my ankle on the left leg and to my knee on the right leg, with a stick in between them. That is when my mom got her first Electrolux vacuum cleaner. She used the vacuum to keep the cast dry.

We always had electricity as far back as I can remember. Anyway, we went to the Harvey school for three years and then were driven to Oak Lake, Manitoba. The neighbours took turns taking us to school. Since I was the youngest in the vehicle, I sat in the front seat with the driver. My worst times were riding beside our closest neighbour, who smoked big fat cigars. I haven't liked the smell of cigars since.

We finally got to drive to school on our own. Dad bought Gary a Volkswagen (VW). The six of us piled into the VW, and off we went. Mom and Dad were foster parents, and so for most of our lives, we had other children staying with us in our home. Tim, Kevin, and Jackie Campbell were raised with us. So, Gary and Tim rode in the front of the Volkswagen, Jackie and I rode in the back seat, and Colleen and Kevin rode in the baggage compartment behind the back seat. When Gary graduated from school, we finally got a school bus. We walked half a mile to catch the bus. I remember it was -40° F, and we walked out to the building that we used as a shelter while we waited for the bus. It was warmer standing outside the shelter than it was inside. Dad finally got the car started and came to rescue us, but the inside of the car was still cold. Thankfully, the bus showed up soon afterwards.

Our house was 40 feet x 40 feet and was built of stone around 1900. It was a two-story house with a full attic and a full basement. The stones were at least 2 feet wide x 3 feet long. There was a widow's walk on the top of the house. I remember, when I was younger, holding pillows against the windows when it hailed outside. One year, when most of us were out, we came home to discover that all the windows on the north side of our house were broken. My foster sister Jackie and her friend had stayed home because Jackie was sick. They said that when the window broke in the bedroom where they were, there was enough force that the glass blew down the stairs. They cleaned up the glass as best as they could.

Finished High School

I finished high school at Oak Lake Collegiate in 1967. The day I wrote my last exam, I got on the Greyhound Bus and headed for Alberta. I worked cleaning cabins at Vermillion Crossing, which is halfway between Banff and Radium Hot Springs. I lived in Banff, then moved to Calgary, and then back to Banff. My girlfriend Carol and I went with her father to a cabin in the Big Stone area. We rode horses to find stray cattle that had got mixed with the neighbour's cattle. That is where I met my future husband for the first time. His horse was trying to buck him off, but he managed to stay on. Carol and I rode her horse into the slough waters sometimes when the weather was hot. We took turns jumping off him into the water to get cooled off. It was a very hot summer. Carol came up with the idea that we should wash our hair in the slough water. She told me to go first. I looked in the water, and there were all kinds of swimming things in it. It took a while for me to get the courage to do it. I got it wet, then I put shampoo on my hair and stuck it into the water. Lo and behold, all the little swimming things left, and I had the softest hair I ever had. Carol had decided she wasn't going to wash her hair there, but I told her if I had to do it, she had to do it too.

Carol moved to Brooks and got a job at the Horticulture Centre. She convinced me to move too, and I got a job there as well. I got engaged to Bill McKillop in March of 1974, and we got married on November 23 of the same year. We farmed with his parents, John and Agnes McKillop. Bill worked for the Laughlin Brothers in Youngstown as a mechanic and farmed as well. I looked after the cows, but he did the feeding in the wintertime. We later bought the ranch from his mom and dad when they moved to Brooks. Shortly after they moved to Brooks, John came down with lung cancer and passed away before we had the children. I helped with the swathing one year and didn't do a very good job. I didn't know how to raise and lower the swather table that cut the hay and left it laying in swaths in the field.

When we did any fencing on our property, we would take our meals to the field with us. My parents came out quite often to visit, as they still lived mostly in Manitoba. They had a house in San Juan, Texas, that they used for the winter months. We moved a house from Calgary to the farm, so they lived in our older house while we moved into the newer house. In 1977, our oldest son, Jonathon, was born in Brooks. In 1979, our second son, Max, was born, and in 1981, our third son, Michael, was born. Our daughter, Jolene, was born in 1983. Mom and Dad helped us on the farm, too. Dad drove the tractors and helped with many things, and Mom often did the cooking and sometimes babysitting when we were all out in the field.

I remember having to go out to the field to check on the cows when they were calving. Bill was away, so I took the suburban, loaded up the kids, and went checking. I stopped, and one of the front tires and the opposite back tire fell into holes in the ground. I couldn't go anywhere. I had Jonathon watch the kids as I walked back to the house and got the car and a chain. I got the suburban out and now I had two vehicles in the field. I asked Jonathon if he would drive one of them, but he didn't want to, so I drove one a little way and then went back for the other one. We got home with both vehicles and the kids, all in one piece.

Fixing Fence in Winter

One time, I had to fix a fence with the kids in the winter. The
weather was cold, so I bundled them up and let them play in the
snow while I hammered in the staples that held the barbed wire in
place on each fence post. Thankfully, it was a short fence. We also
built more fence lines in which all of us went out, except Grandma
Gompf, who stayed home to make supper for us. We worked in a
convoy, using water to put into the holes so that the posts would
go in. That fall, at the 4-H meeting, the kids were asked about their
fun summer. Max said it was fencing as we worked as a family, and
he figured it was a lot of fun.

It was my role to take the kids to hockey in Jenner. All three boys were on the same team. Jonathon was nine, Max was seven, and Michael was five. Jolene started figure skating at three years old. She said to me, "Mom, my leg hurts." So, I told her she had to use both legs to skate, not just one. Then she was off. We would go ice fishing on Blood Indian Dam. The adults would fish, and the kids would play hockey or just skate on the ice. I was kept busy with the kids, as Max and Michael took guitar lessons and Jolene took piano lessons, all in Jenner. This would happen in between their power skating and skating lessons. We were kept busy on Tuesdays and Thursdays with all these activities, as well as 4-H Sewing and Dance lessons on Wednesdays. I was the 4-H Project Leader for 3 years in Cessford, Alberta, under the Dusty Plains 4-H Multi Club. Jonathon took the 4-H cooking project; Max and Jolene took part in the sewing project; Michael was a member of the horse project.

We sold our ranch at Big Stone in 1993 to Bob Olson of Jenner. We asked if we could stay until 1995, when Jonathon graduated high school, and he said that was okay. The Christmas holiday break in 1994 saw us buying a motorhome and heading to San Juan, Texas, with Bill driving his mom, myself, and the four children, plus a friend of Jonathon's, Scott Mickler, in tow. We made meals while on the road, as we didn't want to stop too often. Bill's mother Agnes would hold one pot of Kraft Dinner on the stove, and I would hold the other pot with wieners on the other stovetop burner. Then the children were able to dish out what they wanted to eat, as well as getting Bill some food to eat while driving. After the pots were empty and in the sink, Agnes and I could sit down quietly and enjoy our meal. We did this all the way to Texas, just stopping for fuel along the route. We stopped in northern Texas to get burgers at a fast-food place for a treat. The workers at this restaurant could not believe my order for so many people. The cook came out to the Motorhome to see there were 7 of us there. After we got the burgers, our kids thought the burgers were bad: the beef was corn-fed, so it tasted different than our beef back home. Yet, they were all hungry enough and believed me, so they ate the burgers down with a couple of gulps.

Michael and the Camera

Bill was getting tired and had driven a long way without stopping, so we stopped at a yard that was very decorated for Christmas. Bill had a very restful sleep, as did all the rest of us, and we headed out again the next morning. I told Michael to take some photos of the beautiful decorations the night before with my camera, and he ended up using the whole roll of film. They were very nice photos, all 24 of them. We arrived in San Juan, where my parents had their home and were waiting for us. We had Christmas Day in the backyard, as the weather was very good and warm. We then borrowed a friend's van and another friend's motorhome, and we all headed for Padre Island. The kids liked it so much they wished we had spent all our time there. Padre Island is off the southeastern edge of Texas. The bridge to get there is Port Isabel. We spent about five days there. We travelled into Mexico, and the kids were able to play in the ocean. The comments from the American tourists and workers there were, "Those crazy Canadians!" To us, the water was not too cold. We also set off fireworks at night, and the grandparents were in on it, too. It was a great time. After the Christmas holidays were almost over, we headed home. We got to Custer's Last Stand on New Year's Day. The kids went exploring. They found lots of memorials, and I think that brought to life a little bit of history for the kids. We made it through the border with no problem. I asked the border guard if he wanted to see our birth certificates, and he said, "No, you look more stressed than the kids."

In April of 1995, we bought our home in Millicent, the former home of George and Margaret Charlton. We more than doubled the population in Millicent when we moved there with everyone in our family: my mom and dad, Bill, our 4 children, Jonathon's friend Scott, and myself. We also had many children who visited and spent the night. I would check the porch floor in the morning and see how many extra shoes were there. We had roughly 30 kids who stayed with us off and on when our children were still at home. Bill quit working for Laughlin's when we moved.

Bill had a self-loading bale truck and taught Jonathon, Scott Mickler, and Shaun Soppit to drive truck. Bill began to drive for Ralore Trucking Company in the winter when there was not much bale hauling to do. He also hauled cattle for Dafoe, Grace, and Roberge Trucking companies. Some of those kids who hung around our place now drive semi-trucks and others are mechanics. We did a good job of teaching them about responsibilities and holding down a job.

I went back to Medicine Hat College Campus and upgraded my Business Administration. Bill and I got jobs as security guards on a pipeline by Princess, Alberta. We later went to Jenner and then Sundre as security guards. Bill got the job of Head of Security, so he spent his time checking on everyone and trying to keep up with the boys running the bale truck. After we were done in Sundre, I worked at the Calgary Post Office as security. That was during one of the postal strikes. I was offered a full-time job but decided I wanted to be home. I got a job at the Heritage Inn in Brooks doing the night audit. However, I was so tired of working at night, so I changed jobs and worked for Brooks Farm Centre. I worked there for 18 years. In 2019, I retired at the age of 70 years. I had a lot of wonderful comments from the public when I said I was retiring. I was in the back room, so I didn't see too many people or things that went on at the Farm Centre. One time I remember was when Charlie Charlton, one of the bosses, was moving an air seeder and caught the power line, putting the power off. They hooked up a generator, and I got to work in the front that day so I could use the generator to answer the phone. I did totally enjoy all 18 years there.

Gail Loved Family Life

I loved being a wife and mother, and I loved working on the ranch. Many times, it was hard, but I think it makes one a better person when things are not always easy. We had the great joy of spending quality time with my parents, as well as Bill's. We continued being around them as they grew older and looked out for them when they retired. Our children learned so much from having their grandparents around them constantly.

I started quilting, a hobby I garnered from my Grandmother Lincoln, who also lived with us in the summertime and with her other daughter's family in High River in the wintertime. (After her husband passed away when I was a small girl.) When her other daughter passed away, she then lived with us all the time. My days now are filled with quilting in the winter months and watching the Brooks Bandits hockey team. In summer, I garden and look after the dogs and cats. I love camping and looking after my grandchildren. I have 10 grandchildren: 2 who have graduated high school already and 8 who are school age. We helped raise 2 of them for 10 years. It was a great privilege. They have now moved away, and we miss them very much as our age, aches, and pains creep up on us.

Top left: Julianna, Cheryl, Max
Bottom Left: Jonathon, Mackenzie, LaWanda, Colton.
Top Right-L-R: Michael, Payton
Bottom Right-L-R: Wayne, Jolene, Aunt Frances McKillop, 94 yrs, Diamond, Autum
Middle Photo: Max, Michael, Jonathon, Jolene

We sold our home in Millicent to Kyle and Emily Torkelson in 2023 and have now moved to Mannville, where our son Max lives with his family. Jonathon married LaWanda Eldridge of Taber, and they live in Hanna, Alberta. Max is married to Cheryl Blonjeaux of Innisfree, Alberta. Michael's partner is Tiffany Oswell of Lloydminster, and Jolene's partner is Wayne Tomlinson of Brooks.

We can look back with pride on all we have accomplished. When we worry about all our problems, I remember that someone else has gone through much harder things than you and I, and they survived. I have had two incidents of whiplash from vehicle accidents, and the second accident led me to have my left hip replaced. That was 14 years ago, and so far, I am doing all right.

Bill passed away on December 25, 2023, in the Hanna Hospital from a long battle with lung cancer. He said he wanted to die on Jesus' birthday, and so God granted him his wish a few minutes after 12 am Christmas morning. He is buried at the Patricia Cemetery and will be missed by all who knew him.

Chapter XV

Determination & Dedication

Our Mother, Frances (Hausauer) Good

Story by Diane Good, daughter of Frances

Frances Hausauer was born on October 22, 1925, to her parents, John Jr. & Elizabeth Hausauer. She had a sister, Sophie (born 1928), who married Art Witke, and two brothers: Cecil (born 1926), who married Guila Barton, and James (born 1931), who married Evelyn Glock.

Frances' dad owned a butcher shop in Irvine with his dad (John Sr.), his brother (Edward), and his brother-in-law (Ed Glock). During the Depression, around 1930, there was so much money owing from meat sold in the butcher shop that they had to quit. They threw their account books down a well next to their shop.

In 1933, John Jr. bought some land and moved their house there, just outside Irvine on the south side. They worked very hard to build up the farm. The crops were poor, so cows were milked, and the children would put cream cans on a wagon and pull them to the Irvine CPR station. When they were older, Mom's brother Cecil would ride his bike into Irvine to make deliveries of milk and cream. Her mom (Lizzie) made butter, took it to the store in Irvine, and exchanged it for groceries. Chokecherries were also picked and sold. They had a horse to help bring in the cows for milking. Mom helped bring in the cows and did some of the milking, as she was the oldest of the children. As the other kids got older, they helped too.

They sold their place and moved back to Irvine for about one year. Then they moved another house from Irvine to south of Irvine, where they lived while Mom attended Irvine High School. That house was later moved back into Irvine, close to the Museum.

Frances' mom was a great seamstress: she made her own and her children's clothes without a pattern. Every spring and fall, she would order material from Eaton's catalogue to make clothes for them. My mom remembered her mom making a winter coat and hat for both her and her sister, Sophie. Her dad was very handy, too. He would buy second-hand bikes and repair them. He also made stilts, and they all learned to walk on them. During the summer holidays, Mom worked in a Chinese restaurant. If there was a dance in the Magnet Theatre (the old dance hall), they would make sandwiches and serve them at midnight. Mom and Sophie sang and yodelled at numerous events in the community. She also sang with a group of girls called the "Dizzy 8." When they were young, they used to play "Cat's in the Cradle," which is done with a string.

Mom finished school in 1944. Because of the war, the Normal School in Calgary offered a 3-month course for teachers. They needed teachers since many had gone to war. After Christmas in 1944, she went to the Gaetz School, south of Eckville, and taught 27 children, grades 1 through 9. In September 1945, she taught at Hazel Dell, which had 16 children. The following year, 1946/1947, she started at Hazel Dell; however, in late October, the Inspector of Schools asked her to exchange schools with another teacher. She went to the Alhambra with 50 students and taught grades 1 through six. She then applied to teach in Irvine and got a job teaching Grades 1 & 2 in September 1947. Wherever she taught, she walked to school each morning, though she caught a ride where possible.

Mom then married Harvey Good in June 1948. She was 22, and Dad was 23. She moved to the ranch 17 miles SE of Irvine. They had no power for the first years; later, they bought a wind charger with batteries. After that, they got power with the wind charger and had electric lights in the house. Then Calgary Power came to the area in about 1956, which gave them electric lights in the house. Later, Mom could use an electric iron, which was so much easier!

In the fall, they butchered a cow and a pig, so she canned meat, including sausage. They had a cow for milk, so she made butter and cottage cheese. We had chickens for eggs, and she purchased 100 broiler chicks yearly, which she butchered and canned. Feeding the chickens, gathering the eggs, cleaning the chicken house, and butchering would have been Mom's responsibility. But as we kids got older, we helped. When the electricity came, she could freeze chickens. She loved that luxury.

She baked bread every week and canned many, many, many boxes of fruit. One year, she canned over 100 quarts of saskatoons, which was lots of wild berries to pick. Her sister-in-law Gladys Elliott would have come out to help and picked saskatoons for herself. Mom also picked chokecherries to make jam. She made her own soap for washing clothes, rendering pork lard, and storing it in big jars that were kept in their dirt basement. We remembered them telling us that they would store their meat down the well: it was the only way to keep it fresh. They did have a root cellar, where they would store potatoes, carrots, etc. Most years, she would have had a garden so that they could enjoy vegetables through the summer and winter.

Mom Cleaned Coal Furnace

Mom cleaned out the coal furnace. It was a messy job, with lots of cinders to get out of it, creating lots of dust. Then, she reloaded the furnace with the new pieces of coal. She cooked 3 big meals a day, some of which were delivered to the fields. Floors were scrubbed on your hands and knees. After that, wax was applied, and then an electric floor polisher was used to get the proper shine. Those floors looked great!

Dad would go to town and hire whomever he could get to help if the winter was severe. The same was true at haying time. Haying was a lot of work, so extra help was most welcome, as the hay bales were loaded manually onto hay racks and manually unloaded and made into stacks of hay. Whenever they had a hired man to help with the work, he lived and ate with them. So, Mom also did his laundry and kept his bedroom clean.

In the early years of their marriage, they would cut down trees in the Cypress Hills for fence posts. They were cut to size and put in a vat with bluestone and water so they would last longer.

They had four children. Thomas (Tom), who lived from 1951-1988, married Cindy Henchel, and they have one son, Jeremy. Diane was born in 1953. June was born in 1954 and she married Bob Thomson, and they have a daughter, Becky, and a son, Travis. Lastly, Kathleen (Kathy) was born in 1964; she married Robert Ziegenhagel.

In the winter, during the early years, they would stack bales around their house to help break the cold winds. For entertainment, they curled in Elkwater. Then curling began in Irvine, and they curled in Medicine Hat, too. They also loved to dance in Elkwater and Irvine, which was a regular occurrence then.

Some of the things we, as her kids, remember:

- Christmas suppers with our neighbours and families.
- They got their first phone about 1965, a party line with their neighbours.

We heard stories of our grandparents on Dad's side. In 1918, they ran a wire along the fence line from one yard to another, which was about a mile and a half away. It was used as an old-fashioned telephone, setup between those two families. They kept in touch, so if one was sick, the other could help with chores. They owned land together, so they could plan to check cattle & fences. This was used by our grandfather and his brother.

Mom was one of the first ladies in our area to get her driver's licence. She just needed to drive 100 miles to get her licence. No proof was needed that she had driven there. She was able to help more at the farm by picking up parts and getting supplies from town.

She did the bookkeeping, and they both read the papers & agriculture magazines.

They always had food for meals when visitors dropped by.

Fresh fruit was our treat as kids. Plus, Grandpa Good would bring out fruit, as Mom had asked him to do that instead of candy. We got a fresh supply whenever they came.

A special treat when it was just us women coming home from Medicine Hat was bologna on fresh bread with a Root Beer for the drive home! No dishes, no mess.

We made our own Root Beer and Ginger Ale for a few years until we had a few explosions of pop going everywhere. That was not a fun thing to clean up!

Purchased another Ranch.

In 1970, they purchased a ranch south of Medicine Hat. Moving to a new place always brings on new learning experiences. They had never had flood, wheel moves, or pivot irrigation before, but Dad & Tom learned it all with help from hired men and neighbours. They trailed cattle 16 miles south in May and then trailed them home in October.

The weather was an unknown factor. If you were bringing cattle home in the fall, snow could blow in along with freezing temperatures. Most of the years, moving the cattle was a family affair on weekends. However, sometimes, if they knew the weather would be miserable, Dad, Mom, Tom, and hired men moved the cattle as Diane, June, and Kathy were at school or work. Mom didn't help much in the corral, but she drove a vehicle filled with food, coffee, or tea! She would throw in extra jackets and, of course, remind everyone to take extra clothing!! In the spring, it wasn't uncommon to have the cattle safely in the field only to have a blizzard blow in a few days or weeks later. Dad and Tom would check on cattle with snowmobiles or whatever they could.

In the late 80s, Dad had a bag cell phone in his truck. However, for it to work, the truck had to be running, and the phone needed to be constantly plugged in. If you were in a coulee, you had no reception. Dad or Tom would call Mom, and then if she needed to, she would go and tell whoever wasn't in the truck, such as Dad, Tom, or the hired men, what they were to bring and where they were located. In later years, they all had cell phones.

We remember Mom making great roast beef dinners for branding, as all the women did! She would feed everyone breakfast early on branding morning, probably around 5:30. After those dishes were done, she would start making flapper pies! She had made the fruit pies earlier, and they were thawing. In the early years, most people didn't have much extra space to feed the crew, so sometimes they were served in a small garage, the basement, or, on lovely days, outside. So that morning, Mom and one or two of her daughters would set up tables and chairs and get everything ready for everyone to return from the branding. The branding crew was usually done by lunchtime so that they would be ready for a roast beef dinner and those beautiful pies! Supper was generally chili, salads, and any remaining pies and squares.

After Tom's passing, Dad took over management again, with Cindy and Jeremy there to help. Dad and Mom got all three of us girls involved in ranching. Dad passed away September 9, 2015, at 90 years of age, and Mom passed away January 9, 2017, at 91.

Chapter XVI

Money Mastery Method System & Resetting Poverty Mindset

By Dorothy Louise Beasley

Have you ever found yourself wondering why some individuals effortlessly navigate their financial journey while others struggle to make ends meet? The answer lies in their approach to money management. Successful people are methodical, finding a systematic way to handle their finances that goes beyond mere budgeting.

That said, the *Money Mastery Method* is not just a system. It's a transformative approach that empowers you to take control of your financial destiny. Developed and perfected over 16 years, this method covers everything from creating a household budget to investing your extra income wisely. T. Hark Eker has a similar money management system called the *6 Jar Money Management System*.

But why should you invest your time to learn a money management system? The answer lies in the tangible results it produces. Results that belie the fact that possibly you feel like you can never have enough, be enough, do enough to make enough money to get ahead.

The poverty mindset is like being stuck in a mental prison. It makes you constantly doubt yourself and think there's no way out of your situation. This mindset stops you from seeing opportunities and makes you feel hopeless about ever changing things. It also makes you rely too much on others instead of believing in yourself. And sadly, it can keep poverty going in families and communities from one generation to the next. It's really important to realize how much this mindset holds you back and to work on breaking free from it.

1. **Understand the problem:** Recognize if you have a poverty mindset. It's when you always think there's not enough and opportunities are rare. Remember, many people struggle with negative thoughts about money, so you're not alone.

2. **Change your thinking:** Challenge negative thoughts about money and replace them with positive ones. For example, instead of thinking "I'll never get out of this situation," tell yourself "I can find ways to improve my life." When you hear negative words in your head like "money doesn't grow on trees," counteract them with affirmations like "*I learned this Money Mastery System and I always have money left over in the bank each month.*"

3. **Find positive influences**: Surround yourself with people who have a positive outlook and are successful. Their mindset can rub off on you and show you new possibilities.

4. **Get support:** Reach out to people in the business of saving money, open a bank account and begin to save on a monthly basis using the Money Mastery System. Talk with life coaches, or create a Money Management support group with successful people who have experienced poverty in the past and they overcame it. They can guide you and cheer you on as you work to change your mindset. When negative thoughts creep in, realise they are there as they think they are keeping you safe, in familiar territory. But those thoughts do not serve you and you can tell them to sit in

the back seat of the car you are driving and ask them to be quiet, as you are learning a new way to live your life.

5. **Share new affirmations:** Reach out or form your own support system, other family members who are on this new path too. Possibly some friends that are a positive successful bunch who also believe in themselves and would love to work with you supporting each other.

6. **Maybe try an Experiment:** Come up with positive affirmations around money and then copy them onto a piece of paper and tack it to the bathroom mirror, and other places around the house that you are in, so you see it many times a day. Say those positive affirmations every day as if you believe them. Eventually you will begin to believe them and your life changes, could take a week or a month, but if you keep on doing it your life will change. Those positive ways of thinking about yourself can help you reframe how you think about money.

   a. My financial situation is improving day by day and I am so grateful.

   b. Money is a positive force in my life, and I am happy to receive it.

   c. I am so happy I am attracting new streams of income into my life every day.

   d. My bank account is a reflection of my grateful and abundant mindset.

   e. I am grateful for the abundance of money flowing into my bank acct each month.

7. **Stay strong**: Learn to bounce back from setbacks. Instead of seeing obstacles as roadblocks, think of them as chances to learn and grow. Use affirmations like *"I have money coming from multiple sources each and every month to pay my bills. I have money left over to put into the emergency fund, and that empowers me towards abundance."* Now, think up ways you can create other sources of income.

8. **Push a pause button**: When you see yourself slipping back into the old pattern of doing things. Ask yourself to put all thoughts about disaster on hold for 3 days. During those 3 days, write down things that could be solutions, ways to solve the challenges and get you back up into staying strong. Write down anything that comes to mind, whether it is logical or not. At the end of the 3 days, look at the challenge and see if you should still push the panic button or if a solution came up that works and you are back on track and building a life of abundance.

9. **Set goals:** Decide what you want to achieve in the short and long term. Having clear goals gives you something to aim for and keeps you motivated. Use affirmations to reinforce your goals and beliefs in abundance every day.

By using affirmations and taking small steps like these, you can begin shifting your mindset away from poverty and towards abundance. Picture a life where you not only believe in yourself, you also meet your monthly goals of still having money in the bank at the end of the month to grow your abundance mindset.

The Money Mastery Method is not just theory. It's a proven system that has allowed individuals to consistently have money left at the end of each month, paving the way for a secure and prosperous future. Whether you're starting on your financial journey or looking to enhance your current approach, the Money Mastery Method is your guide to achieving lasting financial success. Get ready to embark on a transformative journey towards financial mastery—a journey that begins with understanding and implementing the principles of the Money Mastery Method.

Create eight individual accounts: one chequing account and seven other individual accounts within a savings account (The bank will do it for you that way):

1. Future Freedom Account

2. Education/Travel Account

3. House Pymt/Ins Account

4. Savings for Emergency Account

5. Community Support (Give)Account

6. Car pymt/Ins. Reg. Account

7. Monthly Fun Account

8. Essential Monthly Exp Account

These account names are only suggestions, so you can change them up as you please, but attempt to keep roughly the same percentages for each account. Keep 8 accounts so you can pay all your expenses each month and have money gaining momentum in the other accounts. Then you can honestly say this affirmation each month: "I have an abundance of money in my bank accounts each and every month." See what happens as the year goes on and you have accumulated an abundance that can be invested from the Future Freedom Account. (Future Freedom Account could mean a down payment on a house, retirement, in case you lose your job, or have an illness, etc...)

Once you have these accounts set up, have your bank split up your paycheque/s into those accounts and your chequing account as soon as they go into the bank. I recommend the following percentages and always pay yourself first into the Future Freedom Account. Say your combined income is $8000/month:

1. Future Freedom Account: 10% of the total paycheque/s = $800

2. Education/Travel Account- 10% = $800

3. House Pymt:18% of total paycheque/s = $1440

4. Savings for Emergencies- 1% of total paycheque/s =$80

5. Community Support Account: 1% of total paycheque. = $80

6. Car Ins/Reg. Account: 10% of total paycheque/s = $800

7. Monthly Fun Account: 5% of total paycheque/s = $400

8. Essentials Account: 45% of total paycheque/s = $3600
(food, veh. pymts, ins/reg, supplies, clothing, CC Debt)

The Money Mastery Method will allow you to pay for all your expenses and still have money at the end of each month, as well as money that you can invest into your Future Freedom Account. Invest the maximum amount each month from the Future Freedom Account into a higher interest bracket so that the Account is growing each month (GIC or other investment account that is not too risky.) You can change percentages as you wish, this just gives you an idea of how to set it up. Only spend from the accounts which are designated monthly payment accounts, leave the rest to gain interest in a Monthly Savings or Investment account.

In the real world, this method empowers individuals to break free from the paycheque-to-paycheque cycle, offering the assurance of a secure financial future. By following this method, one not only meets their current financial obligations but also builds a solid foundation for financial mastery and prosperity. The key lies in the commitment to doing the systematic approach outlined by *the Money Mastery Method*—a journey that begins with understanding and implementing its principles for enduring financial success.

The article was originally found on a website called "Investopedia" by Matt Danielsson, revised to suit the reader and the author, yet still has similar information as was first written and updated in December of 2023. I changed up the order of the habits as I figure that HEALTH needs to be Number One in all our minds and added another habit as I figured it is a great habit too. I once did this and I believe there was over $60 worth of coins deposited in my future freedom bank account.

1. **Take Care of Your Health:** Good physical health can prevent expensive medical bills and lost income due to illness. I put this as #1 habit to form, as your health is the most important of all. Learn to look after yourself FIRST, then when your cup is full, Momma is happy and so are the rest of the family.

2. **Write Out Your Financial Goals:** What would you like your monthly bank account to have in it at the end of the month, at the end of the year? Be realistic, double the amount left in there right now and then imagine it is already there. As you work through these next few steps you could surprise yourself at the end of the year.

3. **Make a Monthly Budget**: Develop and adhere to a monthly budget to ensure all bills are paid and savings goals are met.

4. **Pay off Credit Cards in Full**: Avoid high-interest debt by paying off credit card balances each month.

5. **Create Automatic Savings:** Set up automatic transfers to a Savings Account if you have extra in any account each month and for your Future Freedom account to ensure you consistently save without having to think about it each month.

6. **Start Investing Now**: Begin investing early to take advantage of compound interest, which can significantly increase your funds over time.

7. **Watch Your Credit Score:** Regularly check and manage your credit score as it affects loan interest rates and insurance premiums.

8. **Negotiate on your Purchases and Sales:** Don't hesitate to negotiate prices to save money, especially with small businesses.

9. **Stay Educated on Financial Issues:** Keep informed about financial news and changes in tax laws to optimize your financial decisions or make sure your Financial Advisor at the bank lets you know what is happening.

10. **Maintain Your Property:** Regular maintenance of your possessions, such as your vehicle, house, lawn mower, farm equipment can prevent costly replacements and save money in the long run.

11. **Live Below Your Means:** Adopt a frugal lifestyle, define your needs, and wants, and what you would love to improve your financial health.

12. **Get a Personal Financial Advisor:** Once you have accumulated a significant amount of wealth, consider hiring a financial advisor to help manage and grow your assets. If you have a Business Financial Advisor for your small business, he can help you too. They are no longer one and the same person.

13. **Collect extra change coins from pockets or change purse:** Put them into a roll for coins and as they fill up, exchange for new ones. This also gives you a sense of abundance in your mind. Then store the rolls of money in a large jar and at the end of the year, you may take them to the bank and deposit the accumulation of monies into your Savings or Future Freedom Account where the money is growing.)

Chapter XVII

Minds of Their Own

Gena LaCoste (née Armstrong) and her mom, Verna Armstrong (née Mullen)

Imagine growing up on the wide-open southern Alberta prairies in the 50's! The older I get and the more I travel, the more I realize what a magical stroke of luck it was to be raised in that place, at that time, by those people.

My dad was raised east of Elkwater. In 1946, he & his brothers bought a place south of Bassano to expand their ranching operations, The East and West Ranch.

My mother grew up at Makepeace, which is north of Crowfoot, about 20 miles. Her dad, an Irish immigrant, was what they called a "long rein skinner"—a teamster who hauled grain and other freight with 20 horse hitches of his favourite breed, Clydesdales. Mom said that her dad's herd of about 200 very good horses was what kept them in relative comfort through the brutal years of the depression and dirty 30s.

Verna Armstrong

Being ahead of her time, my mom fought her dad's wishes and became an RN, graduating from the Royal Alex in Edmonton in the mid-40s. She was recruited from her job at the Vancouver General to come home to Bassano and be the "Matron" of that bustling little hospital. Sadly, for the hospital administration, she and Dad ran into each other not long after her arrival back home. She then made the transition to ranch wife and mother—of five kids in nine years. I was the oldest of that pack of brats. To say that experience marked me for life is an understatement. We had a lot of freedom as kids, lots of pets (including wildlife), lots of human eccentrics, and lots of incredible experiences.

When I was a kid, I was mostly intent on escaping the house and being where the action was: moving cattle, checking cattle in the feedlot, helping hay, and visiting the cow camp with my dad. That last one was a regular thing for me, starting when I was 18 months old and my sister Kath was born. That trip was 25 miles of gravel and prairie trail. That route took us down to the two-room shack on the Bow River so we could bring groceries to Scottie, our grumpy old cowboy.

My dad's younger brother, Arnold, was our closest neighbour, and when I was two, he married Aunt Shirley. While I've become known primarily as a Western artist because of the predominance of that genre in my body of work, there's also the influence of my mother, Verna, and Aunt Shirley on all our lives.

As I've reached middle age and become so interested in health and nutrition. I've become increasingly interested in why previous generations were healthier in many respects than we are today. I appreciate more and more the contributions that women like Verna and Shirley made to their families. Their capacity for work was absolutely staggering.

Year in and year out, these women did an incredible amount of work. To start, they fed their kids, their husbands, and the hired men—twice a day—plus haying crews, threshing crews, and, later in life, the combining crews (My dad made breakfast). My mom and Aunt Shirley dealt with the milk and cream from the milk cows twice a day. This included separating and shipping the cream, plus making butter. They both grew enormous gardens with all the vegetables we'd need for a whole year. They canned pickles, relishes, tomatoes, jams, jellies, blanched, and froze the beans, corn, and peas. That's quite the list of activities!

This is hard country for gardeners. I often think of my grandmothers and what they must've thought when they first attempted to feed their families out of that hard prairie sod and the vagaries of prairie weather. My maternal grandmother was an Irish girl from the Ottawa Valley who came west to cook for various work projects going on to open the West. She had a family of 5 kids as well. Mom remembers trying to defend her mother's garden against the hoppers, army worms, and drought through the 30s. It makes me wonder if the West would've been settled at all if it weren't for women like her.

Without the work ethic and skill set that these women possessed, I'm afraid they would've just punched the railroad through here and continued to the coast where conditions were more favourable to habitation, leaving the Palliser Triangle to the First Nations.

Painting by Gena LaCoste- Western Artist

This recipe is an old favourite; This is a great recipe to throw together when unexpected company comes in the door just before lunch time or dinner.

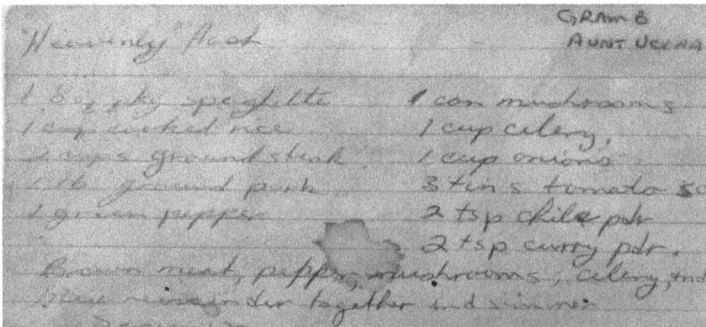

Chapter XVIII

Genuine Integrity & Grit

Margaret Owen's story, as told to Louise in a recorded interview done in Margaret's home in Patricia in late 2022- 2023.

Margaret was born November 7, 1934, in Slovakia, the second child of Joseph and Maria Vrbicky. When she was 18 months old, she moved to Canada with her parents and a brother. Her father wanted the family out of the country since war had been declared, and he was not in favour of what was happening. They came by boat and landed in Nova Scotia, Canada. From there they moved to Coquitlam, British Columbia, and bought a farm, mostly fruit.

They lived there for two years, and then her dad got the itch to move again. He liked to travel. From there, they moved to Scandia, Alberta. That was a big move and included three children, as one of Margaret's younger sisters, Mary, had been born in Coquitlam. They kept on moving after that. Margaret says, "I'm sure he was a gypsy. Quite often, it was because they were looking for something different." In 1940, they bought an irrigated farm in Scandia and lived there for two years before moving to Beamsville, Ontario. Her dad bought a farm there, and another sister, Betty, was born in 1946. Then they moved back to Alberta that same fall, to a place west of Olds, Alberta. They moved two or three different times during that time in Alberta.

"I felt sorry for my mom," Margaret says. "Sometimes, she never unpacked before Dad decided to move again. We moved to Imperial Colony, Alberta, just north of Patricia, and bought a farm there in 1950. That is why we ran out of money sometimes, as Dad always bought the land." Her mom always had a big garden, so they had plenty of canned vegetables and meat. They milked cows and grew crops to sell when the weather was conducive to growing good crops.

I asked Margaret if they went to school at all during all those moves. Margaret said that schooling was a challenge, too, since they moved so much, "I remember going to school in Imperial Colony up to Grade 8," she recalls. "I boarded out in a dormitory in Brooks for Grades 9-11 and came home on weekends. I met my future husband, Donald Owen, at a dance in Imperial Colony."

Margaret's dad worked for Bob Irwin and the Otto Elsbett Family, south of Patricia, when he first came to the area. Later, he was at the Bar 4T, southeast of Patricia, where Dean Wright was manager at that time. They had moved from Imperial Colony and now lived where Shauna and Will Henrickson live, a couple of miles south of Patricia.

Meanwhile, Margaret was at school in Brooks during these moves. "When I got into Grade 12," she says, "I had no place to stay on weekends to finish my schooling as my family had moved again. I would have liked to have finished high school. It just wasn't possible. That's the way the cookie crumbles."

Margaret began working at the Patricia Hotel during the weekends. Then, her dad moved the family back to Rolling Hills and worked for the E.I.D. as a ditch-rider there. He worked in that position for quite a few years, as he had finally found a job he liked. Betty, her youngest sister, graduated Grade 12 in Rolling Hills School. Her sister Mary, brother John, and she had all moved away from home by then. Then, her dad retired from the E.I.D. in 1972. At the time, her brother was living up north. "This is a good story," she says, explaining why her dad never got a chance to fully retire. "My brother John needed help, so Mom and Dad moved up to the Fairview/Peace River Country."

County of Newell & Marriage

Margaret began working for the County of Newell when Bob Scammell, Des James, and Louise's dad, Gordon Douglass, worked there as County Counsellors. They had a machine that printed out the property taxes for everyone who lived in the County of Newell at that time. It was in a back office, so she wasn't really in the public at all. She just worked with this machine and did odd office jobs. She did this for maybe two years, 1955-56, and then got married to Donald Owen on June 22, 1957.

L-R back -Jim Henry, Jim Westwick, Mary, Margaret's sister, Alice, Donald's Sister Donald & Margaret

Donald and Margaret went to live near Patricia, Alberta. They moved into a small trailer, which they rented from Fred Wielizcko. They moved the trailer into Don's parents' yard, just west of their house. Don bought a truck and trailer in 1957 and hauled cattle, grain, and treated fence posts that were used for fencing people's property. In 1959, he bought a larger truck and trailer. He put in many long hours hauling grain for local farmers and cattlemen from Gleichen, Wainwright, Empress, and Acadia Valley, to name just a few places.

Margaret then worked at the Patricia Hotel again. The managers at that time were Dunc and Elsie Ramsey. In the spring of 1958, they began building a house on what was called the Carlburg Place, a half mile south of Donald's parents' place. This land was owned by Don's parents, but they gifted it to the couple when they got married. The foundation of the original house, built in 1925, was still there. They built the house on this foundation. That fall, they moved into the house. It seemed like so much more space after living in the small trailer. She started out feeding the Hereford bulls at home since Don was too busy trucking. Margaret also learned how to milk two cows. Donald's brother and dad looked after farming the land.

She used to feed ten 2000-pound Hereford bulls that were in the corral. She was petrified of them. She had to fill two 5-gallon pails with grain morning and night. She would set the pails down, open the corral gate, pick up the pails again, go through the corral gate, put the pails down again, shut the gate, pick up the pails of grain again, and then run to the trough where the bulls' trough was situated in the middle of the corral. She would spread one bucket out in the trough in a long line and then spread the other one out as fast as she could before the bulls walked up to the trough. She said there was one bull who liked to chase her, but she was lucky in that he never caught her. When she told Don that one of the bulls liked to chase her, he didn't believe her. He found out the truth one day when he was feeding the bulls himself. This particular bull chased him, and Don had to jump up on the fence to get away from it. He shipped the bull out as soon as possible, so Margaret didn't have to worry about it anymore.

On May 30, 1959, Lenore was born. Their way of life changed overnight. August 28, 1960, they got a double surprise. Their second baby arrived early and turned out to be a set of twins: a boy they named Zane and a girl they called Kim. To their dismay, they found out the newborns were allergic to cow's milk. Margaret could not breastfeed any of her babies due to a previous breast operation. Kim was sick off and on the first year. She kept on throwing up after drinking the canned baby milk formula and ended up in the hospital. They figured out she was also allergic to the canned baby formula milk, so Margaret had to take goat's milk into the hospital to feed her. She would pack up the other children and drive into Brooks, which was 30 minutes drive from their farm. It was not an easy task, but she did it because it needed to be done. She did it every day for that first year, on and off, until Kim was strong enough to come home and stay there. The children all drank goat's milk after that.

She recalls buying about four to six nanny goats and one billy goat so that the nannies would have babies and keep on giving the family milk. She remembers having goats tethered around the yard for a few years until the children no longer drank so much milk and ate more solid foods. Some of the kid goats would jump up on the cars—sometimes even into the front seat if a door had been left open.

Children Plus---- Used Washing Machine

Margaret had four children within three-and-a-half years. Ross was born on November 26, 1961. In 1961, they were gifted a quarter of land north of Don's parents, another wedding present. Don sold the truck then, as they now had enough land to get more cattle and go farming on their own. Their last child, Neil, was born on April 9, 1967, 6 years after Ross. Margaret was a busy woman for many years and still did the chores outside, too. Don's mother, Lucille, helped her quite often.

She recalls that "Donald got a washing machine from Bobby Thompson. It washed the clothes, but there was no wringer on it, which meant the clothes had to be wrung out by hand. It was just with an electric motor on the washer part of it. The wringer was an attachment to the washing machine. It sat on the top with two rollers attached. The person operating the machine had to pick up each article of clothing and shove it into the rollers. Not too much clothing could go in at once, as that would jam the rollers up. The two rollers would squeeze the water from the clothes. There was an electric motor that turned the rollers, which wrung out of the clothes as they were pulled through. Jeans or blankets would have to be wrung out more than once since they held a lot of water." Donald got it for a good price, but Margaret really could have used a better wringer. It would have made things a lot easier.

The house that was so spacious three years earlier seemed to have diminished in size as the children grew bigger and older. The fun continued as Margaret still did all the animal chores on the Owen farm. I had to do the work outside and the work in the house. "Everything had to be done," she says, "so I just did it." While she was out doing the chores, the children would take things out of the cupboard and then hide in the cupboard. They were just being kids. They sometimes spilled syrup and cornflakes all over the floor.

Margaret milked two cows. She would get one half-milked and then run into the house to see what the kids were doing, then run back out to the barn to finish milking the cow. She would do the same with the other cow and finally get both milked. She had chickens—two hundred chickens that they butchered for their meals. She froze some and canned some, which was a lot of work. She made nine loaves of bread each time. She canned the vegetables that grew in the garden—beets, carrots, beans, etc. And she made jelly and syrup from the wild berries that she picked. Saskatoons, chokecherries, whatever berries were available.

There was water available to water the garden, thanks to irrigation water coming through their yard in a ditch. The water was used to irrigate the field crops all summer. She remembers having raspberries, strawberries, and plum trees in the backyard to water and then harvest. Then, the plum trees were sacrificed so Don could build a set of corrals out there. They were beautiful big trees, all torn down. "It was heart-breaking to see them out of the ground and gone," she says, "but you gotta move on."

Donald was trucking all the time, making money to buy cattle for the ranch. Meanwhile, Margaret continued working at the Patricia Hotel, too. Lucille, her mother-in-law, would look after Lenore (the oldest child), and Margaret would take the twins while they were still in their little cribs. They slept most of the time while she worked at the hotel. There, she made enough money to buy groceries. Nothing was ever charged at that time, and she says one knew how much to spend, and that was the way it was. They had eggs, chickens, milk, and meat. She remembers the milk cows freshened at the same time, and so she canned 210 quarts of fresh cow's milk.

Canning Milk & Preserves

She put the milk into the quart jars, sealed them shut, and then boiled them in a hot water bath for four hours. "None of them spoiled. I am amazed now when I think of it," she says, "When I think about all the things I did, I wonder how I did it all. When you are young, you just do it as it needs to be done." Donald was home at night sometimes, but mostly, he was gone day and night, trucking cattle and grain. He trucked grain from Saskatchewan and cattle to Calgary. Sometimes, the kids went with Donald in his big truck. This gave Margaret a break, and they really enjoyed going with him.

Donald's mom was good: she would come over and babysit the kids whenever she could. The good thing about the summer was that it was warm enough for all the children to be outside. Margaret could garden outside, and the kids would be out and about in the yard.

Once, a neighbour came over while she was in the garden weeding. "Do you know what your kids are doing?" she asked.

"No," Margaret replied, "not exactly. They are just playing in the yard."

"Yes," the neighbour said, "but maybe you need to come and have a look." They had taken a box of laundry soap outside and sprinkled it around the sprinkler that was watering the lawn. They were jumping around in the soap suds that had piled high all around the sprinkler. Margaret said she thought about the cost of the soap, but there was nothing she could do about it then. And besides, they were having so much fun!

She couldn't be with the children all the time. "Kids will be kids, and that is what happens. They made up their own fun, and it worked out okay! No harm done; the kids all survived." She remembers washing diapers in the irrigation ditch that went by their house before she had a washing machine. Then, she would wring them out and hang them on an outside clothesline. It took them a long time to dry since she couldn't get all the water out of them when wringing them by hand. It was much better after she got the wringer washing machine.

She also found another way to use the wringer washing machine: shelling peas. It worked well, and left the shelled peas in the washing machine tub, while the shells went out onto the ground or into a bucket. Those she fed them to the chickens or cows. It saved her a lot of time, as it took a long time to shell peas by hand.

Eventually, Donald had made enough money to buy the amount of cattle he wanted, and so he quit the trucking business. He was at home helping Margaret by then and ranched full-time. He milked the cows when he wasn't busy farming the land or doing something with the cattle. She still worked full out doing everything else and did what needed to be done if Donald was out in the field at milking time, for instance.

Children's Schooling Plus

The children all started school in Patricia. They got on a school bus early in the morning, and Mrs. Jessen was their first teacher. As they got older, they were all interested in sports. They all took an active interest in baseball. The girls were also members of the Patricia Girls' 4-H Sewing Club. As soon as the children reached grade seven, they changed schools, and a school bus took them another 20 miles to the Duchess school. The girls continued to play baseball and 4-H, then later took up volleyball in the school sports program. The boys were active in hardball, volleyball, hockey, curling, and rodeo. The boys even did some bareback riding in the local amateur rodeos.

In 1975, they were still farming and loving the ranch, so they built a twenty-foot addition onto their house. They really loved the much-needed space. It was completed in time for Margaret's parents' fiftieth wedding anniversary.

The children all graduated from high school, and Lenore went on to further studies at SAIT in Calgary in Tourism. She is married and has children of her own: one girl and one boy. Kim became an RN. She is married and has three boys. Zane lived down in Arizona for a few years and was employed with Alberta Gas Trunk Line for many years. He came back to Alberta and now lives in Brooks. Ross is farming in the Patricia area, married to Brenda Charlton, and they have two grown children: one boy and one girl. Neil is also still living in the area and is the handyman in Margaret's house. He comes by and fixes the little things that need to be repaired. He was married and has Bennett & Keira with his first wife, who passed away from cancer. Neil remarried Sarah, who had two children, Dallas and Erin. It is a good fit, a well-adjusted blended family.

Don and Margaret took time out to enjoy life after the children left home, doing some travelling as well as ice fishing, curling, salmon fishing on the west coast of Canada, and, of course, playing cards—especially the game of crazy eights.

Margaret suffered from some health issues, losing a leg and having other complications with breast cancer later in life. In fact, the same breast she had trouble with as a young woman. She manages quite well with the help of family who live close by. She is in a wheelchair and has home care come in twice a week to help her out. She and Don are still happily married and living in the same house they built so long ago.

**Donald and Margaret's 60th Anniversary- 2017 with their 5 grown family,
L-R: Ross, Neil, Lenore, Kim, Zane**

Don just celebrated his 90th birthday in March 2023. He still drives around to see what is happening in the community, picks up the mail, and visits friends in the neighbourhood. Margaret is 88 years old and still enjoying life.*

*Louise took some of this information from a local history book where Don and Margaret had written out their family history many years ago, *Spurs and Shovels Along The Royal Line*. They mentioned in their story that they felt very fortunate to have been living in this friendly community, where neighbours and friends help one another as they work towards a better future for themselves and for those to come.

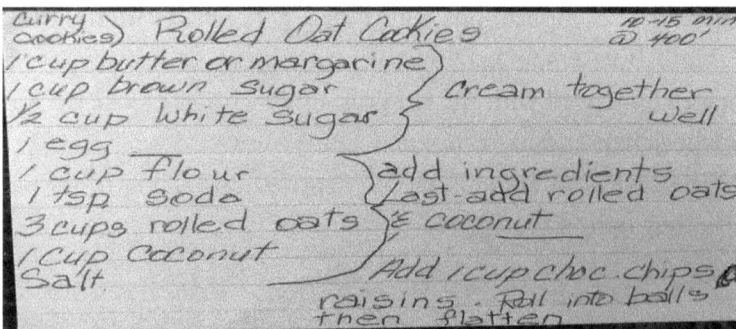

Margaret's Recipe for Yummy Rolled Oat Cookies—Very Good and Easy!

Chapter XIX

Be the Change We Want to See!

Written by Dorothy Louise Beasley

In my exploration of women's experiences, I discovered the profound influence of shame-based thinking, a universal challenge that affects individuals across various roles and cultures. Both men and women grapple with shame, often rooted in cultural beliefs. Feelings of humiliation, disgrace, and embarrassment arise when we experience shame. We also see other people doing things that we weren't allowed to do, and then we feel shame for them, too. Have you ever heard the words "shame on you?"

There are various forms of shame:

- The feeling of inadequacy when we underperform in an area where we believe we should excel.

- The embarrassment that arises from making a mistake in the presence of others.

- The hurt of being excluded from a desired social circle.

- Not to mention the internalized shame that lingers after experiencing abuse or abusive trauma.

- Being ignored, feeling invisible in a room full of people.

- When we burst out in anger when we see other people being treated unfairly or what we perceive as being treated unfairly. "Shame On You."

In the ranching industry, women were sometimes conditioned to see themselves as inferior, perpetuating a cultural bias. Judy Schultz's book *Mamie's Children* sheds light on ordinary ranch women in Canada and reveals the historical stigma surrounding their capabilities. The perception that women were inferior to men persisted for decades, impacting voting rights and societal standing. Women in rural areas often silenced their personal victories, driven by such shame-based thinking. This silence contributed to issues such as depression, alcoholism, drug use, infidelity, and other mental health struggles.

Shameful thinking—expressed through negative words and actions—often led to emotional, mental, and physical abuse, too. With shame-based thinking, we mentally beat up ourselves first, and then other people can tell that we are shaming ourselves by our words and actions. Those other people who have been shamed as children know it is safe to abuse others by using shame, and it becomes a vicious cycle of abuse. It is all unconscious abuse: simply a way of life for people who didn't know how to act any differently. As human beings, we act according to what we know and what we learned as children. There is no blame involved, as it has been a way of life for all of us who have been shamed, which is a large population in the world today and in the past up until now.

Websites like Healthy Way and Inner Tune highlight the lifelong impact of childhood beliefs. Shame-based thinking, passed down through generations, harms our self-worth and contributes to our belief that there is something wrong with us. Yet, these faulty beliefs have nothing to do with us or our situation. They come from and belong to our ancestors. In my case, perhaps I had an ancestor back in the 1600s, or further back, who had good and grave reasons for shaming, declaring that children were to be seen but not heard. My caregivers heard those thoughts from their parents as they had heard it from their parents.

As an example of how faulty beliefs linger beyond their usefulness, let me tell you a story. There was a family who cut the legs off their Thanksgiving turkey every year. One year, a little girl asked her mother, "Why are you cutting the turkey's legs off?" Her mother didn't know why: it was simply what her mother did. So, the little girl found her grandmother and asked her the same question. The grandmother gave the same answer: she did this because *her* mother had done it. Luckily, the little girl's great-grandmother was still alive. When asked, she explained that she had cut the legs off her turkeys because her roasting pan was too small to hold the whole bird.

Now, that is a funny story. Yet, that is precisely what we have been doing with those sayings that we pass down from generation to generation. They might have served the people in the past, but they no longer serve us now. It is time to become aware of those faulty beliefs and ask about them.

Understanding core beliefs is vital, as they shape our reality and behaviours. Negative core beliefs, like those rooted in shame-based thinking, impact our abilities and actions. They often hinder our personal growth and positive experiences. We **all** have faulty belief systems in our subconscious—perhaps even hundreds of them—which persist into adulthood and affect our self-respect, self-trust, self-worth and self-confidence. Positive core beliefs, on the other hand, empower us, shaping a reality filled with growth and positive actions.

Ordinary ranch women, as depicted in *Mamie's Children*, carried extensive responsibilities and challenged the notion that they were "by all standards just ordinary." In the past, women were told they were shamefully "bragging about themselves" if they wrote a story about their experiences. Other women thought their stories were not good enough: they were just ordinary ranch women of no consequence in the grand scheme of life. Some women right up until now still believe this, considering their extraordinary lives and stories to be unimportant. In their minds, they just did things they had to do—the things that needed to be done every day.

Yet we know their stories are very important. They contain so many insights about how much we can do, from right where we are, with whatever we have available. What these ranch women have accomplished throughout their lives is nothing short of amazing.

As I reflect on my experiences, the impact of shame-based thoughts during childhood remains vivid. Caregivers often instilled the belief that "children are to be seen but not heard," fostering feelings of smallness, sadness, anger, and invisibility. In turn, these feelings influenced my ability to express my opinions and emotions as an adult. Sometimes, to hide the feelings of shame, I would voice an opinion, which would be a self-defeating measure. The opinion would come out wrong, and then others would ignore me, laugh at me or say that I had no business expressing what I felt; my opinions were not wanted or appreciated. It was like I was invisible, and my voice wasn't working. Sometimes, when the little me inside couldn't stay quiet any longer, I would burst out with anger, and then when no one asked why or seemed to care, I would punish myself in some way or another for being so stupid in thinking anyone even cared, "Shame On You" Louise for making a scene.

It may seem like "bipolar" disorder, but it is the feelings of shame about myself, letting faulty belief systems rule my life through negative self-talk. Listening to other people in my life who do not feel good enough either, so they hit out at others to draw them down to a lower level, like bullying behavior on the totem pole of life.

This horrible feeling we have about ourselves, is very debilitating, and feels like we are in a deep hole and no one can see, hear or care about us, me, this is how I felt; I thought it was normal, that everyone felt this way. On the totem pole of life, it felt like I was under it, weighted down by feelings of guilt, and with the pain of not feeling loved, cared for, I wondered quite a few times why I was born. I wondered what my purpose was if no one saw me, didn't want to hear my opinions, and/or didn't want to hear me speak. I was most times afraid to speak out in case they abandoned me completely.

This is also what happens as we get older in life and where elder abuse comes in. We still feel those feelings and even though our original abusers are no longer around us, other people take their place and begin controlling our lives. Recently I talked with a friend, who realizes she is being emotionally abused by some of her children and their spouses. Now a neighbour who professes she wants to help my friend is using shame-based thinking to control my elderly friend's comings, goings, what she does with her personal belongings, etc.... The neighbour is helping my elderly friend to move out of her house and is telling her what she can keep and what she cannot keep and then is taking her belongings and taking them all somewhere else, to sell possibly?? Some things are being saved for a garage sale, but new clothing and other valuable items are disappearing. Some of her children are not even coming to help her move, they are staying away; they have threatened her to change her Last Will and Testament so that they receive all the assets. That is abuse. No one deserves this kind of treatment and she has done nothing bad towards them whatsoever.

Elderly abuse is on the rise in Canada, mostly because the elderly are afraid to speak up. Sometimes feeling invisible, unloved, uncared for, is easier than dealing constructively with those people. Especially if they have always felt unworthy, they no longer know what or how to feel happy, joyful or grateful. This shame-based abuse continues until they die, unless they let someone they trust know what is happening and who is able to then get them help and support. Once the elderly person begins to feel differently about themselves, perhaps a friend gets them into a program that builds their self-worth, self-respect, self-trust, self-confidence, then they can gain complete recovery. The advocate can help the elderly and other women who are younger to realize they are valuable and worthy from the time they are born, up until they die. All people: men, women, & children have experiences to share, regardless of age. Once we are supported with friends who love us for who we are, our little person within us begins to feel loved and supported too. Shame-based abuse at any age is uncalled for and is absolutely of no use to anyone on earth, be it abusive behavior against people or any living thing.

Unless we continue to have ongoing support, we fall back into that old pattern of thinking. Which I did last year, as I was around some of those same people who I allowed to make me feel unworthy again. One of those people said to me, "Oh, I heard you talking, but I ignored you because nothing you say is of any value." Responses like this seemingly justified why I should be seen and not heard. This cycle repeats itself until I began to learn about repatterning those negative thoughts. I must keep vigilant on what I am thinking about all the time.

I began reading a book called, *I Thought It Was Just Me, (But It Isn't)* by Brene Brown and became aware as to why I acted the way I did. As I began to become aware of my thoughts, I learned how to repattern them with positive thoughts. These new expansive thoughts allowed me to feel that I more than deserved to speak. **"I deserve to be seen and heard. Voicing my opinions and ideas allows me to feel great! When I speak out loud to others, they are happy that I am speaking up for myself, too. It is important for other people to hear me speak about my opinions and suggest ideas to help others. It is okay to agree to disagree, too, as that allows us each to have our own opinions; this is more than okay."**

As I kept reading the book *I Thought It Was Just Me (But It Isn't)* by Brene Brown and studied her teaching about shame and shame-based thinking, I learned that Brown experienced shame as a child, too. In the book, she has many examples of other women who have experienced shame-based thinking. She said that some people still think that some shaming is a good thing. So, she looked for different shame patterns to see if any of them were of any value for disciplining or anything else. What was her conclusion? "Absolutely not!" She says there are no correct ways to use shame in any shape or form, as it creates so much distress in a child on up until that child is a woman and messes up their minds. It affects them their entire life until they learn ways to repattern those toxic thoughts into forgiveness and believe that they have always been a special person—the person God created them to be. A unique and very gifted person who is loved.

So now it is time for **Forgiveness** for using shame as a form of discipline as parents, teachers, and caregivers, me included. We didn't know any better, so now, say to yourself, as I say to myself, **"I forgive myself and others in my life for believing that shame** would help me discipline my children. I forgive myself for enforcing it, belittling them, not allowing them to have their voices to speak their truths."

We are all free to repattern those toxic thoughts into affirmative, expansive thoughts about ourselves. We are free to let our children know that we love them and want them to be able to voice their opinions and be heard. Befriend your fears of what you can do, from where you are, with what you have. Take time to forgive yourself, then move forward with affirmative actions that are for you and your family's highest good.

As Mary Morrissey states in her new book called *Brave Thinking*, "I make time for the things that matter most in my life. We all get twenty-four hours. We all make time for what we decide we're going to make time for. I make time for the things that matter the most to me."[1]

Here is an Experiment You Can Try:

As mentioned above, the act of repatterning our shame-based thoughts empowers us to live as our authentic selves. Express yourself as you were born to do, as God gave you a voice, so you can speak for yourself and be heard. Write out a different story that says all the above and then begin to say it twice daily. Read out the story of how you would like to remember it and how empowered you now feel.

Here is your chance to transform beliefs like "children should be seen but not heard" into "children deserve to be seen and heard,

---

[1] Morrissey, M. (2023). *Brave Thinking: The art and science of creating a life you love.* Page Two, p.138.

as their thoughts are very important to hear." "Women deserve to be seen and heard, especially when they have all their mental faculties intact. Women, no matter what age are more than capable of making their own decisions about their lives; what they do with they possessions, their money, and what they want to be, do and have." Replace "Women" with "I" in these statements above. "I more than deserve to be seen and heard, as I have all my mental faculties intact and I have made and continue to make responsible decisions for my highest good." (This is a perfect affirmation for women who are being bullied/controlled as grandmothers.)

If you have a child, a grandchild, or if the little child within you is still feeling like she/he shouldn't be heard, then repattern this saying to read, "You, little Louise, little Dorothy, deserve to be seen and be heard, as your voice and the words you speak are very important to hear. You have a right to be heard, as you and I, as the adult you, have a right to be heard. What we have to say is important for us to speak out loud and for everyone around us to hear."

I found a few amazing quotes by Henry David Thoreau. He puts it like this:

"As a single footstep will not make a path on the earth, so a single thought will not make a pathway in the mind. To make a deep physical path, we walk again and again. To make a deep mental path, we must think over and over the kind of thoughts we wish to dominate our lives."

I believe that we, as ordinary Canadian ranch women, can become the change we want to see in the world right now. Begin it. **I have chosen to share this knowledge as I want shame-based thinking to be universally exposed as a faulty belief.** Once the light is turned on and shame is exposed for what it truly does to people's minds, the darkness surrounding it disappears. So now all

"I want to do is shout—shout out loud", as the song is sung. Because I was shamed and emotionally abused all my life, I have become stronger and have more perseverance, determination, courage to walk out and keep moving forward. I am becoming healthier in mind, body and spirit because of the support I continue to receive from my mentors and friends through my personal growth programs., I continue building my self-respect, self-confidence, and self-worth. As a result of continuing to change my way of thinking with affirmative words, I am also continuing to forgive myself and others, as those are the crucial first steps. Another great quote from Thoreau: **"To have made even one person's life a little better, that is to succeed."**

If you need help identifying your own shame-based thinking, I recommend checking out the resources below. They share some great affirmations that you can read and choose from. Write your favourites down on index cards. Then, tape the index cards to your bathroom mirror or to the fridge. Write down at least three affirmations and say them out loud to yourself while looking into a mirror. Do this at least twice a day for 90 days. You will be surprised by the results at the end of that period.

Henry David Thoreau: "Every oak tree started out as a couple of nuts who stood their ground."

Book Recommendations

Shame & Guilt- Masters of Disguise by Middleton Moz MS.

I Thought It Was Just Me (But It Isn't) by Brene Brown

Mamie's Children by Judy Schultz

Brave Thinking by Mary Morrissey

I will end this chapter with the following words:

The good inside of all of us is wrapped in a layer of apathy, and we forget how much potential we have within us, in each one of us, to change the world for the better of ourselves and our children and thus bring about oneness.
–Shari Arison

Chapter XX

Community Mindfulness & Fun Adventures

Shirley (Burrows) Armstrong, written by her daughter Kerrie (Armstrong) Kusler

Shirley was born to Ralph and Billy Burrows of Countess, Alberta, in 1934. The Burrows farm was typical of the era, with chickens, turkeys, pigs, milk cows, beef cattle, heavy horses, and saddle horses. There was an outhouse, an icehouse, a frigid water well with a hand pump, and a woodpile. Billy grew a huge garden and put up 500 quarts of canned meat, vegetables, and fruit each year. Shirley grew up riding her horse to school until seventh grade. She had an older brother named Ralph Jr. School life was pretty good. The students took care of any bullying that happened around the schoolyard. A bully would be taken out behind the barn and dealt with accordingly. The bad behaviour did not re-occur.

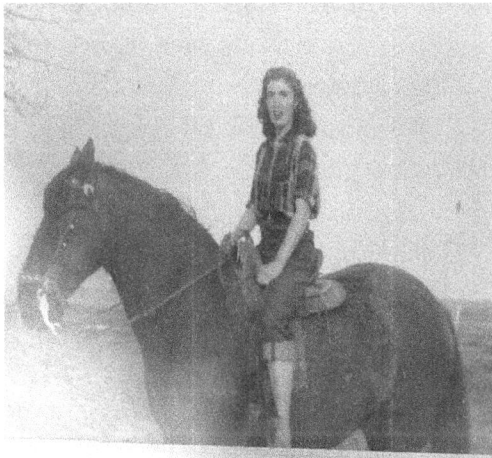

She remembered horse races on the way home from school. If she happened to fall off, her horse would not let her catch him. He would let her almost reach the dragging reins and then walk ahead. In this process, she would wind up walking all the way home. Because all the classes were in one room, Mom enjoyed tuning in to what the class above her was learning. If it was nice out, the teacher often said, "Let's go play ball." No one ever objected to that. However, there were no spontaneous family outings just because it was nice out.

The Second World War was raging. Evenings were spent around the radio, where the whole family gathered to listen to the news from the front. Grandpa always listened to Wilf Carter in the morning. That is how Shirley knew it was time to get out of bed. Their house was heated by warm air rising from the kitchen through a floor vent. On frigid mornings in the winter, a glass of water would be frozen on the windowsill. She would play in the closet because it was warm in there.

Shirley loved her bicycle. While she was learning how to ride, her brother took her out on the road. He sent her whizzing down the hill, and she went over the edge into the creek. She managed to grab a rail and was found swinging over the water, frantically holding onto her bike with her legs. She figured Ralph needed to rethink his teaching technique. Shirley learned to love the animals she looked after, grow a garden, and do everything that farm kids had to do in those days.

4-H Youth Group

She took it very hard every time she had to sell her 4-H steer, a project steer calf (8 months old) that she fed and cared for from November until May of the following year. Then, they would haul it to the nearest town, weigh it in, and enter it into the District 4-H

Beef Show and Sale. Shirley tamed it down, halter broke it to lead, washed and combed the hair, and got it all ready for the show day. She took it through a show ring, which would have been a sort of corral lined with panels to keep the animals in the ring. There was a Quality Beef Judge in the ring who looked at the animals and picked a winner for the best finish (meat and muscle) on the beef steer. Then, the 4-H members would be judged on their grooming steer as well as how they handled the calf in the arena. This would be the showmanship part of the show. Then the Grand Champion Quality, Grooming and Showmanship Ribbon would be awarded as well as Reserve Grand Champion for each of the three events, from the total number of 4-H clubs showing animals that day. After that, the sale would begin, and all the 4-H steers shown that day would be sold to other people for beef to eat. It was most times a sad day for the 4-H members, as they had grown to love their project steer calf. The 4-H member received a cheque for the sale of their steer calf to pay for the feed it ate, and when lucky enough to have funds left over, that money was put into the bank to help with future secondary schooling or some other worthwhile project.

Shirley did some silly things in her life and lived to talk about it. One day, she and some friends were at the "Little Dam," where they saw some boys swimming across and back. If they could do that, she thought so could she. However, she weakened halfway back and had to be rescued by one of the fellows. In another escapade, Shirley had a friend with beautiful long hair that she usually had braided. The long braid hung down her back. One day during school hours, Shirley must have been bored. She thought to herself, for a joke, "I will cut off this braid of hair," and so she did. Her friend was sitting in front of her in the schoolroom. The old school desks were set close to each other in vertical rows. So, it was easy for Shirley to grab the scissors from her desk and cut off the braid. Her friend remembers that to this day, as she is still alive, and verified the story.

Life went on, and Shirley graduated from high school and went on to secondary school to become a telephone operator. It was a great disappointment for Grandma Billy when, after graduating high school, Shirley chose to work as a telephone operator instead of entering nursing school. Her paycheque was $90.00 per month at the time. She met and became lifelong friends with Maude Knight, a true, hardworking Irish lady who was married to Bob Knight, an employee of the McKinnon Ranch.

Family Life & Living Creatures

Shirley and Arnold Armstrong were married in August of 1953. It was funny because lots of people did not know they were dating. *Shirley's dress and veil cost around ninety dollars. Of course, Grandma left no stone unturned for their wedding. She also supplied gladiolas for the occasion. We carried on that tradition when two of Shirley's grandsons, Winston and Daniel, got married. Shirley supplied gladiolas for those occasions. Mom and Dad settled at the Teigland place, south of Bassano, about fifteen miles. The yard was about one and a half miles away from the Bow River. The place had been purchased by Dad and his brothers (East and West Ranch).

One evening, Mom and Dad were victims of a chivaree. A bunch of their "friends" snuck into the yard after their lights were turned out. These "friends" surrounded the house, went in through the windows and doors, and upset their bed with them in it. Mom, being extremely modest, was thoroughly embarrassed. At the time, there were thousands of little frogs in the yard, a phenomenon caused by rain at just the right time. Someone thought it was a great idea to bring in a pail full and dump them on the kitchen floor.

I, Kerrie, came along in 1954, followed by my brother Bill in 1956. Grant was born during a raging dust storm on December 1, 1959. Mom had thoroughly cleaned the house before she left for the hospital and was annoyed to find the house full of dust when she arrived home with her new bundle.

Mom had a tabby barn cat that hated Dad. At least once, while Dad was milking the cow in the barn, this tabby barn Tomcat went up into the hayloft and urinated right over where Dad was. As you can imagine, the pee dropped through the floorboards onto Dad's back. The air was blue! I'm surprised that cat got to live.

A particularly spectacular electrical storm came through the yard one hot summer evening. Mom was enjoying the beauty of the lightning as she walked back from the barn after milking the cow. Suddenly, there was a terrific strike right in the yard. That lightning bolt got her attention, and she beat a hasty retreat to the house, losing most of the milk out of her pail.

The Teigland yard had a washhouse with a modern bathroom, warm running water, and a wringer washing machine. Luxuries!

There were batteries in the washhouse basement that stored 32-volt electricity from the wind charger. This dictated the sort of appliances one could run. If there was no wind, then there was no power. Their telephone was a fence line affair, connecting them to Bob (Dad's brother) and Verna Armstrong's place, just south of Bassano. Mom had a propane stove and refrigerator and a trap door leading to a dirt cellar below the kitchen. The little bunkhouse where the hired men lived had a small cast iron coal and wood stove to keep them warm in the winter.

Home Cooking, Kids & Sticky Blueberry Pie

Mom tried serving her first batch of home-baked beans to the hired men when she was first married. Eating them was like chewing bullets: Maybe not enough water, tomato juice, or other liquids were added to the bean pot, or maybe it was not cooked enough. The old Scottish range rider, Scottie Lewis, offered words of encouragement: "By Gaaad Shiardddley, those airdd the best beans I evairdd et." Eventually Mom learned how to make a good pot of baked beans.

Mom and my Aunt Verna did the meals for the big projects, including branding, cattle weaning, and the trail rides where we moved the cattle down to the river camp, which was called Scottie's. In the early years, Dad would set up a tent, and, along with the use of Scottie's shack, the branding meal was hauled and served at the river.

On one occasion, before the invention of Tupperware, Mom had all her blueberry pies lined up in the car's back window. We kids were relegated to the back seat. Well, Mom hit a pothole on the prairie trail. Sticky blueberry pie down our backs was not a happy thing. Another year, a severe hailstorm struck just as we were all sitting down to dinner. Everyone scurried for cover with plates or cardboard boxes held over their heads. Rescuing the food and stuffing everyone into that little shack was quite a challenge. On occasion, if it rained, the road out of the river valley would become impassable.

Moved Closer to Bassano, Gardening, Cooking

In 1960, Arnold and Shirley moved since there was no school bus where we were. They purchased the Ben Plumer place south of Bassano, Alberta. Mom regretted the move away from the river, but the unlimited water supply for her and Dad to create a massive park: expansive green lawns and flowers, plus a garden, provided great joy. They joined community activities. Mom and Dad were members of the local Masons and Eastern Star, which took a lot of dedication. Fundraising to build the Bassano Centennial Hockey Arena took on a life of its own. Dad was usually involved whenever there was an event scheduled that had to do with fundraising or politics.

Mom sold cream and cooked for harvest crews, hired men, bake sales, hockey clubs, catering clubs, brandings, and whomever else that she deemed hungry. This theme continued throughout her whole life. She canned a huge garden each year. What she could not use, she gave away. One time Mom thought she should grow strawberries and send them to Calgary to a farmers' market. I told her she should not be required to kill herself off crawling around weeding and harvesting and generally wrecking her back for the Farmers Market in Calgary. She listened, but instead, Mom took it upon herself to grow pumpkins, gourds, and squash, with enough extra produce to decorate the church each fall for the Thanksgiving Service. The picking, cleaning, hauling, and decorating took more energy than the planting, watering, and weeding. This tradition carried on for at least forty-five years.

She also supplied giant loaves of homemade bread for the altar and then served that with fresh raspberry jam for the luncheon afterward. My Aunt Betty Anne also shared her artistic genius and did the floral arranging and decorating each year for the occasion. Once Mom and Dad were closer to town, she taught Sunday school and served as a member of the Church Session as a Church Elder. Her daily writings often included a prayer that fit into whatever was going on in life on the ranch.

Over the years, things change, and sometimes for the better. Mom purchased an older motorhome and referred to it as Old Bluestripe. This rig enabled her to haul the meals, usually roast beef, potatoes, gravy, buns, salads, pickles, pies, squares, extra chairs, water, and coffee, which she made on the motorhome stove. Eventually, they built a log cabin at the river, a nice addition to the work and fun days down there.

Bluestripe was always a welcome sight on cold, windy days when they were weaning the calves at the corrals south of Lathom. The little motorhome afforded the crew a nice place to warm up while they were served a hot meal. Mom eventually replaced Bluestripe with a newer version of the same because there was no way she was retiring from her job.

Mom often employed a gal to help with the garden and housekeeping during the summer. These gals got to enjoy our ranch life, including some unexpected experiences. One day, one of these helpers named Linda was there washing windows. Mom and Dad got into a heated discussion, probably because Mom had asked Dad to do some dreaded chore. While he walked away, Dad called Mom an "asshole" under his breath. Mom returned the favour, calling Dad the same as he got in his truck and drove away. In a matter of minutes, up drives my brother Grant on the quad. He was in a surly mood and busy expounding (with very colourful language) on some problem he thought he had. Then he drove away, too. "Yup," Mom said, "And then assholes get married and beget little assholes!" Linda thought she was going to fall off her ladder, she was laughing so hard.

Marriage, Ranch Split, Tragedy

I, Kerrie, got married to Bruce Kusler in 1977. The East and West Ranch went through a necessary split in 1982. Dad and his three brothers all had sons who wanted to ranch, and it was expedient to make a new plan. Tragedy struck the family when Bill passed away after a plane crash on the Bow River in June of 1983. Mom went through an incredible amount of stress.

Grant married Marilyn Wood in 1983. They extended the ranch to include part of the Carl and Pat Block place. Mom and Dad welcomed five grandchildren starting with Winston Kusler in 1981, Daniel Kusler in 1984, then Grant and Marilyn's girls, Alisha in 1985, Laura in 1987, and Rae Lynn in 1988. Sadly, Grant and Marilyn's marriage did not last.

1996 saw our family take part in the Western Stock Growers 100-year celebration. We were a group of thirteen people with two wagons, four heavy horses, and ten saddle horses. The legendary trail ride across the British Block was made possible by the monumental effort of many folks. Mom was ecstatic to be part of the fun-filled historical adventure. She even had two outfits designed for the occasion. Mom borrowed a horse one day and rode for several hours. All her grandkids were along, and she said it was one of the best things she's ever been a part of—an unparalleled experience of a lifetime.

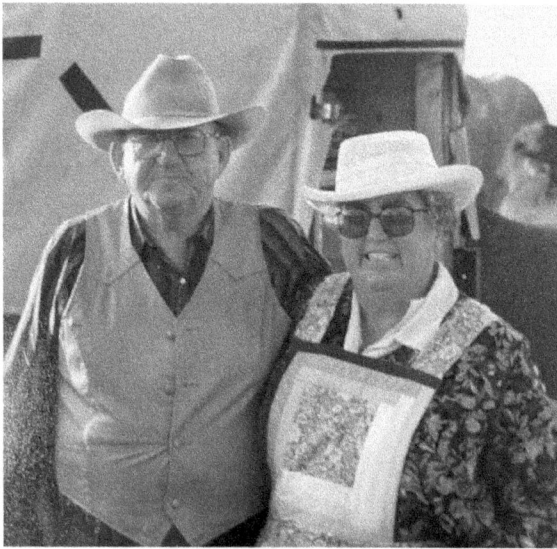

Arnold and Shirley Armstrong 1996

Shirley with Chuck Wagon used by their family on the 1996 Trail Ride

Shirley with the two-horse team that pulled the wagon above.
She loved the whole experience, fun without the work with her family.

COMMUNITY MINDFULNESS & FUN ADVENTURES

#1 Community Supporter

Mom received the rural yard beautification plaque from the County of Newel in 2005. She was chosen as "Woman of the Year" by the community, and in 2009, she was the Parade Marshall for the Bassano rodeo. Grant installed a sign for Mom: "Bow Cattle Cook House." Instead of slowing down a bit, she took the sign literally. She would help cook for her extended family's brandings along with her own. She figured Darwin Wood could not survive without her saskatoon pies. She sent treats to the Church youth group every week, made lunches for her granddaughter Rae Lynn's high school friends, etc. She had a lovely shop in that yard and hosted many events, particularly the Masons' picnics. If a day went by when somebody wasn't at her table for a meal, she felt lonesome. Mom liked to "justify her existence," as she put it. It was fun for her to help Alisha cook for her combine crews. Alisha, having four little kids, certainly didn't turn down the help.

One day, Mom was running a little late. She gets across the highway and puts her "pedal to the metal" as they say. Seems the RCMP were out on the Countess Road that day. When asked why she was in such a big hurry, she replied, "I'm late to feed the combine crew!" The fellow probably thought he'd heard it all until he met 80-year-old Gramma Shirley.

One of the ranch chores that Mom took on after moving to the Bothie place was to salt the heifers. She'd take her Tahoe to the mill and have it loaded with salt blocks. I was sure we'd find her out in a pasture somewhere, with her foot crushed underneath a salt block. She got a little "gator" (side by side) and took great delight in checking heifers, picking twine, and hauling clippings from her 5-acre yard.

Mom bought herself an electric chainsaw. No tree or hedge was safe after that. The guys at the Bassano Dump would cheerfully help Gramma Shirley unload a pile of branches that would defy the law of gravity off the back of her antiquated Ford.

The year Laura got married, she thought it would be a great idea for Gramma Shirley to have a Holstein and five pail-bunters** to look after. (Mom loved milk cows and wouldn't say NO!) This was Laura's idea of how to make money to pay for her wedding, so Mom dubbed the bovine "Honey-Moon." I'm surprised that she did not fire up her old cream separator. Mom once had a Brown Swiss that she named Bonnie after the lady she had purchased her from. Bonnie had a heifer calf that Mom named "Pinky" (Apparently, Brown Swiss crossed with Black Angus results in pink calves).

Several things Mom was famous for were her dill pickles, sticky buns, chili sauce, raspberry jam, and, of course, her gladiolas. There wasn't a week went by that she hadn't produced at least one batch of buns and maybe a couple batches of her oatmeal cookies, all before 10:00 a.m. She'd manage two hours of weeding in her garden during the early hours before it got too hot. Mom would run water on her yard around the clock if it were very dry.

Often, if there was a grieving family in the community, they would be presented with ham and a couple dozen buns, plus a bouquet of gladiolas. If there was a pending bake sale, she would bake for three days so that she could donate to the fundraiser. For the fall church sale, she would arrive with copious amounts of fresh produce and several jars of her home canned preserves.

Mom's hobby of growing gladiolas proliferated into about 700 bulbs. If someone was having a celebration or a friend was ill, they would be presented with a bouquet. If she had extra, the lodge and the hospital were lucky recipients of the splendid bouquets. She used to say that her gladiolas were her ministry. You can only imagine the devastation when one morning she discovered deer had gone in and nipped off the top of each "glad" before they had started to bloom. The following spring, Bruce and I built a ten-foot page wire fence. That stopped the four-legged marauders! In 2017, when Mom, Aunt Betty Anne Burrows, and the family celebrated the 100-year anniversary of the Burrows farm, Mom was able to provide many cream-can bouquets for the occasion.

Halloween was a well-celebrated occasion for Mom. Without fail, about 40 popcorn balls were manufactured. She loved to dress up and hand other delectable treats to all the bus drivers at the school where we were. Christmas was also a very special time of year for Mom. She loved attending Christmas church programs at both Bassano and Gem. Outdoor lights and having a real tree were very important. Hours were spent making sure every piece of lead tinsel was hung correctly. She loved the smell of a natural tree and decorated her home with real holly, cedar, and Poinsettia. Mom loved to send and receive Christmas cards and did not miss a year. Of course, she spent many days baking Christmas cakes, cookies, and candies for the family and the Eastern Star fundraiser.

Gramma Shirley—Cat Lady

Gramma Shirley could be referred to as a cat lady. One of her favourites, a tabby Manx, was named Mrs. Dionne. Unsurprisingly, her first litter consisted of five kittens. Mrs. D. was full of personality. If she wasn't getting enough attention, she would stand in the kitchen and grab Mom by the leg. If Mom was working on her daily diary or writing Christmas letters, Mrs. D. would plop herself right on Mom's writing paper. Mrs. Dionne spent many hours keeping Mom company while she enjoyed hockey and baseball on TV. Of course, this famous feline's progeny is still sought after. One of the most famous is my fifth-generation cat, Missy. She has many strong traits, so when I moved her to Mom's place, Missy easily became part of the household. 12-year-old Missy suffered a severe injury that was probably caused by being attacked by a hawk. It was very expensive to repair. Missy still serves as an excellent mouse control officer at the main yard.

Mom had some great young ladies work for her: Sharon, who stayed on for ten years, then Shawn, and then a Filipino gal named Leslie. When the great-grandkids started to arrive, Mom would often wind up looking after them as their mothers were out and about doing farm chores or moving cattle. Fortunately, Mom had help as she was getting up in years. None of Mom's employees were afraid of work, as there was always plenty of it in the yard and household.

She Loved Sports and Canvassing

I cannot finish this story without mentioning that my mom loved all sports. She was raised going to many baseball games, as her dad did not miss a Sunday pitching for the Duchess Dukes and many other community teams. Both of my brothers played hockey, and Mom and Dad put on many thousands of miles, hauling little league teams to wherever they needed to be. Mom did not miss the puck drop for the opening face-off of my brother's games in town. (I considered myself a hockey orphan.) She also made sure that Grandpa got to every local hockey game. He had both legs removed, but with his canes and Mom's dedication, Grandpa would get into the arena and situated where he could enjoy the games. Years later, a heated easy chair section was created at one corner of the arena, and Mom got to watch hockey from there. Mom attended as many rodeo, 4-H events, basketball and volleyball games, and tournaments as she could possibly fit in. She was a great supporter of all activities that her grandchildren and extended family were involved in.

Mom spent countless hours canvassing for the Heart Foundation, a project the Eastern Star Order took on. In 2008, the Bassano O.E.S. celebrated 60 years of being a chartered organization. It was a tearful occasion when the Mary Koehane #96 Charter had to be surrendered. Mom and other "sisters" then joined the group in Hussar. Eventually, she and her dear friend, Jill Maloney, went to Brooks for the last year of Star there. Mom held many offices in the lodge and could do most of the memory work when asked to fill in. Mom was honoured to receive her 65th-year pin and certificate.

Over the years, Mom developed an amazing collection of community history books. For easy access, they were displayed in an antique bookcase in her sitting room. Mom regularly attended local rodeos and many other functions. She delighted in visiting with and meeting new people. Mom would then go home and read up on their respective family histories. Reading was a great winter pastime for Mom. Mom's refrigerator, besides always being well stocked with interesting things to eat, was adorned with little snippets of wisdom. We all found it very entertaining to stop by to review her latest postings.

Most of the words were meant to educate or enlighten her family. My personal favourite: "Each day, I look for small improvements in my adult children." I felt quite insulted until she said, "Oh, that's not meant for you, Kerrie." In her diary, she wrote: "Some days I do wonder at my seemingly 'wise' decisions of a few years ago." I'll leave it to the readers to surmise exactly which ones she was referring to. After Mother's Day in 2005, she wrote, "I guess Grant thinks he crawled out from a cabbage leaf." I believe all was forgiven when he showed up the next day.

In the fall of 2014, tragedy struck the family and community when Grant passed away suddenly. This has taken a toll on the whole family, and now his girls endeavour to carry on the ranching tradition.

Mom continued her work until she was overtaken with monastic breast cancer in November of 2018. She passed away quietly, with family & friends taking turns to be at her side. These days, it seems that no family is left untouched by cancer. Mom was a character, always cheery with a humorous comment to suit most occasions. We gave away 650 gladiola bulbs to the folks who came to her memorial service. The following poem was penned while she was helping her community put together a local community family history book.

"Old House" by Shirley Armstrong

Poor Old House,
Where No One Lives,
Entrusted To Care,
No Body Gives.

Sagging Door,
Windows Agape,
Bereft of Laughter,
Decor and Drape.

If You Could Talk,
A Story to Tell,
Of a Little Bit of Heaven,
Turned To a Dusty Hell.

Your People came,
With Hopes on High,
Their Hearts in the Soil,
Their Eyes to The Sky.

Woe to the Day,
The Soil was Turned,
Sad the Lesson,
Is too often Learned.

There are some parts,
Of this Thirsty Land,
That Should Have Been Left,
In God's Own Hand.

Photo: Shirley picking raspberries in her private patch.

The following saying suits most folks: "When the elderly die, a library is lost, and volumes of wisdom and knowledge are gone."

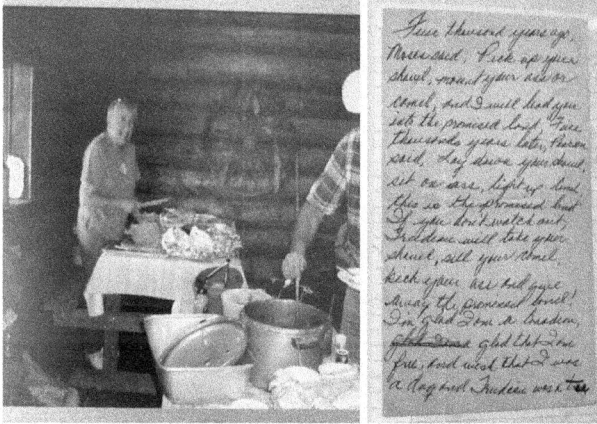

Shirley had a sense of humour and what she wrote was well thought out, as you can tell above; like writing poems and writing about what she felt.

(Author's Add-ons to describe some words that may not reflect what they mean without an extra explanation for those people not familiar with ranch life and what we do extra with baby calves sometimes.)

* Communication and transportation were different back in 1953, so people didn't see each other very much as they were too busy working. Hence some people didn't know they were dating. (Explanation for people who are unaware of the great distances between families.)

** Pail-bunters are baby calves who don't have any mothers, so the milk is in a pail with a nipple on it, and the calves suck the milk out of the pail.

Recipes used by Shirley many times while she cooked for family and friends.

Potatoe Salad Dressing,   Gram B

3 eggs
1 tsp mustard   } mix well stir until
1 tsp flour   } it comes to boil
3 tbsp sugar.
salt + pepper   } use with milk.
1 cu vinegar.

MEXICAN WEDDING CAKE

1 c butter   / 1/2 c berry sugar
2 c flour   1/4 tsp salt
1 c nuts   1 tsp vanilla

Make into small crescent shapes and bake at 350° for 15 min. Roll in icing sugar when cooled.

Shirley Armstrong

Dill Pickles
   Boil together 1 qt vinegar
                 3 qts H2O
                 1 cup pickle salt
Pour over cucumbers for dills, place
jars
To each 1/2 gal jar add: 2 heads dill
                         1 clove garlic
                         1/4 tsp alum

---

put 1/2 tsp allspice and 4 whole cloves
Pour in boiling vinegar + seal.

Chapter XXI

Facts About the Livestock We Raise

Written by Dorothy Louise Beasley

Information from a Canadian Living Magazine while I was making up my Vision Board a week ago, 2024. The magazine is from 1995, so a little bit dated, but the information is not much different today.

Information is taken from the most recent 2024 Canada Beef website as well, www.canadabeef.ca

Today, all the hype is about how bad cows are for the climate. The news channels and social media defame cows for all our global warming. In this article done up by Helen Bishop MacDonald who is a Registered Dietitian for the Dairy Bureau of Canada, Helen talks about "Your Health" in this magazine. She devotes a whole page to talking about cows and the milk they produce, as well as the fertilizer they spread out on the fields for free.

I will share some of this information here just to let the people who read this book know that the cows we raise are not causing our climate to change that much. According to the article she produced, it says this: "Have you heard that the methane (a greenhouse gas) cows produce is responsible for global warming?" She got some facts from the U.S. National Academy of Sciences, which show that all the ruminants together, which includes cattle, sheep, deer, buffalo, giraffes, goats, camels, etc., produce less than 5% of total greenhouse gas production.

She goes on to say that cattle use land for grazing that is unsuitable for growing crops that are produced for human consumption. The dairy cow turns that grass into milk, which feeds the world. The ranch cow feeds a new baby calf that grows up to be meat for us to eat or another cow/bull calf for breeding and creating more female cows. The manure is recycled for fertilizer on the pastures or field crop areas. Or, in days gone by with our pioneer families and some other countries, cow manure becomes odourless when it dries and is used as fuel for heat and as a building material.

In this article, Helen also states that Canadian milk didn't contain preservatives at that time, 1995, so it was and probably still is amongst the safest, most inspected foods in the world. I am not sure if this has changed in the last few years, as raw milk usually only lasts about four days in the fridge, whereas the milk we buy in the store these days lasts for a month or more. It must contain a preservative of some sort, possibly a healthy one!

Raw milk is still the best form of milk to drink, although health authorities beg to differ. One can find this milk on our livestock ranches in the springtime when we milk out a ranch cow to feed a calf unwilling to drink on its own. It must be relatively healthy as our pioneers drank it all the time, and the baby calf sucks it out of the teat straight from the mother, and it is a healthy calf!

Milk contains practically every vitamin and mineral we need to survive. Apparently, it has more calcium than 12 sardines in the can with their bones softened. A single serving of whole milk is said to have more thiamine, riboflavin, and niacin than bread made from 100% whole wheat. Milk contains potassium, almost as much as a banana. Researchers studied the Vitamin A in broccoli and found that milk contains three-quarters of the Vitamin A that is in broccoli. Lean ground beef was compared, and milk has one-third less fat. Also, milk has 45% of our daily requirement of Vitamin D. (This information taken from Canada's Food Guide when drinking whole milk.)

A study done by Canada Beef just recently has similar findings to the studies in 1995. The Canadabeef.ca website states, "The topic of beef and health has been extensively studied. Two large studies, one in Europe[2] and another in the United States[3], found no association between eating fresh red meat and any cause of death, including heart disease or cancer."

Canada Beef website also states that "Research shows there's no reason to avoid fresh red meat when following a heart-healthy diet and watching your cholesterol." A partial quote from Canada Beef states, "Researchers from Harvard University conducted a test, and they found that eating 100 grams of fresh red meat per day is not linked to the development of heart disease."

Red meat is a concentrated source of essential vitamins and minerals. It contains vitamin B12, protein, iron, and zinc and has the same calories as fish.

Canada Beef states that "In the US study,[4] investigators made a couple of other interesting observations—namely that adults who ate red meat more often: (1) tended to eat vegetables more often, and (2) tended to have smaller waists and lower body weights."

---

[2] Rohrmann S et al. Meat consumption and mortality – results from the European Prospective Investigation into Cancer and Nutrition. BMC Medicine, 2013; 11:63.

[3] Kappeler R, Eichholzer M, and Rohrmann S. Meat consumption and diet quality and mortality in NHANES III. Eur J Clin Nutr, 2013; 67(6):598-606.

[4] Ibid.

The same information from the Canadian Magazine, inform-ation on butter and cream, which are a part of milk. It says that butter and cream contain very small amounts of saturated fats, very unlikely enough to cause your body any damage. It says that one-third of saturated fats have no effect on blood cholesterol, and 36% of the fat in butter is monounsaturated. It also states that six of those small pats of butter have no more cholesterol than 100g of fish, chicken, or veal.

The Canada Beef website, Canadabeef.ca, is quite interesting to read, and if you want to know more about the beef we raise and maybe find some recipes for cooking beef, please check it out. (Louise met the brand-new President of Canada Beef and a couple more of the Board Members at a Manitoba Beef Producers meeting recently and was privileged to visit with him for a while.) The website includes information about eating a balanced diet. It says to eat whole, fresh foods: eat many different fruits and vegetables, as you will receive many benefits from eating a variety of these foods. Foods also in high fibre grains and lean proteins. It's the quality and quantity of your food choices that count, says Canada Beef.

So now we can eat better, feel better, have extra energy and good health to enjoy eating what we like, and live life to the fullest. Our Alberta and Saskatchewan Beef is where our Canadian ranch women know where to find the best beef in the world. They cook it up from scratch, with basic ingredients and tools, add a sprinkle or two of love, and put everything together into healthy, nutritious meals. Then serve their families and friends also with love for the ranching industry and the livestock, vegetable gardens, wild and tame fruit trees, and bushes we pick from each year that provide us with food we love to eat and thrive upon.

All great things are preceded by chaos.
–Deepak Chopra

What lies within us and what lies behind us are small matters compared to what lies within us. And when we bring what is within us out into the world, miracles happen.
–Henry David Thoreau

Chapter XXII

About The Livestock, An Ordinary Annual Ranch Work Schedule, Politics & Self-Sufficiency

Written by Dorothy Louise Beasley

Allergies to Animals and Hay/Grain

I was raised with animals all my life up until I had my first child in 1976. I became dangerously allergic to cattle, horses, sheep, chickens, goats, rabbits, dogs, cats' dander; their hair proved unhealthy for me. Hormonal changes occurred that changed some of the chemistry in my body. Before that I rode a horse every day in my child and teenage years and helped with the cattle round-ups, riding horseback, processing the cattle right up until a month before Elsie was born. After her birth, I wore a N95, breathable mask over my nose and mouth and had inhalers whenever I was around the animals. If people who came into the house had been riding a horse or processing cattle, I can still recall what it was like when my lungs filled up with that dander, within seconds. I had to leave the room and get my inhalers and then sit quietly for quite a while until I could breathe again. Sometimes I had panic attacks, then had to quieten down, take slow even breaths, and see if I could catch a breath or two.

Sometimes I drove myself into Brooks, the nearest hospital, which was a 45 mile drive away to get oxygen and medicine to help me breathe air into my lungs again. Can you imagine a livestock cattle ranch woman allergic to all the stuff that pertains to the ranch? I wore a heavy duty mask when helping outside and whenever I was in an indoor arena with cattle or horses. I recently found out that I am gluten intolerant, and when I cut gluten out of my diet, my allergies to the animal hair dander and dust are almost non-existent. The inflammation around my lungs and other parts of my body is greatly reduced. My husband Carl has asthma too; he is allergic to tree/plant pollens, grain dust, mold, hay dust, but not to the animals. So we were able to complement each other. I could rake the hay, but I still wore a mask if it was dusty hay and he could work with the animals. I helped with the animals too, but wore a mask and didn't touch any of them either. I used a stick to push them up in a chute and made sure I was up wind from them in a corral. I managed, as the work needed to be done and someone had to be there to do it. It was okay; I learned what I could do and what I couldn't do. I have also learned to breathe deeper, to calm my nervous system, in through the nose, out through the mouth.

Different Breeds of Cattle

In Canada, there are many breeds of beef cattle. It began with the Texas Longhorn, which was trailed up from Texas to graze the long, tall native grasses of the Canadian prairies when it was first settled. These cattle were able to graze a little, drink water, and traverse the thousands of miles and many months it took to get them up here to Canada. Then once the European, Scottish, and English immigrants began arriving, the Hereford, Shorthorn, and Angus breeds came on boats, the first to arrive from overseas. These cattle were small and not as hardy as the Longhorn. Yet, they survived. Then came larger framed, exotic breeds such as the Simmental, Charolais, Gelbvieh, Black & Belted Galloway, Speckle Parks, Limousin, Maine Anjou, South Devons, and Santa Gertrudus. Today, crosses of all these different breeds, along with crossbreeding among the traditional British breeds, can be found all over Canada. I know I have missed many of the different breeds, but these were some of the ones I recall. These exotic breeds peaked in 1974-75. The A.I. program had taken hold earlier, and there were now many half-blood beef animals as well as dairy cattle bred to these exotic breeds. The Beasley family originally began with sheep, then bought Hereford cattle back in 1970. They bought the Sandgathe ranch near Wardlow, Alberta, which came with a Hereford cattle herd. Then, as the exotic breeds came through the Canadian prairies, the original Beasley Ranching Company Ltd bought some Simmental and Limousin and began crossing them. Eventually, in the early 1980s, the Beasley Family decided to go with the black aberdeen angus cattle. We bought a purebred Black Angus cattle herd that fit our likes and wants for a healthy and productive cattle herd and have never looked back. We have a black angus purebred herd as well as a couple of black angus commercial herds, one in Alberta and another one in Manitoba.

BSE in 2003 and Lots of Cattle Unsold

In 2003, BSE hit and so we could not sell anything older than 30 months, so it was indeed a wise choice to have purchased the land in Manitoba. (BSE- Bovine Spongiform Encephalopathy or Mad Cow Disease.) We didn't have any cattle infected with this disease, so we waited it out, which was tough as we had to keep all our dry cows, unproductive bulls, and dry heifers for a few years afterwards. It was tough to keep all those animals fed over that period. There was no income to pay for some expenses, although we could sell the animals under 30 months of age that were being fed in the feedlot at the Alberta home ranch. Markets were few to sell these animals as all the other countries' borders shut down, too. Do you recall reading the other ranch women's stories about how devastating BSE was to the cattle industry and our ranches?

Cattle Terms

Some readers from urban areas may not understand all our cattle terminology. We have five different types of cattle animals: a cow, a heifer, a bull, a steer, and a heiferette. The female cows/heifers have certain jobs to do on the ranch: get pregnant, keep healthy, carry calves around in their wombs for 9 months, eat lots of grass, drink water, sleep every day all spring and summer long, then eat harvested hay, silage, greenfeed and water for the winter months. Then, whenever they're due to calve, produce a healthy baby calf. The mother cow/heifer feeds her baby calf healthy fresh milk every day for 6-7 months. She keeps it safe from predators and then is forced to wean it in October or November so she can begin to gain weight and get ready for the cold winter months on the prairies. And then do all that over again for the next 12-18 years. The calf will continue to grow after that: either in a feedlot, where it is put onto a mixed ration of grain, or protein pellets, corn, plus hay, and possibly silage feed. The calf will get fat and provide meat for the hungry humans, or out on pasture, where it can become a year older. At first, the yearlings will be penned together and fed only enough to maintain their body weight for the winter months. Then they're put out onto pasture to gain weight or sold to a feedlot to fatten for beef the following fall. These animals may be steers or heifers. If it is a steer, it fattens better, and its body does not turn into a muscular, heavy-duty breeding machine. A steer has its testicles removed when it is a calf so it doesn't become a bull.

Now, you may ask why we would castrate a bull and make it into a steer. Bulls are the male animals. Their job is to breed the cows, which usually begins when they are two years of age. Some ranchers use their younger yearling bulls to breed the younger heifers. Most ranchers don't want all their male bull calves to grow up and breed all the cows, their mothers: that would be called "inbreeding." So, we pick out the best disposition, good-looking bulls with good sound feet and legs that move easily and sell them at a Bull Sale. They are purchased by other ranchers who want their cows bred to those gentle disposition bulls. The rest of the bull calves are castrated.

Now for the heifer, which is a young female cow. If she is healthy, calm in temperament yet protective of her calf, has good feet, a nice compact udder with small teats, enough milk production to feed her baby calf, and a healthy, thick coat of hair for winter, she is mostly likely kept with the herd. Otherwise, she goes into a pen in our feedlot and is fed out for beef, too, or left as a yearling to be sold after another season eating grass. Sometimes, the heifers are spayed and then fattened for meat; they are called heiferettes. This keeps them from accidently getting bred in a mixed-gender feedlot corral. (Sometimes, in a feedlot, many different ranchers have sold their animals to the feedlot and so there could be the odd bull in the same pen as a heifer or cow, then that animal could have a calf while being fattened, which produces an unwanted calf. Then the calf is sold to a rancher who needs a calf to replace one of his that has died at birth.)

The Seasonal Cycles of Cattle Ranching

A heifer and/or cow is bred in July if you want a calf born in April, as pregnancy lasts 9 months and 4 days, or 283 days. If you want your calf crop born in January, February, or March, then she needs to see the bull or be artificially inseminated in April or May; a March calf would be bred in June. In our herd, a few replacement black angus heifers are chosen to replace any older cows who did not have a calf this year. They are usually bred a little bit earlier than the cows, but not much, as the cold and snowy weather are not conducive for having live calves born in a snow drift and kept alive. (Even during April, in the past, we have cold wet snowstorms that occur, and the little baby calves are brought into the house kitchen to be warmed up and then taken back out to their moms.) We do not have barns and such to calve them in. We have April calves in Alberta and May calves in Manitoba, as the snow stays longer in Manitoba. (The weather is drier out here on the prairies, not wet and damp like it is in Europe and the eastern provinces of Canada, so we do not need to house our cattle in barns during the winter months.)

No Barns for our Cattle, They Weather the Storms

Most ranchers have 200 or more cattle to raise, and so it is challenging to house that many in barns at one time. The barns would get too hot and begin to sweat, causing the calves to come down with pneumonia. That said, if there are no trees, bushes, or hills to shelter away from the cold winter winds, we build wood shelters for them out in the pastures. We spread out straw for the cattle to lay on to protect their udders and other parts of their bodies during the cold winter days and nights. Other breeds of cattle put on extra hair as well to protect them from the cold weather. For example, this past January/February (2024), our temperatures were as low as -40 to -45 degrees Celsius.

The work to keep these beef animals alive and well is spread out over a 12-month period to manage a healthy and fully productive ranch herd. (If we had sheep, goats, llamas, or other animals the work would be apportioned out the same.)

When the snow flies in the fall, and the cattle can no longer pick at the grass or the other alfalfa/grass hay materials left in the fields, they are brought together and fed fortified protein pellets, grass/alfalfa bales, silage, greenfeed bales, or whatever the rancher has stock-piled for winter feed. This feeding schedule goes on all winter until the snow disappears in April of the following year. Possibly in February, the rancher separates his thinner (not as well-performing) cows from the main herd and feeds them more during this time. Once there are not so many of them fighting for the same food, they begin to get more to eat and are packing more weight to feed their hungry calves in the upcoming spring.

Around the end of April or May, whenever most of the cows and heifers have calved, they are moved to other areas of the ranch, away from the calving areas. The rancher sorts off any late calvers—cows that have lost their calves due to being stillborn or because of a backwards calf that can't calve quick enough. Sometimes, the calf just dies before it is born or after it is born. All these cows—in addition to the cows that have not calved yet or that never got bred—are sorted away from the mothers and babies and moved to another field.

Summer Pasture Rotations and Processing Hay & Cattle

The cows and calves are split into smaller bunches and moved out to other pastures, where they graze for a month or so. The whole family, plus some neighbours, will help to move these cattle out to their summer grazing fields. The bulls are rounded up from the field they wintered in and tested for semen to see if they will be able to breed the cows or if they are no good. A veterinarian is hired to come out and test the bulls with a specific machine for that purpose. The ranch woman, or a neighbouring ranch woman, prepares a lunchtime meal for the workers during this bull semen testing day. She either takes it out to the corrals for the five to six people to eat, or they come in after the bulls are all finished and enjoy their meal inside, with time to relax after all the work is done.

ABOUT THE LIVESTOCK- CATTLE,
AN ORDINARY ANNUAL RANCH WORK SCHEDULE,
POLITICS & SELF-SUFFICIENCY

Calves are born in April at our home Alberta ranch and in May at our Manitoba ranch. This involves about 150 replacement heifers and about 700 mature cows in Manitoba and about the same in Alberta.

The crops are prepared and seeded around this time, May, once the ground warms up a bit. It's important to do this before it gets too late, or else the crops will not mature on time. The vegetable garden is planted in late May, sometimes first week of June and even then sometimes it freezes down in Manitoba. There are lots of other tasks to do, as well. A trip to the veterinarian clinic to purchase all livestock vaccinations, for the mature cows and calves before the end of June branding. Many trips to town for salt and minerals for the cattle. Daily checks to make sure the cattle have fresh clean water to drink. Moreover, processing calves to prevent sickness, clipping on identifying ear tags, and castrating the bulls. Those male calves are given a shot of painkillers at the same time to lessen the stress on them. The sun may be hot that day, or it could be raining. A nice, warm, dry garage is very welcome if the cowboys have been working in a cold rain all day. The garage is cleaned out and filled with picnic tables, and all kinds of home-made salads, meats, potatoes, vegetables, and desserts are set out buffet style on this major processing day called "Branding Day." The calves used to be branded with a hot iron for identification purposes, but this is no longer done on a regular basis. It is basically a processing of the calves to prevent disease and too many bull calves at breeding time. These keep the animals healthy and go through the animal's body way before it is used as meat. We also select replacement heifers out of the calf herd, as many as we think we will need for the following year to maintain the same number of cattle each year.

Maintaining Healthy Cattle

The salt and minerals are placed in big rubber tires that have been cut in half. The cattle eat the salt/mineral mixture to keep them healthy. During the summer, we must clean corrals of all manure at the home ranch in Alberta—usually hiring someone with specific equipment to come in and complete this work. They spread this manure on the fields, in the fall, before working it in and preparing the ground for seeding next year. This allows the manure to break down, heat, and ferment to create natural fertilizer. In Manitoba, we do not keep the cattle in pens; they are out in the fields all winter, so we only must harrow the pastures to spread the manure out evenly on the fields for the spring grass growing season.

We also move the yearlings/cow-calf pairs to community pastures in Manitoba, putting out salt and minerals for them, too. This goes on all summer, checking to see if Community Pasture Managers need more salt & mineral brought out. The salt and mineral tires are regularly checked to make sure the cattle always have access to these nutrients. This means travelling to four or five different pastures to put out salt and minerals. In the Manitoba and Alberta pastures, we also check fences, as trees may fall upon the fences and break the wires or fence posts, so they need to be cut off the fence lines with a chain saw and so the fence can be repaired. This happens quite often.

We must check the cattle in the home pastures every day— morning, noon, and night—to make sure they are all doing well. We mostly use horses to do this, though we use quads, or trucks if salt and minerals need to be taken out, too. The cattle become used to the horses, the quads, and the slow-moving trucks. We also check to see if there are any predator kills, as the wolves, bears, and other large carnivores are feeding their young at this time of year. (Fresh beef is easy to catch and provides healthy protein to their young pups, cubs, etc. and we lose about 40 animals each year in Manitoba to these large carnivores, mostly wolves and some coyotes.)

In July we will check the fences, as trees fall on them in Manitoba on a regular ongoing basis and the cattle could escape, or next time if there are any staples missing, wires broken due to cattle escaping, elk or moose going through the wires, etc. We'll also check to make sure bulls are getting around the fields to breed the cows and that there are no sick or injured animals in the pastures either. Cows need to be moved to different pastures, so there is enough grass for them to graze and gain weight.

By now, it is the middle of July, which means it's time to harvest the hay, make bales, and store it in stacks for winter use. This takes at least three tractors: one to pull a swather or disc-bine that cuts down the hay, one to pull a rake, that rakes the hay windrows together, and another one to pull a baler. The flat deck or stack mover equipment is used to pick up the bales out of the field and move them to a stackyard, where they are stacked and stored for winter use. This harvesting takes about two weeks from start to finish, if none of the machinery breaks down and it doesn't rain. Then we let the grass grow again and we may be able to take a second cut off the fields, depending on moisture and heat.

Around mid to end of August we might be swathing a second cut of grass hay for the haying projects, and the greenfeed is getting ready to harvest as well. Silage, which you learned about during the stories in this book, may be ready to put into the pit in both Manitoba and Alberta. Calves can have creep feeders put out in the fields to supplement their milk program. Creep feeders are filled with grain, and little amounts of grain come out at the bottom of the feeder, so the calves learn how to eat grain. This can be oats or barley, eaten whole to get them used to the taste of these grains and begin to increase their weights as well. The men repair farm equipment as needed—tractors, tires on rakes, combines, and swathers—before stowing them away for winter months after harvesting is done.

Fall Harvesting & Preparing Cattle for Winter

In September, we pull bulls from the pastures and put them out on some green, renewed, fresh pasture so they may gain weight before winter hits. In October, we finish late fall, such as combining oats and baling greenfeed. We stack the bales in stackyards to keep away from deer and elk. Then we gather up yearlings and ship them back to our Alberta home ranch, to begin feeding them up in a feedlot to fatten for finished beef animals.

We process calves before taking them off their mothers in October. This causes them all less stress and the calves are much calmer when they go through the chutes again later at weaning time. Finally, we separate and ship bulls that were unable to breed any cows and have been fattened all summer on grass or grain.

During this weaning and processing we vaccinate the cattle again for other diseases they may acquire in a feedlot with other animals. In addition, certain bugs may require a booster shot from when they got one in June or July.

November and December Tasks

In November, we sort out all cows that have dried up at weaning time—whether they did not have a calf, lost a calf in calving season, or had their calf eaten by a predator. These are now cows we will sell. These would have fattened on grass for the last few months if they lost their calves earlier on in the calving season or if they have just lost their calf due to predators.

ABOUT THE LIVESTOCK- CATTLE,
AN ORDINARY ANNUAL RANCH WORK SCHEDULE,
POLITICS & SELF-SUFFICIENCY

The other cows who raised calves are pregnancy tested in November or December. The Veterinarian comes out again and tests the cows to see how many have calf foetuses in them or if they didn't get bred at all. The ranch woman provides food for these workers, too, possibly four to six workers who are there all day, so they get two meals provided for them that day. She may be one of the helpers, so she may prepare the meal ahead of time, too. (The Veterinarian comes about 9 am and is there all day until dark pregnancy testing the 800 cows. The 150 replacement heifers have been preg-tested previously.) More cows will be shipped when they are found to be dry and were not bred that summer.

December, all cows are trailed back to the home quarter in Manitoba, next to the main ranch yard; heifers are in the pasture a few miles away, where there is a water trough and a water well pump, so they get water every day too. Predator dogs are moved to the cattle feed supply to keep the elk and deer out of the hay bales. Heifer calves are moved to a nearby feedlot in Manitoba to be fed hay and maintained there until Spring. Bulls are also moved closer to the main yard for easy feeding. The same procedure happens at the Alberta home ranch; feedlots are filled with custom and our own calves and two year olds to be fed and fattened for meat.

From there, everything repeats, as if the same year is repeated 99+ times. The calves and cows and bulls begin the winter-feeding program again, and the whole process continues year after year. Hopefully, we get a few feet of snow, too.

As you can see, there is a lot of work involved to keep these livestock ranches moving forward with the times, prices, weather patterns, lack of water and grass, varying market prices, and always increasing costs of producing the beef as well as the feed we give them. The cost of machinery, fuel, utilities, seeding, corrals, fencing materials, harvesting machinery plus trucks, tractors, trucking costs, minerals, salt, vaccinations, drugs to prevent and cure animal sickness, etc.—nothing is free; everything costs money. When a cow is sold, one piece of our cow herd is gone and so that cow will no longer produce a calf for us to use again. We hope and pray that our livestock provide us with income to pay all our expenses. Even back in the days of our forefathers and mothers, as you will note from the next addition to this chapter, a friend of mine who didn't want her name mentioned has some points to ponder as to "Why would we do it if we didn't always make a profit?"

One Co-Author's Perspective

People look at farmers and ranchers and think that we are making a fortune. What they do not realize is that our forefathers and mothers put their hearts and souls into agriculture for years. They raised their families, made ends meet, and somehow scraped through many hardships. Severe droughts, world wars, grasshoppers, poor commodity prices, high interest and government overreach makes things challenging for ranchers. Competition for agricultural land is growing fierce. The price is driven up by big corporations, environmental interest groups with huge public and government backing, foreign interests, and high interest rates. Young people trying to make a start in agriculture and small family farms are not able to compete.

Folks do not do well with rapid change. Can we afford it? Our accountants and lawyers can barely keep up with the new rules and laws that constantly come across their desks. Some are changing careers because they are frustrated. And the Big Question: Can we afford the Global Warming Agenda that our world governments have implemented as another way to burden our society? (This is the end of her essay.)

Politics, Big Corporations, Money Talks

There used to be a law against people or corporations buying land in Alberta if they didn't live here. Somewhere in the past 80 years, our Alberta government removed that specific Act and added exemptions for the benefit of growth in Alberta. As quoted from the Alberta government website, the Agricultural and Recreational Land Ownership Act was designed to monitor and control the foreign acquisition of prime agricultural and recreational land (controlled land) by non-Canadians. However, the Act does not discourage non-Canadian investors who wish to come to Alberta to invest in or to build new manufacturing plants, processing operations, recreational developments, or home subdivisions or to expand existing developments.

Now, we are being taken over by foreign ownership as there are no restrictions whatsoever against foreign countries buying our land. They can own livestock feedlots, shut 'em down and then bring in all their own country workers, and send all profits back to their home country. Or buy more land and more livestock ranches here in Canada and we become dependent on the government of the year. One piece of land sold for 50 million dollars recently by a large corporation from a foreign country. I recently was asked to write up a Draft Policy about this to the Alberta UCP Government, which I did so we will see if it comes to pass or not.

We, as ranchers, sure cannot compete with that kind of money, so it may be inevitable that foreign ownership could become the norm. They have bought up most of our feedlots now and are working at getting our meat packing plants bought up too. Foreign monopolies could also be the norm, if they also take over our livestock markets. They could ship our Canadian livestock commodities back to their countries to sell.

The news these days is always negative, the Chaos before the Quiet of a well-run machine, such as our world when all is done for our highest good!

Who knows what the future holds for us, unless we stand together as Canadians and speak out. Maybe challenge the provincial governments, as well as the federal government to keep our land under Canadian ownership or at least demand that people buying our lands and businesses, need to live here and the food stays here too. This is my opinion since I learned what it takes to speak up and go for what I believe is right for our country. All our opinions matter, but we also need to become the change we want to see, cut away the violence, berating of each other, and live in peace, support and gratitude for all that we have become, what we do and all that we have right now, at the present time.

I hope the Federal government party has changed with the next Election in 2025 and our next Prime Minister will care about our country and its people. I hope the new leader of our country, Canada, will love, support, and care about all the provinces and reinforce the fact that our prairie provinces, especially Alberta, as well as Saskatchewan and Manitoba, play a vital role as part of Canada with their small carbon footprint. Also, I hope that the new Prime Minister appreciates that all our industries here in Canada, plus the family-run, back-to-basics lifestyle within the livestock ranching industry are all working full out to provide Canada with the best service, compassion for everyone in creating a win/win towards world peace.

Dissecting the Cost of Meat versus the Profit for Producer

We would possibly **receive $1.50/lb for a live weight 1500 lb grass-fed cow ($2250.00)**, which would go to make lean hamburger meat. Say hamburger meat is $3.99/lb, and it would probably **dress out to 750 lbs** with half of that making hamburger while the rest would be soup bones. (Soup bones boiled in water create beef broth) So, **375 lbs hamburger X $6.97 = $2613.75, and the soup bones are worth $17/lb x 375 lbs =$6375.** That healthy cow bought in the store, cut and wrapped, would cost you **$2613.75 + $6375 = $8988.75.** The above price that we received live from the pasture, with deductions **subtracted for trucking, $100** gives **the rancher $2250- $100 = $2150 net price. The difference** between grocery store prices and what we received per cow **is $6838.75. <u>Rancher receives a $2150.00 net price versus the net price of $8988.75 that the store receives.</u>** (There may be some deductions off this store profit, yet you can see that the rancher is not making a profit off this beef animal.) Water is sometimes added to the hamburger and other cuts, so it weighs up more at the grocery store. Water evaporates, leaving a much smaller amount of meat once it is cooked.

Drink Water to Match Your Body Weight

Also, I was reading a book about keeping us healthy by drinking water with every meal to keep hydrated. Rule of thumb is to drink your body weight in water, which means you take your weight in pounds, change it to fluid ounces, and then divide the number by eight to calculate how much water you are supposed to drink every day in eight-ounce glasses. Not coffee or juice, but water; plain water, just like the animals drink. The author of this book, Dr. F. Batmanghelidj, M.D., says at the top of the front cover, "You Are Not Sick, You Are Thirsty." So possibly, if we ate more red meat from cattle and drank more water instead of taking so many medications and other beverages, we would live longer, healthier lives. The book is called *Your Body's Many Cries for Water*. www.watercure.com.

Ranch women serve their families and friends nutritious, healthy, back to the basics food with love which makes it taste so delicious. Love for the ranching industry, the livestock we raise, vegetable gardens, and the rural communities who create support structures that work both ways. We honour the places in the wild where we find an abundance of berries, such as saskatoon, chokecherry, wild raspberries, strawberries, hawthorn trees, and bushes that we may pick. We make jams, jellies, syrups, and canned berries for ice cream toppings, cheesecakes, pies, etc. We are privileged to eat the meat and vegetables we raise, to live where our pioneer ancestors lived, and to be able to raise our children and grandchildren under the umbrella of the Canadian livestock ranching industry.

Suggestions for Self-Sufficiency and Self-Reliance

Now, what if we, as ranch women, taught other women how to become self-sufficient? We have the skills to teach other women about backyard gardens, preserving the food we eat, move forward to cooking meals from scratch, as I cook in my kitchen and you cook in your kitchen, and we have fun exchanging cooking skills, thoughts, and ideas about what else we can do, with what we have, from where we are.

I have a website called www.grandmaskitchen.ca where we can support each other, swap recipes, create friendships, build life skills, connect, collaborate, and communicate together as ranch women helping all women, as we all have or could have common threads woven between us. This book will also be sold there too. If any of you are interested, I am also a Certified Life Mastery Consultant who coaches women to empower them to live their dreams.

Three Dreams Came True

I have had a coach since before COVID to help me get through some outer and inner challenges and faulty belief systems in my life. COVID scared the life out of me. I was worried about family and friends and I knew I wanted someone to help guide me through the pandemic. That coach, Kirsten Welles, from BTI, kept me centred on what I would love to be, do, and have. Now, here I am, having come through it with my dreams still intact and able to celebrate three dreams coming true in the past two years, 2021, 2023 and 2024.

Firstly, I set up a website called www.grandmaskitchen.ca whereby I set up the website as a membership site to help women connect, chat, build a support system for any of the members who want that extra support from women of all ages. I always wanted to be a Chef and so now I have my own cooking show online, showing other people and interacting with them during the show. I pick a recipe and then go online and see who would like to join the show and cook with me in their house. Then I send them the recipe and they go out and buy the ingredients and we pick a cooking day and we all cook the meal together. It is so much fun and we all learn something new and connect in a safe and happy environment. We cook on Zoom and there is a recording at the end so you can always go back and cook with me again whenever you want once you sign up as a member. I love the way we are all communicating, collaborating and connecting and we all have food ready for meals when we are all done.

Secondly, a long-awaited trip with my cousin Jacqui from Scotland, where we travelled to New Zealand to meet, connect, and make friends with around 20 cousins we didn't even know we had until we began researching their whereabouts. Dream achieved! My mom always talked about relatives in New Zealand, as two of her dad's siblings went over there back in the early 1900s and their descendants are still there now. She always wanted to go but when I asked her, she said "I am too old." She was 68 at the time. I went when I was 68, so I proved that I could do it, she possibly could have too. (I took my 80 year old cousin to Scotland with me in 2017, so being old is not a factor when you want to live your dreams.)

Third Dream Achieved: I have written a book that I have dreamed about for over 30 years, another dream achieved! I wanted and needed that extra support to keep me from letting fear get in the way and stop me from beginning the book up until now, as the FEAR stopped me up until now. The fear said, "Who wants to read a book you wrote? What do you know about writing books? What will people think about you bragging about yourself." I asked that little voice of Fear that kept getting louder and louder as I made the decision to write the book, as it was my dream and nobody was going to stop me, to sit at the back of the bus. I told it I would talk with it in 3 days, I continue to push the pause button on my thinking. Then I tell that negative voice that is trying to keep me safe in a world that no longer serves me as it used to, and ask it to be quiet for those 3 days, then I will talk with it and let it know I am safe and going to be okay, it will all work out and the book will get written and published and I am still alive and well. I can do this, I am doing this and now I did it and the dream has been achieved. Yahhhh!!

I would not have been able to achieve all these amazing dreams without the help of supportive friends who are also partners in believing, as well as transformational life coaches who have helped guide me to a more fulfilling and joy-filled life. I am now planning Prairies Voices Ranch-Women Retreats to be launched in July/2024 for 4 days of staying at our ranch, enjoying the great outdoors, seeing animals that live on our ranch, as well as wild animals that live here.

ABOUT THE LIVESTOCK- CATTLE,
AN ORDINARY ANNUAL RANCH WORK SCHEDULE,
POLITICS & SELF-SUFFICIENCY

We will cook together, and learn about preserving foods, picking wild berries and making jams, as well as digging deeper into what we would love to be, do and have for the rest of our lives, enjoying how it feels to live full out, achieving our dreams and doing things that are on our bucket list. You can meet some of the co-authors from the book and connect with them, and have so much fun!

There will be online Zoom cooking shows offered each month on YouTube as well as one LIVE cooking show per month coming soon. Plan is to do speaking engagements at our local halls and other venues wanting to know more about this book. One of my publishers has arranged for me to do podcasts, as well as get myself into local newspaper articles, TV broadcasts. I will be connecting with other women, and talking about the importance of giving ranch women/all women voices.

Promoting this book is #1 on my list right now and getting the words out to as many women as possible. I also want to thank the God within me, as I have leaned into listening to the still small voice that speaks to me in the early mornings, if I am in danger or when I am asking for help and it keeps me strong. We are never alone, as we have the human side of our life, as well as the spiritual being part of us. As we co-create with God, our Higher Power, our Spiritual Soul Self, we can do whatever we put our minds to becoming, doing, and having. Let LOVE versus FEAR guide us each day. as we get better and better at living our best life, as our authentic self.

Epilogue

In this book, you've read stories that recognize the crucial role of Canadian ranch women in shaping agriculture, conservation, and family ranch operations on the prairies of Western Canada. It highlights their historical and contemporary contributions, emphasizing how they handle diverse responsibilities such as child-rearing, machinery operation, bookkeeping, and community involvement.

The younger generation of ranchers—sons of the ranch women featured in this book—are now involved in household tasks such as cooking, house cleaning, doing laundry, and babysitting/tending to children's needs. Yet, strategic planning often remains in the hands of women.

Efforts are made to educate and empower newcomers to the industry, spanning generations and diverse backgrounds. Events like the Advanced Women's Conference in Alberta provide networking opportunities and a platform for learning about ranching life. As technology evolves in the ranching industry, these women prove indispensable with their determination and perseverance. In addition, schools have been established in Alberta to educate young women about ranching and farming, ensuring the continuity of skills for future generations.

This book has delved into the personal challenges that ranch women face, breaking the silence on topics that were previously considered secrets. These previously untold experiences have not only shaped the lives of the women who lived them but have also left a lasting imprint on their families and communities. The enduring connection and love that ranch women have for the land are emphasized, showcasing their commitment to stewardship and sustainable land management.

As I began to write this book and collect the stories, my objective was clear: to get unstuck from my fears and own the courage to choose which way I would look at things. I sometimes listened to the voices of fears that told me I was not good enough to write a book, but I was free to choose gratitude for all that I am becoming and doing—in fact, all that I have and am already.

Every day, then, I look for solutions rather than dwelling on any negative thoughts. Sometimes, I fall off this new way of thinking and begin to pay attention to my negative thoughts. I am not perfect at thinking differently, and if I am not mindful of what I am thinking, then I begin going down the old thought pattern and fear rises and I feel small, on the defence, and opinionated.

That little negative voice in my head sometimes even yells at me through other people's messages and attempts to stop me from publishing this book. I've chosen not to listen to any News on T.V., radio, or Social Media at all and I am okay with that. I have better things to do with my time.

One thing that keeps me busy is designing my life the way I want to live it. I made up a Vision Board, too, to keep me more aware of what I'm thinking about. I notice what I'm noticing around me and know that I can always choose love over fear.

Being mindful of my thoughts at any given time during the day also allows me to be aware of how my actions affect others. I truly love how this book has come together. Through the writing of this book, my co-authors—courageous, independent, innovative, ordinary Canadian ranch women—have been given voices. They speak from the Canadian prairies to you, the readers.

EPILOGUE

Looking forward, the next book in the series will continue with true-life tales of our Canadian pioneer ranch women from the late 1800s. *Beyond the Saddle: Extraordinary Lives of Ordinary Pre-Canadian (NWT) Pioneer Ranch Women* will showcase their legacies and underscore the livestock ranching industry from its beginnings. This second book will recognize the innovative and courageous lives our pioneer ranch grandmothers led during and after the world wars. They grappled with weather challenges, prairie fires, and winter blizzards, all while some lived in tents before they could get a house built before winter.

These hardy, intelligent, hard-working women rode horseback to do most things, yet beyond the saddle, their work ethics, resilience, and innovations contributed significantly to the ranching legacy. I am grateful to the ranch women still among us who submitted their mothers', grandmothers', and aunts' stories, photos, and recipes for this second book of the series.

The final volume in the series will be a reflection on my own life as a ranch daughter, ranch granddaughter, and ranch woman. In part, I'll describe my life of being married for 47 years and raising four hard-working, worthy, and responsible children on the ranch who have grown into successful adults with families of their own. Moreover, I will also intertwine lessons learned on my journey to authenticity. This trilogy of books about ordinary Canadian ranch women will stand as a testament to our enduring spirit, weaving together tales of courage, resilience, and the boundless impact of their stories across generations and landscapes. As these stories are shared, they become a source of inspiration for other women, creating a ripple effect that extends beyond the pages of this book.

There is an addition to this book that will give you an insight into the second book. This story came in during the last part of the editing for this first book, so I decided to make it the first Chapter in the second book, ***Beyond the Saddle: Extraordinary Stories of our Ordinary Pre-Alberta Canadian Ranch Women***. I felt it will give you, the reader, a glimpse into the next book about our Canadian pioneer ranch women's lives, through this sixth-generation ranch family.

Chapter I

Love of Ranching & The Land

J. George & Elizabeth Steinbach Family

Our Steinbach roots run deep in the surrounding area around Bassano, Alberta

By Aleta Steinbach

In a strange way, Bassano is a little isolated. It has natural borders: the Bow River 12 miles south; the main Canal to the east, which cuts us off from Cassils; the Bassano Dam and Siksika Reserve to the west; and a large block of EID land, three Hutterite colonies and some big dryland farms to the north. The rural area around Bassano and Lathom is vast with very few inhabitants, so the farmers and ranchers here are a tight-knit group. They work well together and have each other's backs when needed.

John (George) and Elizabeth (Ma) Steinbach & Family

They answered the call for work on the Bassano Dam: Henry led the little dam workhorse crew. In 1910, J. George (a harness maker) and Elizabeth (Ma) Steinbach arrived in Bassano by train from Iowa. With them were their four sons, Henry, Herman, Joe, Bernard (Ben), and one daughter, Mary (Clarence)Fisher. They had one son Ray. Mary died young of diabetes. Fisher Bridge still stands south of Bassano, where they homesteaded.

The Steinbach homesteaded farther south and was a welcome stop for travellers, especially the LK Ranch crew, to get a warm meal when crossing the Bow River. Bob Knight of that LK Ranch crew told us that the Bar 4 S brand was the first brand registered in the Bassano Post office for George's 4 Sons. He said the kids of Bassano would bike five miles to Ma Steinbach's house in the hopes of getting a cookie. These treats were said to be the size of a plate.

Elizabeth Steinbach

Through the generations, Steinbach men have been very quiet, hardworking folk who kept to themselves and whose word was their bond. Interestingly, they all married women who were outgoing, strong, hardworking members of the community. Their wives either came from local Centennial Pioneer families or, like me, came from far away.

Ben Sr. was 14 years old when he came to Bassano with his parents in 1910, the family all worked together on and off the farm. 1916 is when Ben first decided to become a rancher with his brother, Herman, who had bought some land and built a two-room shack on it. They started out with a few head of horses, 13 heifers, and a bull. (Got this extra information from the Bassano History Book, *Best on the West By A Damsite, Family Histories*.) Ben and Herman broke horses to ride and to drive, as there were a lot of horses in the area at that time. Horses were worth more money than a fat steer in those days. Ben's horse brand was an S hanging reverse L, which Dan Steinbach still owns. In the 1930s, no rain & continuous wind dried out the land, so people left their homesteads and went elsewhere. The land would go back to the Canadian Pacific Railway or be sold for taxes. Ben bought land along the N side of the Bow River that had coulees facing to the south; when the Chinook winds blew, and the sun shone on the coulees, the snow melted, exposing the native grass.

Nora (Boyle) Steinbach, Dr. A. G. Scott
1936.

It was an ideal spot for wintering his two-year-old steers. He sold the steers as grass fed, then trailed them into Bassano stock yards to be taken to the packing house by train. The boys, at 37 plus years, were set, and it was time to start thinking about a family.

Herman Steinbach married Honora (Nora) Boyle, who was an RN at the Bassano Hospital, in 1940. I was told by a workmate that she was the nurse you wanted if you were sick, but she had no time for you if you were just feeling sorry for yourself. Their son Michael married Lorraine, oldest of Bill & Mabel Rodbourne's two girls, in 1965. Her grandfather Frank worked for the CPR and homesteaded at Crowfoot just west of Bassano in 1898. They hand-dug their well 126 feet to get water. Mike & Lorraine still farm that land with their son Lorne, his wife Sherry, and his son Josh, 5th generation rancher last to carry on the name in this area, along with original Steinbach land that is still part of their large family Ranching operation today.

Micheal (Mike), Josh, Sherry, Lorne,
granddaughters Blake & Reese, sister Tanis and Lorraine Steinbach

Magnus MacLean, hired sheep herder Mrs. Strang, hired girl, Mrs. Catherine

Bernard (Ben) Steinbach marries Margaret (Girlie) MacLean, ties with Bassano's first pioneer family.

Girlie's grandfather, Peter MacLean, was born in 1847, and he married Catherine Henderson in 1876. They had eight children: Archibald, born 1877, who disappeared at two years of age, possibly taken by a large bird, a Condor falcon, while playing out in the yard. Their sheep were sometimes taken by the falcons. They also had

Catherine, Ann (who died in Scotland in 1884), Helen, William, John, Archibald the 2nd (Archie), and Magnus MacLean, all born on the Falkland Islands, where they lived for 18 years. They left the Falkland Islands by way of Scotland, arriving in Canada in 1896. *Peter's brother, Archibald, and his wife Agnes, with 11 children, came from Scotland to live with them in 1900 on the Canadian Colonization Co.

They soon searched out a new home six miles northeast of Bassano in 1901. He and the boys built a large home, and the family moved out here in *1902.

They had 3,000 head of sheep, 100 cattle, and several horses. Peter MacLean said that in 1903, Bassano consisted of two box cars at the end of the rail line. The original MacLean home was a favourite stopping place for those going west and north to the Red Deer River. Many cowboys and settlers enjoyed Catherine MacLean's cooking and hospitality. *Peter told his sons, William (Bill), John, Archie, and Magnus, to go and build a shack, which became the first slaughterhouse at the ranch. Then, William (Bill) and Magnus, who both married Riddle sisters, started a meat market in Bassano to sell the meat to feed the Bassano Dam crews. The winter of 06/07 took its toll on the animals.

William (Bill) MacLean married Lillian Riddle. They were married in Calgary in 1912. Lillian's family settled at Bull Pond near Carolside Alberta. *Bill and Lillian had 8 children. Their oldest, Catherine (who died in 1930 of typhoid fever; her dad and sister Jean also had it), Peter (Pete), Margaret (Girlie), Archie, Lillian (Babe), James (Jim), Jean, Norma, rounded out the MacLean Family.

Girlie's older brother, Peter (Pete) MacLean, was born March 21, 1914. He lived his whole life in the Bassano area. He was a rodeo cowboy and became a champion calf roper, team-roper, and chariot driver. He married Doris Milne, an avid horsewoman. They had four children and lived on a ranch east of town. Back in the day, land was notoriously traded by gambling misadventures, and it was common that places were lost and gained in the blink of an eye. In the 1930s, one day, Doris looked out the window, and everything was getting loaded up, and they moved into Bassano. Doris was also a hard worker and known throughout the community for her gorgeous, abundant garden full of vegetables. She always fed her family the many preserves she made from her garden. In later years, when she no longer needed that much food for the winter, she shared her garden produce with those people she liked.

Jim, one of Girlie's younger brothers, and his wife Iona's son, Rod MacLean, is a well-known cattleman with a keen eye throughout Alberta, who still ranches with a good herd of Black Angus cattle a little east of Bassano.

**Gramma Lillian MacLean with grandchildren
Peter, Catherine and Bernard Steinbach**

Lathom Ladies — Mrs. Munro, Martha (Salmond) Cowan holding Judy, Johnny Cowan,
Mrs. Warren, Mrs. Gosling, Mrs. Lore, Mrs. Ben Steinbach, Mrs. Albert Levesque.

Ben and Girlie were married in 1932. They moved closer to Lathom so the three kids, Bernard, Catherine, and Peter, could go to a one-room school. The family had good neighbours and enjoyed living in Lathom. They would trail the cattle from the river land 12 miles back to the home place, eventually moving to the North end of Lathom, where they set up feed facilities for cattle.

School was over for Bernard Steinbach in Grade 8, in 1948 because he had to help his father, Ben, run the ranch. A few years later, young Bernard's dad met Ruth Stuart in Bassano and he went home and told Bernard, "You should take that girl to the movies." It wasn't long and Bernard was married to Ruth Stuart from Turner Valley in 1953.

Ruth's dad, Jack, had left his home in Saskatchewan as a kid on his own and never went back, and her mom's family, the Tuckers, arrived in Alberta in 1890. Blanche Stuart, Ruth's mom, had polio as a kid, which affected her right side.

Gramma Stuart driving Grandson Ben Jr's team with family on the sleigh. I was almost due to calve, as Ben Jr would say, and fell in a badger hole and caught this photo on the way down.

Despite that, Blanche had 12 children, of whom Ruth was second oldest. Blanche managed everything amazingly and never ever complained. Making something out of nothing was one of her greatest skills, and she wouldn't make anything that wasn't useful. Her whole house was smaller than some ladies' kitchens that include all the amenities. Current wives now with only two kids would be stressed out in such a small house. I think the term "Hold my beer" comes to mind.

Bernard and Ruth (Stuart) Steinbach

Ruth, born in 1935, came to Bassano in November of 1951 as a nursing aide. In 1953, she then became a full-time ranch wife of Bernard with a crew of ranch hands to feed. Coming from the foothills, she wasn't used to the big Ranches' wide open spaces and now was getting lost and had trouble getting around to deliver food to the men for the first few years. You could go 12 miles and never leave the ranch, and there were no landmarks, crooked trees, foothills, and mountains to get your bearing. The flat prairie land with endless fences all looked the same, and the wind never stopped.

The first time she was headed to the old branding corrals to feed the crew, she got so hopelessly lost that she just laid on the horn of her vehicle. Some of the cowboys heard her and rode over the hill to save her. She giggles about it now.

Things got rough after a couple of years of marriage. Ben Sr. died of a heart attack in 1955. This brought on the premature delivery of Ben Jr, a baby boy whom they named Bernard (3rd) (Ben Jr.). At that time, the government had a death/inheritance tax, and that winter 20 head of cattle went through the ice on the Bow River and died. They had to dig deep to save the ranch. Ruth says they were young, but they stuck together, holding on to "the cow's tail," and she pulled them through.

Seeding, calving, branding, haying, harvesting, and weaning crews were always needing to be fed. Men worked hard, and if the women didn't feed them hardy meals, it wasn't long before they moved on. That was one thing Ruth had on her side: coming from a big family, she could cook. They always had ranch hands who lived with them and became part of their family.

Bernard was the love of her life, and they had five children: Jacqueline (Jackie), Bernard 3rd (Ben Jr), Thomas (Tom), Daniel (Dan) and Janice. All the kids took part in the everyday chores and grew up handy. One of the fun things that stood out as a family together was a trail ride to the Cyprus Hills that most of the Bassano Ranch families went on. One year they went to BC to Mara Lakes, where the tables turned. Ruth loved the mountains but Bernard and some of the kids were like caged bears because they couldn't see anything. They used to ride to town on Sundays for gymkhana with their MacLean cousins and horseback broomball on the ice in the winter. Winter, once the cows were fed, was the time they went to visit Lathom neighbors and play cards.

It wasn't until 1960 that Peter Steinbach came home and started to be part of the Ranch. Up until then, Girlie did the books, and Bernard and Ruth ran The Steinbach Ranching Co. Peter Married Frances King; her parents were Franklin (Frank) and Mildred King, and their family had come to Bassano in 1909 and operated the Bassano pool hall. Peter and Frances had five daughters: Mildred, Kristine, Josephine, Patricia, and Stephanie. Frances had exchange students from around the world stay with them and cooked many meals for all the farmhands. Peter made some big BBQs, and they were in quite a demand. Peter and Frances cooked beef & beans at community functions, using their homemade BBQs. They were good supporters of the Bassano Community. Peter was the first to set up pivots in our area and was a good farmer.

Bernard and Peter split the operation into two. Bernard operated the cattle and feedlot side, and Peter did all the farming and harvesting, which worked for both growing families. Their mom, Girlie, retired to live in Bassano. The hard times hit again in the late 1970's and early 1980's. Bad government policy brought on inflation. Cattle prices played into that scenario, along with the banks appraising land higher than it should have been. The banks then talked farmers and ranchers into loans for irrigation systems and capital expenditures on the overpriced land values that now had a mortgage on them. Then, BANG! The floating interest rates went up to 24%. So many people lost their places, and some took their lives. This was an extremely hard time to live through, and downsizing was a thing. The boom of Oil and Gas came just in time, saving a lot of Ranching families.

Peter Steinbach (Branding Crew) Bernard Steinbach

Bernard and Peter continued to ranch on their own for a few more years until first Peter passed away, and then Bernard. It wasn't long, and change keeps happening to this day. Of their 10 Steinbach children only, Ben remains ranching here in Lathom, whom I have been married to for almost 50 years.

When it comes to hard times, Ruth says the worst is when their son Tom was killed in an accident. It's something you can't change or fix; the sadness is always there.

When the kids all left home, Bernard and Ruth started travelling with the McKinnons, Armstrongs, and Stewarts to Arizona, Texas, California, Montana, and New Zealand. They loved checking out feedlots, ranches, and rodeos while also just travelling down back roads to see how the cattle and horses looked in other places and what they were being fed.

Ruth was a great community leader—helping with fundraisers and working for the arena. She also joined the Lathom Ladies Club, Rodeo, Catholic Church, and Kinette Club, where she headed up the first Bassano History Book.

Bernard was an astute cattleman and operated a quality Red Cross commercial herd. One of his proudest moments later in life was during a 4-H Show & Sale: Judge Groeneveld talked about the Grand, Res, Jr, and Peewee 4-H Champions, of which all had come from his herd, and to top it off, his grandchildren and great-niece were showing them. Groeneveld stated that "the mother herd these animals come from have good genetics and feet built for this country. What a fine group of Champions."

**Ruth, Bernard, Ben Jr, Yolanda, Suntana, Aleta...
Rita & Mackie Pozzobon front Makayla & Vanessa Steinbach**

Bernard (Ben Jr) and Aleta Pozzobon

I, Aleta Pozzobon, came from Chase, BC, where I grew up—the oldest of six girls and grandchildren of two pioneering families there. My mom Rita's family, the Zinck's, were one of the first farms at Scotch Creek, right on Shuswap Lake. Her dad, Karl, worked on the ferry to pay for the farm. Her mother, Dorothy, was salt of the earth and a workaholic. No matter what she was doing, she always wore a dress and apron; it was only in her later years that she started wearing slacks. My mom and two of her sisters logged and cleared the two hay fields while also helping her mom with all the farm work. My mom left home at 17 to be a cook at a logging camp to earn money. While she was there, she ran a trap line on Crowfoot Mountain. It was then she met her cowboy, my dad Mackie, at a family dance.

At age seven, I lived with my grandparents for a year to go to school. That's when I learned to love sewing. Gramma would make the dough for bread at night, and it would rest on the oven door till morning when she would bake it. Every morning, she would start the stove to cook breakfast, deliver coffee to my grandfather in bed, and wake my aunt, uncle, and me up to eat. Then it was "go" time: we had chores to do before we walked a little over a half a mile to the bus stop. My job was to fill the wood boxes and make kindling while they milked the cows by hand. It was always a competition to see who could make the most foam with the milk. We brought the milk into the separator room where I ran the handle of the separator. They packed out the cream and milk cans down to the ferry to be sold. They also had a purebred herd of Polled Herefords.

Gramma Zinck made everything, and when they slaughtered animals, Dad was always the butcher. Nothing went to waste: things like head cheese, tripe, liver pâté, sausages, jerky, pickled pig's feet, and scrambled brain and eggs were made.

Gramma pulled the garden and picked the fruit; everyone in the family would come and help with the butchering and preserving. She made apple cider, water glass and pickled eggs, sauerkraut, preserves of every sort, cheese, yogurt, and the worst, hands down, was unga butter. Gramma also knit socks, mitts, hats, and sweaters for everyone. She made soap, too. (Louise copied the recipe and attached it at the end of the story.)

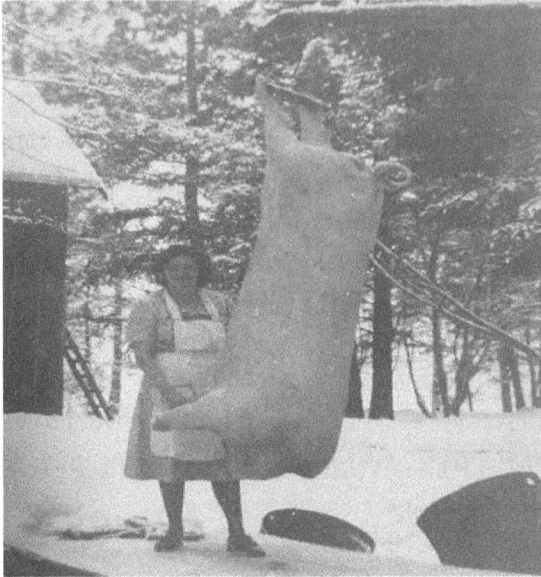

Aleta's Gramma Dorothy Zinck in her dress and apron, cutting up a pig to feed her family. Winter of 1950-51

The grandkids loved it when the tins with the queen's picture on them came out of the cupboard because they were full of cookies carefully wrapped in wax paper.

Gramma was born in Regina. Her father was a wheelwright for the Royal Navy. He worked on the fort in Ft McLeod and the barracks in Regina, where she was born. Great Grampa received the Queen's coronation medal, which was given to me. This past year, my son-in-law Tyler Kraft was honoured with the Queen's 70th anniversary medal. I passed the first medal on to him, and now he has the first and last of Queen Elizabeth's coronation Medals.

Sam Pozzobon Family

My Nono, Sam Pozzobon (his spelling, he taught us), left Italy after their only sister drowned in a canal on their farm. This tragedy drove their mother to drink. (Side note: this canal system comes from Bassano, Italy. Must have always been a part of God's plan for me to end up here.) He had 11 siblings. He and two brothers stowed away on a boat out of Venice, arriving in Canada on his 12th birthday. A Scottish family took them in, and they started working in the coal mines. All three became master blast men. My Nono worked in coal mines across Canada, even working in Drumheller. He ended up in British Columbia as a head blast man for the #1 Highway through the Fraser Canyon. When he quit blasting, he bought three ranches near Kamloops, went back to Italy in 1924, and married a girl the families had arranged.

Nona Assunta never learned much English, but the talents she brought from the old country served her family well. She hated snakes and called them vipers. When my dad was six months old, she was working in the garden and had put a rock on his nightdress to keep him in the apple box. When she turned to check on him, she discovered a rattlesnake was also around the rock. Somehow, it never bit the baby. But that was it: the homestead had to be cleaned out of rattlers. So, they brought in 500 pigs, which cleaned up the sage brush and the snakes, then they sold the fattened pigs. Dad said that, over the years, pigs cleared a lot of ground. The snakes would bite the pigs, but their fat protected them. When they butchered them, you could see the pockets where the snakes bit them.

Nono & Nona raised some tough cowboys, which likely was the last thing she imagined. My Dad & Uncle Sammy broke 100 head of horses one year for the army. She knew what they loved, and she saved the money from raising turkeys to help each one buy their first set of spurs and saddle. Dad was pulled out of school in Grade 6 to feed the herd of cattle for the winter, a day's ride from the home place. He loved math, so the school superintendent would come out once a month to give him work. He even ended up with an engineering certificate. He could do or make anything and was a self-made man, but he loved being a cowboy the best.

**Aleta's grandparents Sam & Assunta Pozzobon,
My Dad Mackie, Freddy, Sammy, Marino & Maria their children**

Resilient Moms and Grandmothers

Our foremothers worked very hard to raise their children. During their time, childbirth was not easy, and there was no way to avoid it. Unfortunately, sometimes, it did not end well. Food was scarce, and extra money was non-existent. A basic need like water had to be packed in with a pail. There was no such thing as a full night's sleep, either: to heat the house, the stove always had to be stoked. Growing, preserving, and cooking food was their life, and they were darn good at it. Many times, they had to carry the load themselves because their husbands were away trying to make money to pay for the essentials to live. Three of our grandmothers died way too young. None of them ever asked or expected much when they were alive, and one thing everybody knew: you did not cross them.

I'm always amazed at how tough they were and the things they had to endure with little or nothing. Winter meant cutting blocks of ice to store in ice houses to keep food from spoiling. Things we take for granted, for them, meant hours of hard work. Somehow, I think what got them through it was that they knew how to laugh, tell stories, enjoy the moment, and then get right back to work.

All our parents went to rural one-room schoolhouses. Some of them have stories of kids they went to school with who were dragged with runaway horses. Stories of death by wind, cold, winter snow, dirt and lighting storms, or getting hung up. Tales of the teachers being very mean. Mom told us about a teacher who didn't like some of the boys and would hang them up on coat hooks by their collars. Then there are the stories about what the kids did to the teachers, like taking a lot of spear grass and aiming for the teacher's wool pants. Girls' hair braids getting dunked in ink wells. Dad and his brothers took a democrat apart and put it back together over the peak of the roof when they were very young. Most of them didn't mind being at school because it was easier than the work waiting for them at home. From the stories I've heard, and I love their stories, this generation of kids liked to joke and play pranks, and the friends they grew up with were lifelong friends. Newlyweds were always a target. Stories of escapades lasted for years, and the longer they lasted, the more they were embellished. Humour was a gift to endure hard times.

Our family of six girls had it a lot easier than our parents and their parents before them. Our dad Mackie always fed out a pen of steers in the winter, and we all had chores. I milked the cow while the other girls had pigs, chickens, horses, and rabbits to feed. There was a massive garden. None of us really liked weeding, which is funny now, as I think it's calming. We had about 20 hives of honeybees, and the hottest job in the summer was extracting the honey. Every week, we each had a day to cook, so we all left home being good cooks. Dad equally had us work with him, so we weren't dependent on anyone.

We went to gymkhanas, rodeos, and turkey shoots with our parents. In the winter family dances were so much fun: everybody danced, grandparents, parents, and kids. The wood stoves in the Hall kitchens had the best smells of turkey, and such great delights with pies on the counters, and the music would play on. It wasn't long before the kids were sleeping on the benches, and the men would go outside to make sure the tires didn't go flat. They always came in laughing; no liquor was allowed inside with women and children.

8 people in a single-cab truck

When I got older and did school sports, there were some parents who came to watch, but not many. I don't think mine ever had time to come, and it was fine. The school bus took us wherever we played, and no parents ever went to away games. Parents didn't have the money then, and there were lots of kids still at home to look after. Another thing that's different today is riding as a family in a vehicle. There were eight of us, and the single cab truck was what we would take to Kamloops to get feed or parts. How we fit I don't know, but I do know my fingers got sore from putting them in the vents trying to hold myself up. Then there was the station wagon. No seatbelts, but mom's arm was always holding someone back when she stepped on the brakes. We did everything with our parents, who did everything together, too. Each of the five houses we ever lived in, my mom designed and then dad built them. The last one was fancy, but the first house mom said was cowboy culture: rough wood floors with apple boxes for cupboards and flour sacs for curtains. She said I was old before I learned to walk as she couldn't put me on the floor to crawl because the first time down, I got so many splinters in my knees that they got infected. That love shack also didn't have power or running water way up in the mountain, so every day, she packed it in.

Now add, right after me, a set of preemie twins and then another, four babies under 2 in diapers, plus she fed dad's logging crew. If that doesn't make you strong, nothing will. Gosh, I admired her. My parents taught us how to make and do things, so there is not a lot I can't do. We did have a few nail-biting moments together. One time, Dad was haying, and Mom took lunch up to him (something you can't say out here in the flat land). I was six, and my little sister was still in a buggy bed when a mad bull started charging us. Mom was so quick-witted that she put the buggy bed into a crook of a tree. Dad spotted her in distress, trying to get us all into safe positions in the trees and beat the bull off. Across the field, he came in the open-air tractor with this wee umbrella above and rammed the bull a few times until he took off. Another time, we were taking a trip to Calgary in our camper, our last family trip all together. We were parked at a campsite in the Pass, and it was hot, so us kids all slept outside. We heard something and thought it was a bear! Mom said, "Go to sleep! It's nothing." Still, we could hear something and soon were all under the truck, where we went back to sleep. In the morning, we woke up to a big commotion because bears had been there and wrecked the other side of the campsite.

The next year, I graduated. The Royal Bank in Chase needed to fill four positions and couldn't find enough replacements. The manager came to the school in January to see if anyone would be interested in a job. As I already had enough credits, the end of that semester was the end of my schooling. I started work at the bank at 17 years old. I started in the accountancy program, and at that time, you had to spend time in a big city bank. There was no way I was going to Vancouver. So, I took a lateral transfer and came to Alberta...

Aleta and Bank Job

On October 1, 1973, I drove into Bassano at noon. It was like the Twilight Zone: the only things on the street were giant tumbleweeds blowing right down Main Street, not a person or vehicle in sight. I drove around looking for someone, and then a siren went off, and people started coming out of the woodwork. I came to find out that everything in town shut down for lunch and supper. Once you got used to it, it was nice. That only lasted for about another five years. I settled right into Bassano, met this fellow that team roped, and started team roping, too. I was having so much fun I decided to get married to Ben Steinbach instead of heading off to Calgary. I worked at the bank during those hard times that Ruth talked about when the interest rates went up from 6% to 24%. As a banker then, you couldn't give out a loan until you called in to head office to get a current interest rate, and that sometimes changed up to a few times a day. It was crazy. Then, it was the worst job to have—when people started defaulting on their loans and you had to call them to come in. For some reason, the bank hired some mean arrogant managers. One day, a nice, elderly farmer came in, went into the manager's office, and left crying. I quit the next day.

The crafty person I am, I decided to open a flower shop, which I then sold when we had kids. From the time I got married, it seemed like we always had a hired hand living with us. While I worked, Ruth continued to cook most of the meals for the men. I did a lot of riding with Ben, not without wrecks. One time, the cows got out, and we chased them in. To get the gate closed, Ben put a rope around it, and I dallied up. I accidentally got the rope under the horse's tail, and he went bucking. Yup, I landed like a sack of potatoes and fractured my back. Water isn't my friend either. I was chasing a cow out of a slough, and my horse fell and rolled right over me. While I was pinned under the saddle in the water, I thought to myself, "I guess this is it." Then, just as quick, I came up, still in the saddle, covered in mud and soaking wet. Still, I finished trailing cattle to the lease. Another time, my horse lost his footing, and we went into the canal, both of us taking a swim. Oh ya, horse wrecks happen, and mad cows are fun, too. Sometimes, they like to boost you over fences. When you're working out in nature, things are going to happen, that's for sure.

A few years after we were married, we were out checking for hot cows in the Artificial Insemination (AI) field. A week prior, we had chased a neighbour's bull back home. Then, one evening, it was super hot and dry, and there he was back again. Ben took after the bull in the rough three-quarter-ton truck, but the bull had his number—he'd obviously been chased with a truck before. The dust was just a-flyin', and I was hitting the roof of the truck, and bump! The bull turned in front of the truck, and now the truck was on top of the bull. Suddenly, we saw another cloud of dust coming right at us, our neighbour, Arnold Armstrong. He jumped out of his truck and reached into his pocket. (I was scared: "What is going down here?") He pulled out a knife and said, "Ben, stay right there! I've been trying to cull him for 2 years, and he always escapes." And so, Arnie (Arnold) Armstrong fixed him. We got the truck off the bull; he shook his head and walked away. The boys had a barley sandwich, and we helped chase the steer back home.

Ben and I have always worked together, whether it's in the shop, branding shed, or pen; whether we're pulling calves, trailing cows, building a fence, or putting in a new water trough in the field or on the range. I wish I could say he even does the books with me, but that's a hard NO from him.

Ben was a successful amateur cowboy, and for 25 years, he managed a pay cheque at the Bassano Rodeo. When it was a Pro Rodeo in 1972, he won the team roping buckle with his great uncle, Pete MacLean. In 1975, the names were drawn out of the hat for partners, and Pete drew my name. He was horrified that he had to rope with a woman. Then we won, and from that time on, we were best buds. The sad part was that they gave out trophies that year instead of the iconic Bassano buckle. The arrival of our first child, Suntana, in 1982 changed how much time I spent in the saddle. She was followed by Yolanda, Vanessa, and Makayla. Ruth hung up the apron, and I took on the cooking duties full-time. Still today, I might start out cooking for two and end up with a dozen or more at our big purposeful table. No problem, and no worries; just throw another plate on the table and potato in the pot.

Most of our Steinbach cousins and neighbours— Armstrong, Evans, Landis, Roen, Hood, and McKinnon families—had young kids of the same age as ours, and we sure did have fun. One -25° Halloween, Neil McKinnon called up and said, "Get the party going! We don't want you to bring the kids out; we're all coming to you." All the families came, each picked a room, and all the neighbour kids went from room to room. It was a warm, spooktacular evening.

The Lathom party line organized a lot of events: prairie-style rodeos, horse shows, jumping competitions, Boxing Day out-of-the-hat curling bonspiels, broom ball at Lore Lake, baseball teams, hockey teams, golf hops, bowling, cribbage, and ice fishing tourneys. However, the unplanned events were always just as much fun. The men would do the morning chores, then say, "Ok, it's cold, but what a nice day! Let's harness the horses to a couple of wagons." Then they'd start at one end of Lathom, stopping at every place and gathering happy people till the day's end, or sometimes till a wagon lost a wheel. There were many misadventures, and the ladies kept adding food as we went. One time, the day after Christmas (Boxing Day), there was a very cold blizzard. The Armstrongs had headed to the river to feed cattle and got stuck on the road. Out rolled the big tractors to pull them and all the oil workers in the area out of the snow. By that time, all the power was out in the surrounding country. Everyone knew we had a wood cookstove, and it was soon put to work for the community. We even had a couple from Australia come along with all the neighbours. We then played games until the wee hours of the morning.

Something that I have inherited through my genes and passed down directly from the women before me was a creative artistic talent. I have shared all the lost art skills that I have gathered in my life with my girls, their children, and anyone who has the inkling to learn. Everyone in my whole crew loves coming and doing things with me. They are getting very good at learning things like sewing, weaving, braiding, leatherwork, making knives, glass, and pottery. Every now and then, they even try the hands at painting and sculpture.

Steinbach Branding Crew Below

Makayla, Remy, Vanessa, Lathom, Ben, Aleta, Yolanda Douglass, Suntana, Navada, Rayla, Jack Lawes/Riata, Dalum Kraft/Dayton, Denym, Danika/GW, Myra, Arlen Murray

Bar 4S cattle brand changes hands

Bernard handed down the Bar 4 S brand to his son, Ben, and the meaning changed just a little: instead of four sons, it's four Steinbach girls. Ben had a saying on his horse trailer: "My best cowboys are cowgirls," and that they are. They are fierce competitors in all sports—roping, rodeo, 4-H, Jr Cattle shows— and won many championships. While they were growing up, we had hired hands and many people from other countries who lived with us, and it gave them a different view of the world. Lathom was a great place to raise our family. They learned how to work and the value of a job well done.

Our children George and Suntana Murray, Dylan and Yolanda Douglass (here in the Bassano area situated on original MacLean grazing land), Tyler and Vanessa Kraft, and Casey and Makayla

Lawes are all working partners in ranches of their own. They are following in their foremothers' footsteps and raising their kids to be great 6th and 7th-generation ranchers.

I see more strong ranch women in the future. I agree with Ruth that being partners together in ranching is the best family lifestyle. It gives you an appreciation for the land God gave us, a love for your fellow man, and a caring heart for animals.

Ladies Groups, Steinbach Women- 4-H Leaders

Our rural community has been known for years for its Lathom Ladies groups from the time of Ma, Catherine, Lillian, Girlie, Nora, Ruth, Frances, and Lorraine Steinbach. Ruth, Frances, and I were all 4-H leaders for numerous years in the Bassano club. One of my proudest moments as a 4-H leader was at the Bashaw provincial show. Seven members of our club went, and each one ended up in the Championship Showmanship and grooming classes; yes, we did bring home the banners. A few times over the years, all four of our girls won the Sr & Jr Grand & Res Championships at Provincial and National level Jr. Shows. They pushed each other to perfection. Steinbach wives have been part of many community, provincial, and national organizations and service clubs, volunteering for churches, schools, and wherever else they were needed.

Our Steinbach Girls roping all double hocks at the same time at Branding)

Many of these families have had lots of girls, and most of them have followed their husbands on their own journey, as it should be. In my Steinbach Story, I have only followed the direct line of Pioneer Ranch women who set down roots in this country and their descendants who still remain in this area Ranching. They have been hardy resourceful women who stand and work with their men so they can make it through anything as a family.

Left to Right: The Murray family, the Douglass family, the Kraft family, Ben & Aleta Steinbach, the Lawes family

*& **Author's Add-on: Louise found some additional information for the story in the Bassano, Alberta History book, Best in the West by a Damsite. This book has one Volume, all on the Bassano and District Family Histories. As you have read above in the story, there are at least two to three generations of Margarets, Catherines, Peters, and Bernard (Bens) in both the MacLean and Steinbach families. This is what happens when people immigrate from the UK, like Scotland, and European Countries, such as Germany, etc. It is so confusing when doing up a family tree. I know myself with our descendants from Scotland. It makes sense to the family members, as they know the descendants mentioned. I just wanted to clarify and allow the readers to acquire a deeper sense of family when they know more about each Peter, Ben, etc.*

SOAP MAKING RECIPE (GRAMMA ZINCK)

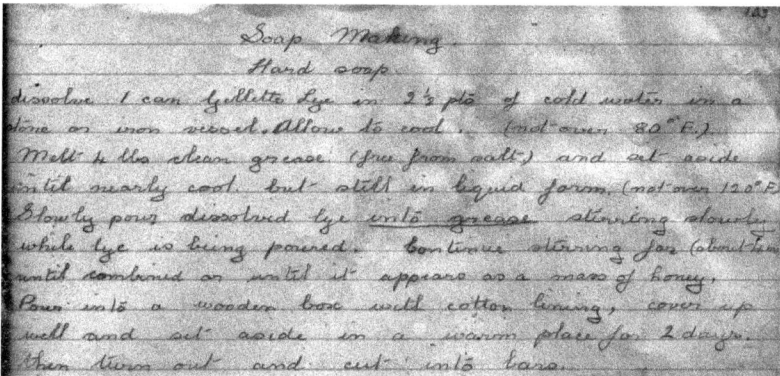

www.ingramcontent.com/pod-product-compliance
Lightning Source LLC
Chambersburg PA
CBHW060249100426
42742CB00011B/1689